APHASIOLOGY

Volume 21   Number 1   January 2007

CONTENTS

APHASIOLOGY

SUBSCRIPTION INFORMATION

Subscription rates to Volume 21, 2007 (12 issues) are as follows:
To individuals: UK £494.00; Rest of World $817.00
To institutions: UK £1175.00; Rest of World $1940.00
A subscription to the print edition includes free access for any number of concurrent users across a local area network to the online edition, ISSN 1464-5041.
Print subscriptions are also available to individual members of the British Aphasiology Society (BAS), on application to the Society.

For a complete and up-to-date guide to Taylor & Francis's journals and books publishing programmes, visit the Taylor and Francis website: http://www.tandf.co.uk/

Aphasiology (USPS permit number 001413) is published monthly. The 2007 US Institutional subscription price is $1940.00. Periodicals Postage Paid at Jamaica, NY by US Mailing Agent Air Business Ltd, c/o Priority Airfreight NY Ltd, 147-29 182nd Street, Jamaica, NY 11413, USA. **US Postmaster**: Please send address changes to Air Business Ltd, c/o Priority Airfreight NY Ltd, 147-29 182nd Street, Jamaica, NY 11413, USA.

Dollar rates apply to subscribers in all countries except the UK and the Republic of Ireland where the pound sterling price applies. All subscriptions are payable in advance and all rates include postage. Journals are sent by air to the USA, Canada, Mexico, India, Japan and Australasia. Subscriptions are entered on an annual basis, i.e. from January to December. Payment may be made by sterling cheque, dollar cheque, international money order, National Giro, or credit card (AMEX, VISA, Mastercard).

Orders originating in the following territories should be sent direct to the local distributor.
India: Universal Subscription Agency Pvt. Ltd, 101–102 Community Centre, Malviya Nagar Extn, Post Bag No. 8, Saket, New Delhi 110017.
Japan: Kinokuniya Company Ltd, Journal Department, PO Box 55, Chitose, Tokyo 156.
USA, Canada and Mexico: Psychology Press, a member of Taylor & Francis, 325 Chestnut St, Philadelphia, PA 19106, USA
UK and other territories: Psychology Press, c/o T&F Customer Services, Informa UK Ltd, Sheepen Place, Colchester, Essex, CO3 3LP, Tel: +44 (0)20 7017 5544; Fax: +44 (0)20 7017 5198; UK.
E-mail: tf.enquiries@tfinforma.com

Typeset by H. Charlesworth & Co. Ltd., Wakefield, UK, and printed by Hobbs the Printers Ltd., Totton, Hants, UK. The online edition can be reached via the journal's website: http://www.psypress.com/aphasiology

Back issues: Taylor & Francis retains a three-year back issue stock of journals. Older volumes are held by our official stockists: Periodicals Service Company, 11 Main Street, Germantown, NY 12526, USA, to whom all orders and enquiries should be addressed. Tel: +1 518 537 4700; Fax: +1 518 537 5899; E-mail: psc@periodicals.com; URL: http://www.periodicals.com/tandf.html

APHASIOLOGY, 2007, 21 (1), 3–8

Ψ Psychology Press
Taylor & Francis Group

Editorial

Issues of access and inclusion with aphasia

Madeline Cruice

City University, London, UK

This special issue of *Aphasiology* examines the issues of access and inclusion as experienced by people with aphasia. It includes research reports that (1) describe and measure communication accessibility, (2) evaluate changes in practice in information or communicative access, and (3) document the social inclusion and exclusion of people with aphasia. It also contains a detailed description of communicative access in practice, and theoretical papers that apply known frameworks or related knowledge bases to the issues of access and inclusion with aphasia. This editorial introduces the concepts of access and inclusion, outlines access in relation to services, information, and work, and provides an overview of current and possible newer meanings of access (namely psychological access). Clinical implications and suggestions for future research are not covered in this editorial, as authors of each paper have outlined their own.

INTRODUCTION

The relatively early development of this field is reflected in the varying individual interpretations made by researchers and clinicians when referring to access and inclusion. A starting point for understanding these terms can be found in dictionary definitions. According to *The American Heritage Dictionary of English* (2000), access is traditionally understood in a physical sense as the means of approaching, entering, or exiting. In more recent times, it has come to mean communicating with or making use of, and also involves the ability or the right to access. It includes both the notion of having access *to* some thing/person/place (e.g., access to the web or "web access"; access to information or "information access"), and access *for* a purpose (e.g., access for making decisions, or access for participating in an event). Various papers in this issue define and illustrate access in different yet related ways, helping us to expand our understanding of what access means in a professional sense. Inclusion, however, seems less well understood, being defined as the act of including or the state of being included (from *The American Heritage Dictionary of English*, 2000). This is but a

Address correspondence to: Madeline Cruice PhD, Department of Language and Communication Science, School of Allied Health Sciences, City University, London EC1V 0HB, UK. E-mail: m.cruice@city.ac.uk

http://www.psypress.com/aphasiology   DOI: 10.1080/02687030600798071

brief definition though, and Bunning and Horton (2007, this issue) and Parr (2007, this issue) devote their papers to discussing and illustrating inclusion and exclusion, and how both are mediated through the societies in which people live. Returning to the notion of access, the following paragraphs review access in terms of services, information (including the Internet), and the world of work.

THE CONCEPT OF ACCESS

The concept of access was originally highlighted by the lack of access, or inequitable access, to direct healthcare services for people with illness or health problems, who have more frequent needs for more regular contact. Specific barriers to accessing healthcare services in the United States are raised by Threats (2007, this issue). Bunning and Horton (2007, this issue) further discuss service provision, and issues of access and inclusive living for people with aphasia and people with a learning disability, and recent research by Law, Bunning, Byng, Farrelly, and Heyman (2005) demonstrates that issues regarding inclusion and communication in consultations with primary care practitioners are shared by people who experience language and learning difficulties.

A second way in which we construe access is through access to information, and this has become increasingly important given the link between information, knowledge, and empowerment (Ramcharan, Roberts, Grant, & Borland, 1997). Access to information is fundamental to initiatives such as shared decision making in medical encounters, and user involvement in service planning and delivery (see Pound, Duchan, Penman, Hewitt, & Parr, 2007, this issue, for further discussion). Worrall, Rose, Howe, McKenna, and Hickson (2007 this issue) discuss in detail the accessibility of written information (particularly about health) using an evidence-based approach. Given that the explosion of information via the Internet enables patients and consumers independent access to and availability of a range of health and medical information, we could qualify information access further to include features of *accuracy*, *appropriateness*, and *timeliness*. For further research into how people with aphasia access the Internet, the reader is referred to papers outside this issue, such as Egan, Worrall, and Oxenham (2004), and Parr, Moss, Newberry, Petheram, and Byng (2005). Related to information access, is the well-discussed notion of *communication* or *communicative access*, which is discussed a little later on in this editorial.

Not included in this special issue of *Aphasiology*, but essential for a balanced understanding of access, is the notion of access to life opportunities, including work or education. Aphasic individuals' access to and barriers in returning to work environments have been studied in detail by a number of researchers, and some of the findings are briefly mentioned here. Focus groups conducted with 22 employers, 14 aphasic people, and 13 speech and language therapists (SLTs), revealed the anticipated barriers to work reintegration as executing work tasks. Specifically these included working conditions, electronic tools, dealing with unfamiliar speakers, levels of productivity (quantity and speed), and attitudes of work colleagues (Garcia, Barrette, & Laroche, 2000). Their study demonstrated that employers, people with aphasia, and the SLTs differed in their thinking as to how to address these barriers. A larger study of 78 people with varied communication disabilities illustrated that some aspects of the workplace can present as barriers (such as noise or tasks requiring speed) regardless of the type of communication disability (Garcia,

Laroche, & Barrette, 2002). Bunning and Horton (2007, this issue) describe other issues that are shared across types of disability. Lock, Jordan, Maxim, and Bryan (2005) conducted focus groups with young stroke survivors and found a range of factors that acted as both enablers and barriers to work, including the rehabilitation process, the employer agency (e.g., employer's attitudes towards making reasonable adjustments in the workplace), social structural factors (e.g., inaccessible benefits system and lack of accessible information about searching for work or training), and personal factors (e.g., determination as an enabler; difficulties with memory, processing information, speech and language, vision etc. as barriers). Further detailed examples of difficulties with work, as well as information and services, are given as individual illustrations from the lives of people with severe aphasia in Parr (2007, this issue), described as "infrastructural aspects of social exclusion".

ACCESS AND THE ENVIRONMENT

In considering access, one is required to think about the environment; for example, an individual's *access to*, and *access in* the work environment, the supermarket, or their GP's surgery. Worrall and colleagues (2007, this issue) elaborate on this person–environment fit model in their paper. The role of the environment in promoting unconscious or subconscious access and inclusion (more often, *barriers* and *exclusion*) is often under-recognised, and the environment is seen as static, lifeless, physical structures and surfaces. Yet, viewing the environment as interdependent with its living users (and thus almost animate itself) aids in recognising and exploiting its true power. Simmons-Mackie and Damico (2007, this issue) discuss how social actions must be perceived as interdependent with context and interactions, and thus issues of access, barriers, and solutions cannot be treated as isolated concepts. One framework for conceptualising the relationship between users and their environment is the International Classification of Functioning, Disability and Health (ICF: World Health Organisation, 2001). The ICF is briefly introduced by Worrall and colleagues (2007, this issue) and then discussed in detail by Threats (2007, this issue) with respect to the importance of context affecting an individual's access. Briefly, one's access and participation in life can be hindered (*barriers*) or facilitated (*facilitators*) by a range of factors. Worrall and colleagues (2007, this issue) expound further how barriers and facilitators can be identified as affecting aphasic people's access in their community, while Simmons-Mackie and colleagues (2007, this issue) note these in relation to healthcare systems.

Access, when used in conjunction with "environment", has had a largely *physical* connotation, in the form of ramps, railings, toilet design, and doorways in built environments. Lubinski's work (1995) on physical access in dementia provides a useful example here, as she describes different ways for improving the physical access of residential home environments for people with dementia (e.g., "orientation friendly" corridors, floors, and rooms; wheelchair-accessible living areas; bathroom and call buttons access; etc.). Because these accessible features are implemented, the resident has *physical access* to (and in) the home environment. This notion of access for participating in environments can be broadened to extend the meaning of physical access, and to also include *psychological access* and *communicative access*.

Accessing the environment and beyond is more than being able to get about (and this may include being able to get about *communicatively* as well as physically), it is about a deeper level of access which constitutes a sense of belonging (Napolitano,

1996), or psychological access. Psychological barriers and access in the environment may be created both by others and by the disabled person. Garcia and colleagues (2002) described how employers viewed the attitudes of colleagues and the psychosocial adjustment, self-esteem, and confidence of the person with communication disability as possibly the greatest barriers to work reintegration. Parr, Byng, and Gilpin's study (1997) with aphasic individuals identified attitudinal barriers to work and leisure including embarrassment, sense of incompetence, loss of confidence, loss of self-worth, anxiety, fear, and depression.

This aspect of psychological access may also be demonstrated in conjunction with physical access or communicative access. Inclusive spaces, environments, and resources (including people) promote conscious or unconscious positive messages about one's importance and value (Napolitano, 1996), and thus exclusive spaces promote the reverse. People may claim their environments provide physical access facilities, but not all have *inclusive design*. For example, what message is being promoted when someone in a wheelchair has to go around the back of a building, past bins, and through the kitchen to get to a room? (Napolitano, 1996). It is likely that the individual using the wheelchair may have a negative psychological reaction to this devaluing and cumbersome experience, wherein the physical access that is provided appears as an afterthought in the design, and possibly a less costly alternative to building a ramp or lift. Conversely, inclusive design in physical environments indicates that the key users (disabled people) are considered at every step, efforts are made to provide for their comfort (particularly seating furniture), and the design fosters a sense of community.

Two papers in this issue describe and illustrate communicative access thoroughly (Pound, Duchan, Penman, Hewitt, & Parr, 2007, this issue; Simmons-Mackie, Kagan, O'Neill Christie, Huijbregts, McEwen, & Willems, 2007, this issue), which is the interpretation of access that has been the most discussed in aphasiology to date. (See seminal work of Parr and colleagues, 1997, regarding barriers experienced by people with aphasia.) In this issue, Simmons-Mackie and colleagues describe how communicative access training targeted at the systems level produced significant positive change in the acute care, rehabilitation, and long-term care systems that were providing services and care for people with aphasia. Simmons-Mackie and Damico (2007, this issue) also provide insights into the values and expectations around communication and competence that underlie the social interactions between people with aphasia and their conversation partners. Raising awareness of the power of communication is needed to aid our shared campaign in raising public awareness of aphasia (Simmons-Mackie & Damico, 2007, this issue; Worrall et al., 2007, this issue).

A similar paper regarding sustainable whole systems change by Pound and colleagues (2007, this issue) describes in detail how Connect have championed communicative access as a pathway to inclusion in their organisation. Their paper gives useful examples about *what* can be done to achieve communication access, and the message of *how* to create communication access is clear. Pound and colleagues' paper also exemplifies *psychological access*, as members of the centre described a sense of belonging. Both communicative and psychological access are also evident in the work of Simmons-Mackie and Kagan (1999), who described how "good" speaking partners use specific techniques to reveal the aphasic person's competence. Simmons-Mackie and Damico (2007, this issue) elaborate on how acceptance and accommodation to nonstandard forms of communication facilitate inclusion of people with aphasia in conversations. Finally, recent research into access and participation in service users and medical practitioners' consultations demonstrates the interdependence of information access, processes of communication, and inclusion (Law et al., 2005).

ACCESS FOR INCLUSION FOR QUALITY IN LIFE

Although access and inclusion are different constructs, they are clearly related, seen as a pathway or conduit for inclusion (Pound et al.), and thus enabling people to achieve quality in life. Researchers Raphael, Brown, Renwick, and others, in the Quality of Life Research Unit (QLRU, 1995), provide an alternative (i.e., non-health) conceptualisation of quality of life (QoL) as *being*, *belonging*, and *becoming*, wherein life (and social inclusion) is constantly changing, minute by minute—a theme reiterated by Parr (2007, this issue) in her documentation of social exclusion and inclusion of people with aphasia. The notion of *belonging* is described as the connections with one's environment in three different ways: (1) with physical belonging in the home, workplace/school, neighbourhood, community; (2) with social belonging connecting with intimate others, family, friends, co-workers, and neighbourhood and community; and (3) with community belonging, which represents access to resources for all community members, namely adequate income, health and social services, employment, education and recreational programmes, and community events and activities (QLRU, 1995). Thus, for people with and without disabilities to feel a sense of belonging or inclusion in their community, they need to find their connections with these environments as *physically, psychologically and communicatively accessible*.

CONCLUSION

Access provides people with aphasia with a number of opportunities: information or communication access for decision making (see Simmons-Mackie et al.); access to be included in conversations (Simmons-Mackie & Damico); access to be socially included in life (Parr) and the community (Worrall et al.); and access for participating and contributing to the development of new services and the running of an organisation (Pound et al.). This issue demonstrates how access and inclusion can be studied at different levels—at a systems level (e.g., Bunning & Horton; Pound et al.; Simmons-Mackie et al.), a dyad level (e.g., Simmons-Mackie & Damico), an individual level (e.g., Worrall et al.), or using a different conceptualisation (e.g., infrastructural, interpersonal, and personal levels of social exclusion; Parr). Authors' contributions illustrate how all endeavours are necessary in developing our understanding and evidence base in access and inclusion.

Although authors have offered different insights into how we can continue moving forward in facilitating accessible and inclusive societies, all the papers unite on two points: (1) it is time to do things differently to achieve greater access and inclusion; and (2) the issues are not specific to people with aphasia, but rather shared with others who have communication disabilities, and indeed people with other forms of disability. Therefore, combining our knowledge bases, experience, skills, and resources will lead to more effective outcomes in communicative access and inclusion than pursuing the road for people with aphasia alone.

REFERENCES

Bunning, K., & Horton, S. (2007, this issue). "Border crossing" as a route to inclusion: A shared cause with people with a learning disability? *Aphasiology, 21*(1), 9–22.

Egan, J., Worrall, L., & Oxenham, D. (2004). Accessible Internet training package helps people with aphasia cross the digital divide. *Aphasiology, 18*(3), 265–280.

Garcia, L., Barrette, J., & Laroche, C. (2000). Perceptions of the obstacles to work reintegration for persons with aphasia. *Aphasiology, 14*(3), 269–290.

Garcia, L., Laroche, C., & Barrette, J. (2002). Work integration issues go beyond the nature of the communication disorder. *Journal of Communication Disorders, 35*, 187–211.

Law, J., Bunning, K., Byng, S., Farrelly, S., & Heyman, B. (2005). Making sense in primary care: Levelling the playing field for people with communication difficulties. *Disability & Society, 20*(2), 169–184.

Lock, S., Jordan, L., Bryan, K., & Maxim, J. (2005). Work after stroke: Focusing on barriers and enablers. *Disability & Society, 20*(1), 33–47.

Lubinski, R. (1995). *Dementia and communication*. San Diego, CA: Singular Publishing.

Napolitano, S. (1996). Mobility impairment. In G. Hales (Ed.), *Beyond disability: Towards an enabling society* (pp. 30–35). London: Sage Publications.

Parr, S. (2007, this issue). Living with severe aphasia: Tracking social exclusion. *Aphasiology, 21*(1), 98–123.

Parr, S., Byng, S., Gilpin, S., & with Ireland, C. (1997). *Talking about aphasia: Living with loss of language after stroke*. Buckingham, UK: Open University Press.

Parr, S., Moss, B., Newberry, J., Petheram, B., & Byng, S. (2005). *Inclusive Internet technologies for people with communication impairment*. Research report retrieved from URL http://www.york.ac.uk/res/iht/projects/l218252051/ParrFindings.pdf [retrieved on 17 September 2005].

Pound, C., Duchan, J., Penman, T., Hewitt, A., & Parr, S. (2007, this issue). Communication access to organisations: Inclusionary practices for people with aphasia. *Aphasiology, 21*(1), 23–38.

Quality of Life Research Unit (QLRU). (1995). *Quality of life concepts: The quality of life model*. Newsletter (vol. 1, no. 1, September) retrieved from URL http:///www.utoronto.ca/qol/concepts.htm [retrieved on 17 September 2005].

Ramcharan, P., Roberts, G., Grant, G., & Borland, J. (1997). *Empowerment in everyday life: Learning disability*. London: Jessica Kingsley Publishers.

Simmons-Mackie, N., & Damico, J. S. (2007, this issue). Access and social inclusion in aphasia: Interactional principles and applications. *Aphasiology, 21*(1), 81–97.

Simmons-Mackie, N., & Kagan, A. (1999). Communication strategies used by "good" versus "poor" speaking partners of people with aphasia. *Aphasiology, 13*(9–11), 807–820.

Simmons-Mackie, N., Kagan, A., O'Neill Christie, C., Huijbregts, M., McEwen, S., & Willems, J. (2007, this issue). Communicative access and decision making for people with aphasia: Implementing sustainable healthcare systems change. *Aphasiology, 21*(1), 39–66.

The American Heritage Dictionary of the English Language. (2000). *The American Heritage Dictionary of the English Language* (4th ed.). Houghton Mifflin Company. Accessed 11 September 2005 from http://dictionary.reference.com/search?q=access.

Threats, T. (2007, this issue). Access for persons with neurogenic communication disorders: Influences of Personal and Environmental Factors of the ICF. *Aphasiology, 21*(1), 67–80.

World Health Organisation. (2001). *International classification of functioning, disability and health*. Geneva: WHO.

Worrall, L., Rose, T., Howe, T., McKenna, K., & Hickson, L. (2007, this issue). Developing an evidence-base for accessibility for people with aphasia. *Aphasiology, 21*(1), 124–136.

APHASIOLOGY, 2007, 21 (1), 9–22

ψ Psychology Press
Taylor & Francis Group

"Border crossing" as a route to inclusion: A shared cause with people with a learning disability?

Karen Bunning and Simon Horton

University of East Anglia, Norwich, UK

Background: A raft of legislation and social policy has been published in the United Kingdom to progress social inclusion for people with disabilities. Access and participation are central to the notion of inclusive living, which is about being part of a community that is sensitive to the ways of living and the needs of *all* its members. However, having a disability means that opportunities are not dealt out in equal measure and occupying a "place in society" is rarely an assured thing. The opposite of inclusion is exclusion. This implies barriers to and remoteness from mainstream activity, where fewer opportunities may be available for self-expression and to influence the actions of others (Scott & Larcher, 2002).
Aims: This paper seeks to broaden the debate on inclusion for people with aphasia by drawing on the documented experiences of people with learning disabilities, the development of practice initiatives, and visions for the future. The extent to which the narratives of people with aphasia find resonance in the life course of people with a learning disability gives rise to a simple question: "Is inclusion a shared cause?"
Main Contribution: Addressing diverse client groups, such as people with aphasia and people with a learning disability, draws out the common experience, despite their separate traditions of service provision. Living with a disabling condition, whether physical, communicative, or intellectual, whether developmental or acquired in type, means that the usual determinants of social inclusion often appear elusive. Review of UK government policy and assessment of its impact on the two communities (people with aphasia and people with a learning disability) reveals the limitations of a single-track approach. The need for collaborative action involving multiple agencies at the mutually dependent levels of self, community, and society becomes clear. Synthesis of the literature and practice development initiatives from the two clinical groups serves to strengthen the ongoing debate. The right to be included is shared by *all* human beings regardless of individual characteristics. It is about having the opportunities to perform roles that are personally meaningful, to develop relationships, to engage in self-determination, and to have presence in the places that other people occupy.
Conclusion: No matter the primary *cause* of the disability, marginalisation is frequently a feature of the lived experience. For people with aphasia, it is the impact of having a communication difficulty on quality of life that leads to disruptions to sense of self, autonomy and choice, social life and community participation (Cruice, Worrall, Hickson, & Murison, 2003). For people with learning disabilities, it is the incremental disempowerment with regard to the uptake of societal roles as maturation takes place (Barnes, 1997). The concept of "border crossing" is pertinent to the cause of *both* groups. It captures the many different ways in which individuals break out of the traditional roles cast for people with disabilities, and engage in self-advocacy. For individuals who grow up with a learning disability "border crossing" is affected by the

Address correspondence to: Karen Bunning, School of Allied Health Professions, University of East Anglia, Norwich NR4 2TJ, UK. E-mail: k.bunning@uea.ac.uk

© 2007 Psychology Press, an imprint of the Taylor & Francis Group, an informa business
http://www.psypress.com/aphasiology   DOI: 10.1080/02687030600798162

surrounding social support infrastructure offered by statutory services, which is informed by targeted government policy. For people with acquired language impairment, the terrain is less clear. After the initial medical crisis has passed, it is the individual's personal context (characterised by the roles and responses of marital partner, family members, work colleagues, etc.) rather than statutory service provision, that affects the degree to which individuals are able to resume former life courses.

The extent to which a person is included is not simply a matter of "inborn characteristics" (Ramcharan, Roberts, Grant, & Borland, 1997, p. 253); rather it concerns phenomena that have been socially engineered. The history of learning disability services provides a good illustration: the institutional care provision of the 1900s up until the inception of new community-based services in the latter part of the twentieth century literally ensured the non-participation of people with learning disabilities in mainstream society (O'Brien cited in Tyne, 1981). Four years on from the publication of the UK government white paper *Valuing People*—aimed at services for people with learning disabilities (Department of Health, 2001a)—there have been a number of practical developments to support access and participation. However, the debate is still open.

The question of inclusion is also relevant to people who experience onset of communication difficulty in adulthood. The social actions of everyday living become far from straightforward. An assortment of barriers may inhibit access and participation, ranging from environmental, such as ambient noise levels, fast rates of conversation, and elliptical turn-taking, to structural, leading to opportunity restrictions and poor availability of support; from attitudinal, manifested in ignorance and lack of comprehension by others, to informational, characterised by inaccessible linguistic code leading to many unanswered questions (Law, Bunning, Byng, Farrelly, & Heyman, 2005; Parr, Byng, & Gilpin, 1997). Factors affecting work integration for people with aphasia include organisational, e.g., task demands and work productivity demands, electronic tools, and use of telephone; and societal, e.g., attitudes of interlocutors, awareness of disorder, and realities of the job market (Garcia, Laroche, & Barrette, 2000). The severity of a person's aphasia may be critical. It appears to correspond to greater social functioning limitations (Cruice et al., 2003) and serves as a predictor for health-related issues (Hilari, Wiggins, Roy, Byng, & Smith, 2003).

BORDER CROSSING

Just how far has the concept of inclusion moved away from simple rhetoric towards the lived experience? A series of questions signal the debate in this review, starting with consideration of the impact of legislation and social policy in the UK, moving on to the role of community action, and finally the process of self-advocacy. The interactions that take place *between* and *at* each level of the ecological system are critical to the debate on inclusion.

"Border crossing" captures the idea of an ecological system where there is interplay between the person and the context. The concept was introduced to the disability literature by Peters (1996). As with the term *advocacy*, "border crossing" does not simply refer to an arbitrary set of standards. It is a process of movement and change across an ecological system of mutual dependencies—at the levels of society, community, and self—where each level exerts reciprocal influences on the other two. This finds resonance in Bronfenbrenner's (1979, 2005) ecological systems theory, which defines the interaction between the changing person and the dynamic context. He identifies a series of subsystems that move in concentric circles from the person outwards to the "microsystems" or different communities that are relevant to individual life course, e.g., family, friendship group, etc. Each microsystem, although not exclusive to the others, has its own "pattern of activities, roles, and interpersonal relations" (2005, p. 148). Surrounding the "microsystem" is the "macrosystem" which Bronfenbrenner (2005) views as the "social blueprint for a particular culture, subculture or other broader social context" (p. 150). The significance of government legislation and social policy as a source of influence over the inner layers of the ecological system is considered in the following section.

LEGISLATION AND SOCIAL POLICY

To what extent is successful "border crossing" dependent on the social infrastructure? Legislation and social policy offer some ways in which the passage of change may be engineered (Dalrymple & Burke, 1995). Review of UK government policy reveals the growing enthusiasm for involving the public in decisions that affect their lives. The creation of a patient-led National Health Service (NHS) stems from observations that, within the system, there are "barriers and blockages, professional and organisational boundaries, vested interests and perverse incentives" (Department of Health, 2005, p. 7). The document is clear in its aspirations for improvements in listening to, understanding, and responding to people, and of the importance of patient and public involvement in everyday practice, which must lead to action for improvement. The exercise of choice is the starting point for this involvement, but further mechanisms are outlined, including Patient Advice and Liaison Services (PALS), patient forums, and NHS Foundation Trust Boards. Changes towards a patient-led NHS will be managed towards 2008 through a number of initiatives, including listening events, stakeholder forums, and continuing discussion with local communities.

These proposals should also be considered in the light of the Wanless Report (Wanless, 2002)—an evidence-based assessment of the long-term resource require- ments for the NHS. The report proposed a more effective partnership between health professionals and the public through reinforcing patient involvement in NHS accountability arrangements. The report led to a huge boost in NHS funding, but "the Treasury made clear, however, that the NHS cash lifeline is conditional on radical reforms in working practices, patients' freedoms ..." (Moore, 2002, p. 993).

The Wanless Report also looked forward to an extension of the UK government's National Service Framework (NSF) approach. A number of NSFs have been published by the Department of Health (e.g., Department of Health, NSF for Older People, 2001b). The aim of these framework documents is to set out a programme of action and reform to address current problems in the delivery of healthcare for specific groups. For example, in the NSF for Older People, the aim of achieving person-centred care requires health service professionals to listen, recognise individual differences and specific needs, and enable older people to make informed choices, involving them in all decisions about their needs and care.

Despite the best efforts of the law makers and policy developers, the reality of implementation is far from problem free. While legislation and social policy provide relevant frameworks to promote change in the prevailing culture, transformation of societal values and attitudes cannot be forced. The operationalisation of the UK Disability Discrimination Act (Department for Education and Employment: Disability Discrimination Act, 1995) has not meant an end to discriminatory practice; rather it has led to a number of cases being referred to tribunal (Casserley, 2000). It could be said that such legislation contributes to consciousness raising among the public, providing both the framework and the impetus for individual challenges to the status quo.

While policy initiatives and action documents set out proposals for a patient-led NHS and highlight a number of key principles—for example, listening and responding to patients, the involvement of patients and public in everyday practice, the exercise of choice—these documents give little insight into the ways in which these principles could be put into operation for people with aphasia (or any other communication impairment). Law et al. (2005) interviewed three constituencies of service users—adults with aphasia, adults with learning disabilities, and young people with specific language impairment—about the degree to which they felt involved in the consultation process with their general practitioners. Feelings of not belonging or being bypassed were commonly expressed. Inaccessibility of information, whether verbally presented or written, contributed to the frustrations experienced. This finds resonance in a study conducted by Cottrell and Davies (2004) who reported that the overriding concern of patients with aphasia was lack of participation in their own rehabilitative care—they felt excluded from ward rounds and discussions. Parr (2004) also found a mismatch between the needs of people with aphasia and the provision of services. For example, service providers typically did not know how to maximise understanding and expression, and as a result, consultation and choice were rarely in evidence. Remarkably, highlighting this deficiency did not ensure the provision of more information and support in communicating with people with severe aphasia. Instead, physical rather than communication needs were prioritised in their training. Cottrell and Davies (2004) stress the need for all healthcare professionals to provide explanations backed up by aphasia-friendly visual aids to involve users at all levels of decision making. Parr (2004) underlines the importance of training and support for communication, which is a fundamental concern, even though it is rarely prioritised over physical issues. With the right level and type of support she argues that people with aphasia can express choices, wishes, and concerns, and engage in enjoyable and productive activity.

Of course, the mediating role of the caregiver should not be overlooked. It is one that affects the lives of people with aphasia *and* those with a learning disability. Partners, parents, relatives, or paid carers frequently fulfil the role of intermediary, providing critical support for individuals in carrying out the activities associated with daily living. Law et al. (2005) recognised the caregiver's role in interpreting the information given by GPs so that it is accessible to the individual who has a communication impairment. However, inequalities in status and social standing in the caregiver–care receiver relationship are usually present (Dowson, 1997). By reconfiguring the person as a "service user", the individual is viewed as a consumer of services and therefore an active agent as opposed to a passive recipient. Exactly how far individual service users can realise their ambitions within "the care, welfare and protection model" and take their place in society is a moot point (Stalker, 2002, p. 50). The agendas of caregiver and service user may be juxtaposed such that access and participation exists only on the terms of the person in a position of power, i.e., the caregiver. The personal views, experiences, and judgements of those recruited to support and facilitate those who experience difficulties may interfere with an honest and relevant advocacy process.

Having a philosophy of social inclusion does not necessarily make it so. There is the matter of defining and developing the technologies to put it into practice. Where is the provision—training and resources, for example—for staff to support the inclusion of people with communication impairments? Where is the provision for the fundamental re-education of values for NHS staff, i.e., training in disability and diversity? These are the "wicked issues" that require address on a number of levels.

WICKED ISSUES

The term *wicked issues* has been more commonly used to refer to the complex problems faced by central and local government planners for which there is no single solution or outcome (Rittel & Webber, 1973). Used here, it refers to the complications that people encounter, the unequal share in community living, the things that disrupt, inconvenience, and disallow fulfilment of personally valued roles. Resolution is achieved through multi-agency collaboration that involves local action at the levels of community and self.

The use of low-technology augmentative communication methods provides a good example of practice that supports interaction between self and community. "Talking Mats" (TMs) have been employed variously with people with aphasia *and* people with learning disabilities. TMs involve the selection of graphic symbols, usually generated from Widgit software (*Picture Communication System*: Johnson, 1994; *Rebus*: Woodcock, Clark, & Davis, 1968) and backed with Velcro^{TM} for attachment to a woven mat. The idea is to support the construction of meaning and to provide a visual record of views expressed. TMs have been used to support client discussions on quality-of-life matters, goals for rehabilitation, and plans for discharge from hospital (Murphy, 2000), as well as facilitating choice, expression of preferences, and making lifestyle decisions (Murphy & Cameron, 2002a, 2002b).

Other examples are to be found in the development of speech and language therapy (SLT) practice for people with aphasia that does not restrict its focus to the individual, but extends to the external environment. The six goals for aphasia intervention proposed by Byng, Pound, and Parr (2000) include identifying and dismantling barriers to social participation, and the promotion of autonomy and choice. The life participation approach to aphasia (LPAA) advocated by Chapey et al. (2001) is consumer driven, and emphasises re-engagement in life, with the therapy context consisting of real-life social interactions, and family members and the larger community as active contributors to the rehabilitation process (Boles & Lewis, 2003). For example, Avent and Austermann (2003) report a case study of a man who was a former physicist, and who developed moderate aphasia. The study explored the potential therapeutic value of increasing participation in life through natural language use with communicative partners during shared learning activities. The authors followed changes to the man's language, psychosocial well-being, and quality of life as he taught science to 4- and 5-year-old children. The results indicated better verbal word retrieval skills within the classroom ("Reciprocal Scaffolding Treatment") as compared with aphasia group treatment. His journal entries also indicated improvements in quality of life. The authors argue that the value of this approach lies in the way the therapeutic context of treatment is extended to include mutually beneficial outcomes for all participants—the individual with aphasia, family friends, and the children taught by the patient.

A study by Lasker, LaPointe, and Kodras (2005) used an innovative synthesis of intervention methods in a life participation model, which involved multi-modal approaches—the application of voice-output technology with the use of residual speech skills. JK, a university professor with aphasia, took part in a simulated classroom teaching exercise. Her teaching and communication skills were rated by students under two different conditions: use of voice-output device and limited natural speech; and use of voice-output device, natural speech, and a Key Word Teaching technique. Students expressed greater satisfaction with the learning process under the second condition. In addition, they commented that JK appeared "more at ease" (p. 408), which was borne out by video recordings of the teaching sessions. The authors comment on the emergence of collaborative word finding between JK and her students. This study demonstrates the benefits of multiple strategies applied to particular situated needs experienced by an individual, which impact positively on both students and teacher.

LESSONS FROM THE LEARNING-DISABILITY COMMUNITY

Unlike the approach taken with people with aphasia, which depends largely on local enterprise, a systemic approach has been taken to the configuration of modern-day services for people with learning disabilities in the UK, starting with the community care legislation that has introduced the development of individual packages of care based on an assessment of need by social services (Department of Health, 1990) and the option to exercise some control over the purchase of resources to meet support needs (Department of Health, 1996). Although the original intentions may have been altruistic, the reality has been rather short of the mark. Care plans containing complex language forms and imprecise implementation methods have restricted the degree to which service users are able to be actively involved in the process. More recently, the publication of the UK government white paper *Valuing people: A new strategy for learning disability for the 21st century* (Department of Health, 2001a) took up the cause for social inclusion by calling for collaboration between all agencies. It set out the UK government's proposals for "improving the lives of people with learning disabilities and their families and carers" through deliberate attention to independence, choice, civil rights, and social inclusion (p. 10). Strong encouragement has been given to service user representation on partnership boards that are responsible for developing local services, and to the establishment of a range of local advocacy schemes.

The main strategy for inclusion in *Valuing People* is through the mechanism of person-centred planning (Department of Health, 2001a), whereby strong collaborations between relevant agencies in partnership with the service user are facilitated. Planning meetings are held, at which the service user is usually present and facilitated to participate in the discussions and decisions concerning lifestyle and occupations (Carnaby, 2002). However, putting a mechanism in place does not ensure inclusive practice. The dispersal of residents of learning disability institutions to ordinary housing in the 1980s showed that inclusion was not simply a matter of community placement (Felce & Perry, 1996). Alongside person-centred planning, there is the imperative to develop workable communication policies and to harness the advocacy process (Department of Health, 2001a).

The use of multiple media provides some valuable and creative options for addressing barriers to access and participation. It allows for the augmentation of meaning beyond the conventional forms of the written and spoken word. The learning-disability community has long embraced the use of augmentative and alternative communication strategies, e.g., Makaton signing vocabulary (Walker, 1980), to promote effective communication. More recently, particularly in the field of special needs education, interest has grown in the use of information and communication technology (ICT) (Stevens, 2004). The work of the Rix Centre at the University of East London in conjunction with Mencap (leading UK charity for individuals with learning disability and their families: http://www.mencap.org.uk) has been instrumental in pursuing this agenda for the learning-disability community. The development of an ambitious Internet Portal to connect the learning-disability community with ICT developers and researchers has heralded the way for further initiatives. It provides support, tools, and inspiration to use the Internet to produce accessible and self-made content, and to exchange views and experiences (see: http://www.thebigtree.org).

A linked development is "Trans-active", supported by Mencap, which is a tool that uses digital photography and a simple Do-It-Yourself multimedia authoring software package to create individual "Passports" (see online example at: http://www.trans-active.org.uk/adult/index.htm). These are interactive multimedia albums in which young people capture their options and choices for adulthood. Importantly, Trans-active has a built-in mechanism for bringing people with learning disabilities into close working relationships with their typically developing peers in mainstream education, who learn how to be good "peer supporters". Collaborative practice in the development and use of the passport supports the communication of personal perspectives. Passports can then be used outside learning settings, e.g., to help people contribute to their own review meeting with professional carers about their future. Inclusion is thus facilitated by the process of interpersonal advocacy whereby the agenda of the service user is revealed through the empowering practice of the peer supporter.

The work of Trans-active is currently being extended by "Project @pple" (see http://www.thebigtree.org/p_apple/index.htm). This is a $2\frac{1}{2}$-year study supported by a major research funder in the UK—the Economic and Social Research Council. The project is part of their People at the Centre of Communication Information Technology (PACCIT) programme (http://www.ost.gov.uk/link/paccit.htm). It is focused on the development of a unique collection of the most effective e-learning tools and materials. In this context, general use of cameras and sound technology, video, the World Wide Web, digital drawing skills, scanning, and even photo-capable mobile phones constitute the e-learning opportunity. It aims to explore different ways of using accessible authoring packages, like the Trans-active passport, for the development of independent living skills and choices for people with a learning disability who find auditory and text-based learning difficult.

For the learning-disability community, the outcomes of using ICT and e-learning are manifold. Computers offer access benefits to people with disabilities, e.g., optional adaptation for input by switch, as well as output options that move beyond text to graphics. Improved integration of pupils with special educational needs in mainstream classes has been reported (Rahamin, 2004), along with enhanced learning and self-esteem (Hedley, 2004). Such initiatives have clearly benefited from research and development of ICT in mainstream education.

In the field of aphasia, interest in computing and ICT has predominantly focused on the use of personal computers in the delivery of therapy programmes, especially in relation to facilitating independent practice of therapy tasks (e.g., Petheram, 1996). The rapid development of ICT, however, threatens to exclude people with aphasia from daily life, where Internet usage is expanding all the time, both in the home and in the public arena (e.g., Internet cafes, public libraries). While research and service delivery in the field of Internet and systems access is in its infancy, there have been some small-scale developments addressing accessibility needs specific to people with aphasia. For example, Blenkhorn and Hawes (2002) point out that work on developing and improving physical accessibility to computer systems is not enough for people with communication impairments. Picture-based systems are an obvious answer for people with reading/writing impairments, but most of these systems have been developed for use by children and are inappropriate for adults with acquired aphasia. Blenkhorn and Hawes discuss the use of "pre-stored vocabularies" or "applications" in conjunction with the use of dynamic screen systems that allow the user to build sentences by picture selection. The use of "HandsOff"—an on-screen keyboard—allows control of the Windows environment with the ability to use published pre-stored vocabularies in face-to-face communication, word processing, and email programmes. In terms of Internet access, Anderson and Nielsen (2001) discuss the use of a system ("myZiteEdit®"), which enables the delivery of technology to the user in terms of their own level of need. For example, if the user needs "sound augmentation" the system can be adapted so that when s/he visits their own personal website the text for the various buttons is read aloud. Adaptation of the system to the user's needs requires an assistant to help determine the appearance of the user's website. Finally, Parr, Moss, Newbery, Petheram, and Byng (2003) explored the issues of access to the Internet using participative and action research methods. People with aphasia were involved in evaluating barriers to accessing information and support of health- and disability-related websites. The study also investigated the potential of the Internet as a means of expressing identity and sharing narrative, when talking and writing is difficult. The key output for that project was a website (http://www.aphasiahelp.org/) which was built to demonstrate accessible design. The authors conclude that the Internet has enormous potential as a vehicle for communication for this group of users. It offers a means of contacting and supporting others as long as barriers to access can be overcome.

QUEST FOR CHANGE

While legislation has the potential to bring more cohesion to social policy on disability, the question of implementation is left, in the main, to local interpretation (Waddington, 2000). The Department of Health in the UK has recently (2004–5) commissioned a consultation on the future support arrangements for patient and public involvement in health (PPI). This was carried out by Opinion Leader Research, an independent survey organisation. Interestingly, in the responses to two of the open questions on the important issues about staff support that should be provided for PPI forums (Q6) and other important issues in the effective working of PPI forums (Q12), only 0.2% (8/4146) of respondents made any mention of disability, or support to enable people with a disability to become involved. Whether the notion of "communication disability" as opposed to physical disability is really understood at all is a moot point.

There are UK Department of Health initiated mechanisms for supporting changes in practice at a local level. For example, *The Essence of Care* (UK Department of Health Modernisation Agency, 2001; 2003) has been designed to support the measures to improve quality, and to contribute to the introduction of clinical governance at a local level. The benchmarking process outlined in *The Essence of Care* is designed to help practitioners take a structured approach to improving practice in a number of areas, including "communication" (added in 2003), "continence", "hygiene", "pressure ulcers", "privacy and dignity", and "self care".

The "NHS Live programme" supports local innovation in the way services are delivered, developing a "bottom-up" approach to improvement to complement other national programmes. Support for front-line patient-centred projects is aimed at improving the staff and patient experience, and NHS Live is claimed to be a proven catalyst for change (Department of Health, 2005). The aim is for staff, patients, and the local health community to work in partnerships to find innovative solutions to patient needs.

Increasing numbers of speech and language therapists are moving towards a more collaborative or social/participation approach to therapy. However, there is still evidence from a number of sources that indicates continued uncertainty about how to translate the principles of collaborative decision making into meaningful and effective interactions with clients (Freeman, 2004). It may be helpful to re-conceptualise Peters' (1996) "border crossing" as a two-sided interface that represents movement for the service provider as well as the service user. Successful "border crossing" is not simply the *physical* presence of people with particular support needs in the places where decisions are made. It presupposes openness to all at the heart of the social infrastructure (Lindsay & Dockrell, 2002).

A QUESTION OF VALUES?

If, as Von Tetzchner, Grove, Loncke, Barnett, Woll, and Clibbens (1996) point out, communication really is at the heart of the relationship between an individual and society, then something needs to done about the shortfall experienced by people who have difficulties in everyday communication. To be included means having an equal place in situations where human engagement happens (Kenworthy & Whittaker, 2000). It implies acceptance of and support for diverse ways of communicating and engaging socially (Bunning, 2004). So what the person has to say through the use of graphic and gestural communication to support impaired language is attributed the same worth as the person who communicates through intact linguistic code. The question is how to foreground communication so that individual difficulties are addressed and personal agendas are heard. Although some programmes have attempted to address the communication problem through training practitioners in new communication behaviours (Silverman, Kurtz, & Draper, 1997), unless there is a concurrent examination of values to underpin practice, actual change may be difficult to achieve (Law et al., 2005).

Values are the guiding principles that capture the vision and philosophy of a community. They underpin the way individuals and community react and interact. Many community services for people with learning disabilities were originally fashioned according to the principles of *social role valorisation* (SRV) where value was given to the many different social roles that an individual may have during a lifetime (Wolfensberger, 1992). These have recently been reshaped to embrace the *Valuing People* statements of intent—namely, "recognition of their rights as citizens, social inclusion in local communities, choice in their daily lives and real opportunities to be independent." (Department of Health, 2001a, p. 10). In the world of aphasia, the London Centre of Connect, the communication disability network, provides a therapeutic environment that reflects an ethos of "live(ing) healthily with communication disability" (Byng, Cairns & Duchan, 2002, p. 98). Similarly, as part of its mandate, the Aphasia Institute in Toronto, Canada, embraces the notion of *communicative access* as key to life participation. The need for interventions to take consideration of both individual and environmental factors is stressed (Kagan & LeBlanc, 2002).

ADVOCACY PROCESS

Advocacy may hold the key to a cause shared by people with aphasia and people with learning disabilities. As a process, it seeks to oppose discriminatory practice and provide a "counter movement to state paternalism" (Goodley, 2000, p. 3). Goble (2002) makes a distinction between *advocacy* with a small "a" and *Advocacy* with a capital "A". The former is "conducted within the limits and constraints of service systems" (p. 73). As such, it falls to the role of professionals and local entrepreneurs to institute changes to services and to make practical responses to government policies and legislation. Also referred to as citizen advocacy, this form of advocacy finds resonance in normalisation theory, later termed social role valorisation (SRV), which has provided the philosophical backdrop for learning disability services (Walmsley, 2002). Citizen advocacy is needed to make up for the inadequacies in service organisations (Clement, 2002) and provides the setting conditions for self-advocacy (Byng et al., 2002). However, on its own and without the contribution of service users, in particular those people who are at risk of devaluation, the seat of power remains firmly with the service provider.

Self-advocacy, or "Advocacy" with a capital A, is "social and political, rather than systemic in nature" (Goble, 2002, p. 73). It is about the mobilisation of resources in response to self-expression by an individual or group of individuals. Self-advocacy frequently involves the review of life experiences, thereby enabling understanding of both past experiences and the present culture so that the future may be influenced (Young & Quibell, 2000). Pound, Parr, Lindsay, and Woolf (2000) describe the use of personal portfolios with people with aphasia at the London Centre of Connect (Connect – the communication disability network: http://www.ukconnect.org). The individual collates information about his/her life that relates to the past, what is happening now, and any future goals, plans, hopes, and aspirations. The individual becomes the "expert witness" and is thus empowered to challenge the present state of affairs (Atkinson, 2002).

Sometimes individuals come together to form a self-advocacy group so that common causes may be addressed. "People First" is a national self-advocacy organisation founded in the UK in the 1970s (see an example of self-advocacy group at: http://www.peoplefirst.org.uk/pflinks.html). It is run by and for people with learning disabilities, providing a forum for social and political commentary, developing campaigns for improved rights, and for educating the general public. Because representation of views is carried out by and for the people to whom it is relevant, it establishes integrity at the heart of the process. Regardless of where the advocacy process stems from, whether it originates from the service user or from the professional (or local service entrepreneur), the main drive is to open the channels of communication so that individuals, who are at risk of *not* being heard, *are* heard. For those in a position to influence the way services are provided, i.e., the professionals employed within the service, there is a need to develop suitable operational policies that look at service accessibility, amenability, and responsiveness to the ideas and commentary of the client group (Mosely, 1994). Thus a sort of service advocacy corresponds to a process of self-advocacy. Naturally, just how service user views are represented demands careful planning in terms of material resources and immediate support from communication partners, so that representation happens in whatever forum it needs to happen. Having access to information is vital if service users are to influence the ways in which services operate (Grant, 1997). Included in this is the right of redress, so that access to complaints procedures is straightforward.

Finally, the point at which self-advocacy and "service advocacy" come together rests on the process of communication. This has been referred to as "interpersonal advocacy", where the locus of power within an interaction is equally dispersed among the interlocutors so that inclusive communication happens (Bunning, 2004). Interestingly, both Stirling (2003) and Shale (2004) outline the benefits of using supported conversation training approaches in the acute setting as part of the process of inclusion for people with aphasia. These interventions resulted in changes in attitude and practice among healthcare staff. However, such a communication partnership is neither swiftly nor easily achieved (Scott & Larcher, 2002). It is dependent on the setting factors of "service advocacy" and the self-advocacy process.

SHARING THE CAUSE?

It is very much the case that the development of devices and strategic frameworks to address the access and participation difficulties tend to be client-group specific and driven by local entrepreneurs. Obvious differences in approach exist: the learning-disability community in the UK benefits from a systemic approach aimed at shaping community social services, which provides a fertile background for "border crossing" to take place, while people with aphasia are reliant on the local enterprise of self, family, and professionals. However, both client groups are users of public services. Of what concern are the origins of a patient's communication difficulties to the general health practitioner? The most pressing need is how to engage in the consultation process, so that the individual has access to the relevant information and is able to contribute at the stage when negotiation of symptoms takes place (Law et al., 2005). If the institutional practices of public services are to be influenced for the better, then surely the most effective way is to pool energies and to galvanise resources for the common good? It may be timely for some mutual "border crossing" by professionals in the two communities!

The concept of "border crossing" is similar to the advocacy process where access, participation, and inclusion are key accomplishments. It is relevant to *both* people with aphasia *and* adults with learning disabilities, and involves a range of collaborative relationships—between people who have experiences and needs in common; between service provider and user; between partners; and between caregiver and person receiving care. A shared cause it most certainly is.

REFERENCES

Andersen, T., & Nielsen, M. B. (2001). Removing barriers to the Internet for people with cognitive disabilities by the use of myZiteEdit®. *Proceedings of the Technology and Persons with Disabilities Conference*. California State University, Northridge, Los Angeles, CA, USA.

Atkinson, D. (2002). Self-advocacy and research. In B. Gray & R. Jackson (Eds.), *Advocacy & learning disability* (pp. 120–36). London: Jessica Kingsley.

Avent, J., & Austermann, S. (2003). Reciprocal scaffolding: A context for communication treatment in aphasia. *Aphasiology, 17*(4), 397–404.

Barnes, M. (1997). Families and empowerment. In P. Ramcharan, G. Roberts, G. Grant, & J. Borland (Eds.), *Empowerment in everyday life – Learning disability* (pp. 241–58). London: Jessica Kingsley.

Blenkhorn, P., & Hawes, P. (2002). Bridging the gap between aspiration and capability and brain injured people. *Proceedings of the Technology and Persons with Disabilities Conference*. California State University, Northridge, Los Angeles, CA, USA.

Boles, L., & Lewis, M. (2003). Life participation approaches to aphasia: International perspectives on communication rehabilitation. *Journal of Social Work in Disability and Rehabilitation, 2*(2/3), 47–64.

Bronfenbrenner, U. (1979). *The ecology of human development: Experiments by nature and design*. Cambridge, MA: Harvard University Press.

Bronfenbrenner, U. (2005). Ecological systems theory. In U. Bronfenbrenner (Ed.), *Making human beings human – Bioecological perspectives on human development* (pp. 106–173). London: Sage Publications.

Bunning, K. (2004). *Speech and language therapy intervention: Frameworks and processes*. London: Whurr Publishers Ltd.

Byng, S., Cairns, D., & Duchan, J. (2002). Values in practice and practising values. *Journal of Communication Disorders, 35*, 89–106.

Byng, S., Pound, C., & Parr, S. (2000). Living with aphasia: A framework for therapy interventions. In I. Papathanasiou (Ed.), *Acquired neurogenic communication disorders* (pp. 49–75). London: Whurr Publishers Ltd.

Carnaby, S. (2002). Making plans: Undertaking assessment and care planning. In S. Carnaby (Ed.), *Learning disability today* (pp. 95–106). Brighton, UK: Pavilion Publishing.

Casserley, C. (2000). The disability discrimination act: An overview. In J. Cooper (Ed.), *Law, rights & disability* (pp. 139–64). London: Jessica Kingsley.

Chapey, R., Duchan, J., Elman, R., Garcia, L., Kagan, A., & Lyon, J. et al. (2001). Life participation approach to aphasia: A statement of values for the future. In R. Chapey (Ed.), *Language intervention strategies in aphasia and related neurogenic communication disorders*. (4th ed., pp. 235–245). Baltimore: Lippincott, Williams & Wilkins.

Clement, T. (2002). Exploring the role of values in the management of advocacy schemes. In B. Gray & R. Jackson (Eds.), *Advocacy & learning disability* (pp. 50–71). London: Jessica Kingsley.

Cottrell, S., & Davies, A. (2004). Supporting conversation, providing information. *Royal College of Speech and Language Therapists Bulletin, 630*, 12–13.

Cruice, M., Worrall, L., Hickson, L., & Murison, R. (2003). Finding a focus for quality of life with aphasia: Social and emotional health, and psychological well-being. *Aphasiology, 17*(4), 333–353.

Dalrymple, J., & Burke, B. (1995). *Anti-oppressive practice: Social care and the law*. Buckingham, UK: Open University Press.

Department for Education and Employment (DfEE) (1995). *Disability discrimination act*. London: Stationery Office.

Department of Health (1990). *The NHS and community care act*. London: Stationery Office.

Department of Health (1996). *The community care (direct payments) act*. London: Stationery Office.

Department of Health (2001a). *Valuing people: A new strategy for learning disability in the 21st century*. London: Stationery Office.

Department of Health (2001b). *The national service framework for older people*. London: Department of Health Publications.

Department of Health (2005). *Creating a patient-led NHS. Delivering the NHS improvement plan*. London: Department of Health Publications.

Department of Health Modernisation Agency (2001; 2003). *The essence of care – patient-focused benchmarking for health care practitioners*. London: Department of Heallth.

Dowson, S. (1997). Empowerment within services – a comfortable delusion. In P. Ramcharan, G. Roberts, G. Grant, & J. Borland (Eds.), *Empowerment in everyday life – Learning disability* (pp. 101–120). London: Jessica Kingsley.

Felce, D., & Perry, J. (1996). Adaptive behaviour gains in ordinary housing for people with intellectual disabilities. *Journal of Applied Research in Intellectual Disabilities, 9*(2), 101–114.

Freeman, M. (2004). SLT talk and practice knowledge: A response to Ferguson and Armstrong. *International Journal of Language and Communication Disorders, 39*(4), 481–486.

Garcia, L. J., Laroche, C., & Barrette, J. (2002). Work integration issues go beyond the nature of the communication disorder. *Journal of Communication Disorders, 35*, 187–211.

Goble, C. (2002). Professional consciousness and conflict in advocacy. In B. Gray & R. Jackson (Eds.), *Advocacy & learning disability* (pp. 72–88). London: Jessica Kingsley.

Goodley, D. (2000). *Self-advocacy in the lives of people with learning difficulties.* Buckingham, UK: Open University Press.

Grant, G. (1997). Consulting to involve or consulting to empower? In P. Ramcharan, G. Roberts, G. Grant, & J. Borland (Eds.), *Empowerment in everyday life – Learning disability* (pp. 121–143). London: Jessica Kingsley.

Hedley, I. (2004). Integrated learning systems: Effects on learning and self-esteem. In L. Florian & J. Hegarty (Eds.), *ICT and special educational needs: A tool for inclusion* (pp. 64–79). Buckingham, UK: Open University Press.

Hilari, K., Wiggins, R., Roy, P., Byng, S., & Smith, S. C. (2003). Predictors of health-related quality of life (HRQOL) in people with chronic aphasia. *Aphasiology, 17*(4), 365–381.

Johnson, R. (1994). *The Picture Communication Symbols Combination.* Solana Beach, CA: Mayer-Johnson Co.

Kagan, A., & LeBlanc, K. (2002). Motivating for infrastructure change: Toward a communicatively accessible, participation-based stroke care system for all those affected by aphasia. *Journal of Communication Disorders, 35*, 153–169.

Kenworthy, J., & Whittaker, J. (2000). Anything to declare? The struggle for inclusive education and children's rights. *Disability & Society, 15*, 219–231.

Lasker, J. P., LaPointe, L., & Kodras, J. E. (2005). Helping a professor with aphasia resume teaching through multimodal approaches. *Aphasiology, 19*(3/4/5), 399–410.

Law, J., Bunning, K., Byng, S., Farrelly, S., & Heyman, B. (2005). Making sense in primary care: Levelling the playing field for people with communication difficulties. *Disability & Society, 20*(2), 169–184.

Lindsay, G., & Dockrell, J. (2002). Meeting the needs of children with speech language and communication needs: A critical perspective on inclusion and collaboration. *Child Language Teaching and Therapy, 3*, 91–101.

Moore, W. (2002). NHS to receive an extra £40bn over next five years. *British Medical Journal, 324*, 993.

Mosely, J. (1994). *You choose.* Cambridge, UK: LDA.

Murphy, J. (2000). Enabling people with aphasia to discuss quality of life. *British Journal of Therapy and Rehabilitation, 7*(11), 454–458.

Murphy, J., & Cameron, L. (2002a). Let your mats do the talking. *Speech & Language Therapy in Practice, Spring*, 18–20.

Murphy, J., & Cameron, L. (2002b). *Talking mats and learning disability: A low-tech resource to help people to express their views and feelings.* Scotland: University of Stirling.

Parr, S. (2004). *Living with severe aphasia: The experience of communication impairment after stroke.* London: Pavilion Publishing.

Parr, S., Byng, S., Gilpin, S., & Ireland, C. (1997). *Talking about aphasia.* Buckingham, UK: Open University Press.

Parr, S., Moss, B., Newbery, J., Petheram, B., & Byng, S. (2003). *Inclusive Internet technologies for people with communication impairment.* Report for the Economic and Social Research Council Innovative Health Technologies Programme, UK.

Peters, S. (1996). The politics of disability identity. In L. Barton (Ed.), *Disability and society: Emerging issues and insights* (pp. 215–234). London: Longman.

Petheram, B. (1996). Exploring the home-based use of microcomputers in aphasia therapy. *Aphasiology, 10*(3), 267–282.

Pound, C., Parr, S., Lindsay, J., & Woolf, C. (2000). *Beyond aphasia: Therapies for living with communication disability.* Buckingham, UK: Winslow Press.

Rahamin, L. (2004). From integration to inclusion: Using ICT to support learners with special educational needs in the ordinary classroom. In L. Florian & J. Hegarty (Eds.), *ICT and special educational needs: A tool for inclusion* (pp. 35–45). Buckingham, UK: Open University Press.

Ramcharan, P., Roberts, G., Grant, G., & Borland, J. (1997). Citizenship, empowerment and everyday life – deal and illusion in the new millennium. In P. Ramcharan, G. Roberts, G. Grant, & J. Borland (Eds.), *Empowerment in everyday life – Learning disability* (pp. 241–258). London: Jessica Kingsley.

Rittel, H., & Webber, M. (1973). Dilemmas in a general theory of planning. *Policy Sciences*, *4*, 156–159.

Scott, J., & Larcher, J. (2002). Advocacy with people with communication difficulties. In B. Gray & R. Jackson (Eds.), *Advocacy and learning disability* (pp. 170–188). London: Jessica Kingsley.

Shale, A. (2004). Beyond common sense. *Royal College of Speech and Language Therapists Bulletin*, *621*, 14–15.

Silverman, J., Kurtz, S., & Draper, J. (1997). *Skills for communicating with patients*. Oxford, UK: Radcliffe Press.

Stalker, K. (2002). Inclusive daytime opportunities for people with learning disabilities. In C. Clark (Ed.), *Adult day services and social inclusion – Better days* (pp. 46–66). London: Jessica Kingsley.

Stevens, C. (2004). Information and communications technology, special educational needs and schools: A historical perspective of UK government initiatives. In L. Florian & J. Hegarty (Eds.), *ICT and special educational needs: A tool for inclusion* (pp. 21–34). Buckingham, UK: Open University Press.

Stirling, A. (2003). Talking partners. *Royal College of Speech and Language Therapists Bulletin*, *614*, 10–12.

Tyne, A. (1981). *The principle of normalisation*. London: Values into Action.

von Tetzchner, S., Grove, N., Loncke, F., Barnett, S., Woll, B., & Clibbens, J. (1996). Preliminaries to a comprehensive model of augmentative and alternative communication. In S. von Tetzchner & M. H. Jensen (Eds.), *Augmentative and alternative communication: European perspectives* (pp. 19–36). London: Whurr Publishers Ltd.

Waddington, L. (2000). Changing attitudes to the rights of people with disabilities in Europe. In J. Cooper (Ed.), *Law, rights & disability* (pp. 33–58). London: Jessica Kingsley.

Walker, M. (1980). *The Makaton vocabulary*. Camberley, UK: Makaton Vocabulary Development Project.

Walmsley, J. (2002). Principles and types of advocacy. In B. Gray & R. Jackson (Eds.), *Advocacy & learning disability* (pp. 24–37). London: Jessica Kingsley.

Wanless, D. (2002). *Securing our future health. Taking a long-term view*. London: HM Treasury.

Wolfensberger, W. (1992). *A brief introduction to social role valorisation as a high-order concept for structuring human services*. Syracuse, NY: Training Institute for Human Service Planning, Leadership and Change Agentry.

Woodcock, R., Clark, C., & Davies, C. (1968). *Peabody Rebus Reading Program*. Circle Pines, MN: American Guidance Service.

Young, D. A., & Quibell, R. (2000). Why rights are never enough: Rights, intellectual disability and understanding. *Disability & Society*, *15*, 747–764.

APHASIOLOGY, 2007, 21 (1), 23–38

ψP Psychology Press
Taylor & Francis Group

Communication access to organisations: Inclusionary practices for people with aphasia

Carole Pound, Judith Duchan, Tom Penman, Alan Hewitt, and Susie Parr

Connect – The Communication Disability Network, London, UK

Background: When speech and language therapists/pathologists talk about inclusion, they are usually referring to a client being included in events outside the clinic or the organisation that provides the speech and language therapy services. This article describes ways in which those providing services for and with people with aphasia can work to involve service users in their own organisations. A communication access pathway to inclusion and user involvement in organisations is presented. This draws on established methods in the field, as well as on methods and underpinning frameworks that require a shift in views about the nature of service provision. The pathway involves (1) targeting situations in which the "business" of the organisation takes place and then (2) designing ways of achieving communication access to those situations.

Aims: The overall aim is to present ways in which an organisation can become more communicatively accessible to service users with aphasia and communication disabilities. We describe a range of involvement contexts and communication access conditions at Connect, a charity in the UK, where we have attempted to increase the engagement and power of people with aphasia in our organisation's business.

Main contribution: In order to show how organisations can create more inclusive practice, we present some of our own projects. We describe four different contexts in our organisation that we targeted for inclusion: (1) making therapy choices, (2) delivering therapy services, (3) providing courses to service providers, and (4) employment practices. For each of these contexts we present methods used to support the involvement of people with aphasia. Some types of support are tried and tested methods arising out of established theories, others are newer to the field and require a shift in thinking and values.

Conclusions: In order to attain authentic communication access for people with aphasia, service providers need to look beyond established theories and practices. The result, judging from anecdotal evidence as well as evidence from qualitative evaluation, suggests that creating communication access in a service organisation can serve as a powerful means for involving people with aphasia and in so doing can improve on the services provided to them.

Traditionally, speech and language therapy has been concerned with the definition, diagnosis, and remediation of different impairments. Around the 1980s speech-language therapists/pathologists began to widen their gaze. This happened when therapists began asking how those with communication disabilities were being

---

Address correspondence to: Carole Pound, Connect – The Communication Disability Network, 16–18 Marshalsea Rd, Southwark SE1 1HL, London, UK. E-mail: carolepound@ukconnect.org

DOI: 10.1080/02687030600798212

responded to. This slight shift of focus can be seen as the starting point of a movement that led to an eventual sea change in therapy practices.

More context-sensitive practices, known in the 1980s as "functional" approaches, grew out of a pragmatics movement that recognised the importance of context in achieving communication success. Therapists began to see communication as consisting of speech acts aimed at achieving a purpose—requesting something, refusing something, accepting something. We began to talk about communication breakdowns as arising not only from how our clients communicated but also from how well those communications were responded to by others (Chapman, 1981; Davis, 1980; Holland, 1980; Prutting, 1982). This shift of focus occurred across the range of therapists' work: with children, people with learning difficulties, and adults with acquired impairments.

Locating the source of communication problems in the context led speech therapists in the 1990s to begin manipulating the context to make communication more successful and congenial. It was then that speech pathologists started to work with partners' and teachers' conversations and classroom lessons to make their discourse more accessible to people with different kinds of speech and language problems (Beukelman & Mirenda, 1992; Kagan, 1998; Light, Dattilo, English, Guitierrez, & Hartz, 1992; Lyon, 1989; Lyon et al., 1997; Manolson, 1992). Paying attention to issues of competence, well-being, and achievement started to widen the therapist's focus beyond remediation.

Another influence on the move towards inclusion within speech and language therapy has come about more recently. It arises from the thinking of those in the disability rights movement who have argued that disability is socially constructed, and that people are disabled by the different barriers they encounter, rather than by their intrinsic impairment. This societal focus and more prominent positioning of the "patient voice" has prompted (or perhaps reflects) legislation requiring organisations to develop policies for providing user access and user involvement. For example, in the UK, Health Service policy has been keen to locate access and empowerment at the heart of its standards on good practice. Policy statements advocate person-centred care, engaging service users in decision making about their therapies, and encouraging people with long-term conditions to take an active role in managing their conditions. One effort of those adopting the premises of this disability rights movement is to work to make everyday situations more accessible, since people have a right to be included in all of society's domains (LPAA, 2001; Pound & Hewitt, 2004). Another related aspect of the movement has been to empower people to have more of a say about what happens in these situations.

These aspirations to more "inclusive" practices have begun to lead to a less paternalistic system of health delivery where patients engage with practitioners about choice and decision making. Specific initiatives that have championed more equal relationships between service user and provider have included Building on the Best: Choice, Responsiveness and Equity in the NHS (Department of Health, 2003), the Expert Patients programme (Department of Health, 2001), the National Service Framework for Long Term Conditions (Department of Health, 2005). There are similar initiatives in the United States, such as Participatory Action Research being promoted by the US Department of Education (National Institute on Disability and Rehabilitation Research, 2005).

The goals of these governmental initiatives are clear: improved quality of life, greater self efficacy, more relevant, creative, and user-focused services. The means and mechanisms of translating policy rhetoric into everyday practice are less explicitly articulated, however. Both health policy and postmodern thinking on organisational development to manage complex change agree on the critical role of language and communication in mediating new ways of working (Stacey, Griffin, & Shaw, 2000). However, if language and communication are at the core of a population's impairment, moving towards sustainable systems of involvement, participation, and partnership will represent no small challenge to services and organisations working towards authentic inclusion of people with aphasia.

Reviewing shifts in and challenges to professional practice, there are two ways to view the influence of the disability movement on services rendered by speech-language therapists. One is that it is a logical extension of pragmatic thinking in the 1980s and 1990s, when context was shown to have a powerful influence on communicative competence. In this view, inclusionary practices involve the creation of contexts where a person with a disability is provided with the support they need to express their needs and to participate in life activities.

The second way to view the impact of the disability movement on professional practices is to see it as involving a paradigm shift in service provision. It depicts inclusion as more than the addition of new practices to an existing toolkit. In this view, inclusionary practices are seen as a fundamental rethinking of values *and* practices, and reframing the relationship between service providers and service users (Swain, Clark, Parry, French, & Reynolds, 2004; van der Gaag & Mowles, 2005).

This paradigm shift might lead an organisation to ask how it can go about changing so that it can create the conditions and infrastructure that will involve clientele in service development and delivery as well as having a say in their use. What can it do to engage with its key stakeholders not just as more empowered service users, but also as collaborators, advisors, teachers, evaluators, and leaders?

We will be arguing in this paper that an organisation serving the needs of people with communication disabilities can use established practices derived from the pragmatics movement for some aspects of inclusion. We feel, however, that to achieve full and authentic inclusion organisations and service providers working for them will need to venture into new theoretical territory. This article offers evidence for how both renderings of inclusionary practices are useful when creating methods for inclusionary practices in an organisation.

COMMUNICATION ACCESS AS A PATHWAY TO INCLUSION

In this paper, we cast the issue of organisational inclusion in terms of *communication access*. In using this framework, we draw parallels with physical access, the metaphor that represents access as a way to get to a destination. Just as a ramp can provide access to a building for people with motor impairments, so communication access can open up services and organisations for people with communication difficulty.

We will be describing the efforts of our organisation to achieve communication access for people with aphasia. We are a small voluntary sector organisation located in the UK, called Connect – The Communication Disability Network. Established in 2000, we have had the opportunity to develop, from scratch, Connect's values, aims, mission, and ways of working. This has allowed us to explore new ways of involving people with aphasia in all aspects of the organisation, from service planning and delivery, to infrastructure, governance, teaching, and research. It has also allowed us to select carefully from older, more traditional ways of doing things, in addition to designing new ways of operating.

This notion of communication access has fitted well with established notions in the field of speech-language therapy. It incorporates the functional notions of the 1980s, where a person's communication was depicted as being purposeful, and successful communication was evaluated both in terms of its intent and responses to it. It also incorporates the work of the 1990s of providing communication support to people with communication disabilities.

Other aspects of our efforts to achieve communication access have required us to create new ways of thinking about and delivering our services. We needed to go beyond a focus on speech act functions and conversational support and consider the organisational culture and priorities. This allowed us to offer the sustainable whole-systems change that was needed to govern our evolving relationship with people with aphasia.

In order to create communicatively accessible contexts, we first reflected on the purpose of our organisation, the services it offers, and the way in which it carries out its business. We found that for many services and contexts we were able to use established ideas and practices. For example, we provided conversational support to:

- make information more accessible, relevant, and engaging;
- offer our users choices, and support to negotiate these choices;
- offer our users the communication support they need in different contexts.

We also designed new ways to involve our users in a range of activities, from service provision to infrastructure and governance. Our aims soon required us to go beyond current practices. We wanted to provide ways, for example, that people with aphasia could serve on the Board of Trustees, provide service delivery, and train stroke service providers. In order to ensure true involvement within each context, we began analysing the dynamics of each targeted context. We went through a set of steps, such as the following, when figuring out how to make a context communicatively accessible to a person with aphasia:

- We explained what's required/expected of people with aphasia and staff for involvement to take place in that context.
- We set out the options for ways in which people with aphasia can be involved.
- We discussed possible involvement and how it might look.
- We negotiated and supported service-users' decisions regarding their involvement.
- We documented what was decided.
- We took stock, checking and reviewing involvement and responses to it.
- We planned next steps in collaboration with service users.
- We worked towards longer-term involvement in different contexts.

The above steps led us to a new set of values and practices. Our focus became one of attaining authentic access of an individual rather than skill enhancement. We also began to focus more on the success of the communicative event than on a person's communication performance during the event. So, for example, a conversation involving a person with aphasia as a co-facilitator might be evaluated by whether the needed support was provided, or how it might be better managed next time by both facilitators. Finally, we began to work alongside the person with aphasia to strategise about common goals rather than delivering a service to that person.

In this paper, we will describe Connect users' involvement in four areas of our organisation: (1) as recipients of services, (2) as co-facilitators of services, (3) as trainers in courses for service providers, and (4) as employees. We will discuss, at the end, some of the challenges that communication access and more systems-based change pose to Connect and to other organisations working to include people with aphasia in their services and structures. We will also include some practical steps for change.

INCLUSION AS SERVICE RECIPIENTS: CHOICEMAKING

Three times a year, service users with aphasia who have passed through an initial "Starters Group" (a 7-week introduction to Connect) attend "choicemaking" sessions in which they select their service options for the forthcoming months. On average 80 clients access each choicemaking session, attending the centre to browse the therapy options, select what they would like to do, and then discuss these preferences and priorities in a one-to-one interview with a staff member. Given the range of activities on offer (an average of 12 different possible groups per session), and the fact that communication impairment makes it difficult for people to take in information and engage in debate and discussion, choicemaking requires careful preparation. Information about the options must be clear and comprehensive, and there must be enough people with communication support skills to facilitate browsing and discussion, and to brief and de-brief the choice-makers. We feel that investing time and effort into preparation for this event is essential, so that people with aphasia have full access to choice.

The process of choicemaking involves several steps:

- Choice-makers view a number of A3 posters, each describing a particular activity on offer. The information is clearly laid out, using straightforward language, bullet points, emboldening, and key words, and supplemented with illustrations. Each poster itemises the themes involved in the activity choice, what is involved, and the benefits as described by people with aphasia (see Figure 1).
- Choice-makers then pick up individual leaflets about each activity to use as physical props in their discussion of options.
- Trained communication supporters (students and volunteers) answer questions about therapy activities. People with aphasia who have previously attended the activity add personal insights about what they liked or didn't like about a group.
- Choice-makers then negotiate choices and discuss decisions in one-to-one sessions, with communication support. They are given accessible written documentation of agreed decisions and priorities.

These different levels and layers of communication support thus provide multiple points of checking and double checking about the choice that has been agreed by client and therapist.

Informal evaluation of this process, drawing from our staff's reflections on more than 200 individual choice-making sessions annually, suggests that people with aphasia take a more active role in selecting and prioritising activities when participating in these sessions. The process allows for different perspectives and priorities to be made transparent. Sometimes choices made are at odds with a therapist's preconceived ideas about what would be in a person's therapeutic

Conversation Group
- A group for people with aphasia

What is the group about?

- Chatting
- Relaxing
- Laughing & joking
- Discussion

Benefits

- Lots of opportunity for **real-life conversation**
- **more confidence** in communication

Who is the group for?

- **People with aphasia** who **have** new ways of communicating
- If you **can follow** others conversation
- If you like a **fairly quick pace**
- If you like a **good discussion!**

Days: Tuesdays

Times: 10.30 - 12.30

Dates: 20th April - 29th June 2004

Number of people: 16

Support: †

Figure 1. Poster for the conversation group.

interests and what a relative would like for them. The physical manipulation of choice leaflets allows people with aphasia to clarify their preferences in a concrete and practical way.

Developing the process of choicemaking has enabled service providers at Connect to sharpen up explanations of what different activities are about, and to be more explicit about the two-way process of negotiating choice. Before this process was established, there was a sense that clients deferred to the experience and expertise of the therapist rather than taking a lead in selecting appropriate activities. Seeing what people choose individually and across a client base of over 80 people provides an overview of the choices that are most popular, and perhaps choices that are missing. Thus the process has helped Connect to manipulate and modify limited resources to best effect.

Finally, there is some evidence that sign-up by choice leads to more consistent and motivated attendance at groups, possibly because there is less scope for misunderstanding the purpose of a group at the sign-up stage.

INCLUSION AS SERVICE PROVIDERS: CO-FACILITATION OF CONVERSATION GROUPS

For a number of years one of the most popular groups at Connect has been the co-facilitated conversation group. This group, typically attended by between 12 and 18 people with aphasia, is led by two people with aphasia. The facilitators are supported within the group by up to four volunteers (without aphasia), and have a short weekly supervision session post-group with a speech and language therapist.

The group is entirely conversation based. Each week social news and current affairs are discussed, as well as themes and topics for discussion that have been decided beforehand. The role of the people with aphasia who co-facilitate the group covers its organisation and the management of group dynamics in order to best support easy, inclusive conversation. Organisational tasks concern structuring sessions, producing the weekly agenda, facilitating the selection of topics, managing the environment, and overseeing the division of group members into smaller groups.

When managing group dynamics, the co-facilitators are involved in a variety of tasks, all concerning conversational support. They assign volunteers and students to one-to-one supporter roles, negotiate with volunteers for the type of help they themselves may require to facilitate particular group members, plan and collect appropriate resources to support the week's topic, and identify ways of engaging quieter members and managing those who are more talkative.

Critical to the success of the group has been the weekly post-group debriefing and problem-solving session. The facilitators meet up with a speech and language therapist, who does not attend the group but acts as a sounding board for the facilitators and volunteers. Together the team collaborate in finding practical, aphasia-friendly solutions to managing group dynamics and keeping the group conversation both lively and engaging for all the participants. Ideas have included a suggestions bin in which group members can deposit photographs, newspaper clippings, and any other items they would like to discuss in future weeks.

The ongoing popularity of the group is one of the key indicators of its success. Evaluation data from qualitative interviews conducted with facilitators, volunteers, and group participants highlight a range of benefits. Group members value the opportunity to chat, have a laugh together, and hang out with friends. Some benefits result from the group being led by people with aphasia rather than therapy staff. Members talk of a sense of "ownership" and a facilitation of more "natural" conversations, because the facilitators with aphasia allow extra time and demonstrate patience. Participants and facilitators reflect on the greater clarity and order that co-facilitation brings to the group proceedings. They also comment that these groups avoid more institutional/therapist-led talk that many have experienced in previous "therapy" groups. Jim, a group member, differentiates therapist-led and person-with-aphasia-led groups, and comments on the sense of liberation they bring: "We was still in the … *guideline* of what the therapy was. Here it *isn't* … although it's there, you – you are more … you talk all the frees and no-one says 'Hold on, you can't do that' …" (Lindsay, Penman, & Pound, 2000).

The co-facilitators themselves report development of skills and a growth in confidence through assuming new roles and responsibilities. In some cases this has also brought increased levels of stress and fatigue, as overseeing the smooth running of the group and the progression of conversation and inclusion for everyone is a different experience from just participating in the group. An additional challenge for co-facilitators has been tackling the perception by other group members that group leadership typically falls to those whose language is intact, whether therapists or volunteers.

For Connect, the benefits of this group are more obvious. At low cost (approximately 30 minutes supervision time each week, plus the initial training of volunteer communication supporters), services have been extended to a group of people seeking long-term access to conversational opportunities. The investment of time in supporting co-facilitators and volunteers has enabled Connect to gain new ideas, and practical, efficient, aphasia-friendly solutions in relation to the management of groups. Finally, the experience has taught Connect not to make assumptions about who brings what to the management of groups.

INCLUSION AS TEACHERS: TRAINING SERVICE PROVIDERS

Connect provides a comprehensive programme of training for service providers. A key area of training, based on the principles of supported conversation (Kagan, 1998), aims to develop the communication skills of stroke service providers. People with aphasia are involved both as trainers and conversation skill evaluators within this programme. Trainers with aphasia learn their skills by taking a 6-week course (six 90-minute sessions).

Trainers choose to volunteer their time for the course and for subsequent training sessions for a variety of reasons, not the least being their passionate commitment to changing people's awareness of the communication needs of those with aphasia. Routine post-group evaluations conducted by the group facilitators with over 40 people who have completed the training programme consistently highlight a range of personal benefits. These include an increase in confidence and communication, typically attributed to practising and analysing good and bad conversations, an expressed enjoyment of opportunities to interact with strangers, a sense of feeling in control, and a sense of usefulness and responsibility through making a contribution to improving society's reaction to aphasia.

Part of the job of the trainers with aphasia involves giving feedback to service providers, and commenting on their conversational skills. The following scenario, observed and recorded during a "live" training session for social care staff highlights the impact that the reversal in traditional client–provider roles can have for some people with aphasia who assume a trainer role.

Jane, a former teacher, gave direct feedback to a course participant, who she felt had talked too fast and too loud. Jane's mediocre rating came as a surprise to the course participant, who had run groups for people with aphasia for over 15 years. While highlighting some of the good aspects of the conversation that they had had, Jane also wrote down the word "patronising". The course participant reported both her surprise at the feedback and her future commitment to checking out her pace and style with the people with aphasia she worked with. When asked what she had thought of this and another training session, Jane replied, "this is the first time in 2 years … me … in control."

From Connect's point of view, the trainers with aphasia provide an important means of delivering user-focused training. First and foremost, their presence demonstrates their expertise and their ability to manage a role other than that of patient or recipient of services. Their conversations with service providers convey an insider perspective of life with aphasia. Service users and providers share information about their individual life stories and interests, and the social relations between them are equalised, at least for a short while.

Many service providers comment on their anxieties about being assessed by a person with aphasia, and about experiencing a new relationship with people whom they typically interact with only as "patients". So, in a relatively short interaction (generally about 40 minutes), the course participants have had the unusual experience of both having to keep a 30-minute social conversation going with someone with aphasia and being on the receiving end of an assessment. The ease and confidence of the trainers with aphasia is not lost on the anxious service providers.

A key aim of Connect's communication skills training is for participants to go away with a range of techniques and ideas to use in future interactions with people with aphasia. We also want them to experience, and remember the experience, of being in a different power dynamic. This is not intended to frighten the service providers (although that is what sometimes happens). Rather, it is to provide a springboard to ways of engaging people with aphasia in different, more equal, and more inclusive relationships.

What are the challenges in involving people with aphasia as trainers, and how can these be overcome? First, clients who embark on training as trainers need to know what they are signing up for. Recruitment of trainers with aphasia starts with a clear brief as to what will be involved in the initial six-session training, who can sign up, and what previous trainers say about the personal benefits. All of this material is carefully drafted onto a recruitment poster presented in an aphasia-friendly format (that is, using larger font, appropriate spacing, illustrations, etc.).

Another challenge concerns providing communication support throughout the training of the trainers with aphasia. Each session is facilitated, and all participants have the appropriate level of support to enable them to engage. Trainees are also offered accessible minutes following the group sessions. Accessible materials (developed and modified by people with aphasia) are used to give specific feedback on trainees' skills in conversation.

Access and support continue as a feature in the "live" training sessions (in which people with aphasia train service providers), with briefing and debriefing sessions before and after any training interactions. The feedback sessions are supported by a skilled facilitator using drawing and key words to check trainers' views on issues such as the balance, feel, and equality of interactions, and the service provider's use of techniques and resources.

In our opinion, and on the basis of consistent feedback from both our trainers with aphasia and the service-provider trainees who come to enhance their communication skills, there are many advantages to running this programme. The input of people with aphasia enables the courses to convey the insider's perspective in a direct and powerful way. The evaluation sessions led by the trainers with aphasia demonstrate by example the important relationship between power, expertise, and competence. In addition, the central involvement of people who live with aphasia ensures that the ideas and language of the course are kept understandable and accessible to a wide audience of service providers, not just those with a professional or speech pathology background.

INCLUSION AS EMPLOYEES: THE WORKING TOGETHER CO-ORDINATOR

In 2002 Connect obtained a grant to support a person with aphasia as a part-time employee. The role of this employee is to ensure that people with aphasia are included in all aspects of Connect's operations.

Recruitment to the new position was carried out so that the process would be accessible to a wide range of people with aphasia. This meant:

- advertising the position in newsletters read by people with aphasia, using accessible language and layout;
- conducting supported meetings for those interested, to explain about the job in communicatively accessible ways;
- supporting people in preparing application materials;
- creating interviews that were accessible to applicants and to interviewers with aphasia;
- asking applicants to identify the communication support they might require to participate in the interview and carry out the job.

From an interested pool of 18 people with aphasia, six applied, and three were shortlisted. Alan Hewitt, a person with aphasia who had previously served as a Trustee on Connect's Board, was recruited to this post. Induction to the post involved talking with staff about Connect's goals and activities, having weekly meetings with Connect's Chief Executive, and regular meetings with Connect's programme coordinators.

Alan's responsibilities related to his role of fostering the involvement of people with aphasia and ensuring they developed a strong voice in the structure, not just the service-delivery aspects of Connect (see also Byng & Duchan, 2005). This included recruiting and supporting people to become involved in aspects of the running of Connect, co-ordinating the *Live-Wire* group (a 14-person user group that meets quarterly to evaluate and suggest ways to involve people with aphasia in organisational strategy and activity), and monitoring the varying types and levels of involvement across Connect's key activities—therapy services, training, publications, governance, research, and development.

The benefits of Alan's role as Working Together Co-ordinator have been apparent at a personal and organisational level. Alan describes the benefits of his employment as contributing to a new sense of purpose and "engagement". He differentiates this feeling of "engagement" in real work from mere "participation" in therapy (Hewitt & Byng, 2003).

From an organisational point of view, the benefits have been significant. Alan's role as a staff member means he has a presence in day-to-day meetings and decision making, allowing him to flag up inaccessible communication, advocate for greater levels of user involvement, and question service-provider priorities and assumptions. For Connect staff, Alan's presence has highlighted the importance of preparation and clarity. It has also led to more frequent (and useful to all) clarification of roles and core purpose in different pieces of work. For example, discussion of strategy within line management sessions has typically led to the co-production of clarifying diagrams and key messages. A way of working that requires attention to the clarity of communication before, during, and after meetings has become a discipline with benefits for all staff. Although requiring additional time, it has been well worth it, because it has opened the way to better organisational practice as well as increased authenticity of user involvement.

Alan's current role is both to coordinate and monitor the involvement of people with aphasia in all aspects of the organisation, and to support the communication access initiatives that underpin Connect's attempts at greater involvement of people with aphasia. Reflecting on his role and the relationship of communication access and involvement, Alan notes, "If it's not clear I can't take part. Nor can lots of others who have aphasia. Communication access is the way in to real involvement ... not just involvement around the edges."

DISCUSSION

Reflecting on the ways of involving people with aphasia in different aspects of Connect's work, it is possible to see a number of patterns emerging. Table 1 summarises the ways in which Connect has tried to ensure that people with aphasia have access to involvement.

In the second column of Table 1 is a list of roles played by people with aphasia once they have been provided with full access to the targeted context. This column is a departure from established practice, since the typical role played by people with aphasia in relation to the service provider is that of client, or recipient of services. In order to support people with aphasia in the various roles listed in the table, we had to rethink our usual model of service delivery. We no longer served as expert service provider, but rather as collaborator, facilitator, and coach. This required a major shift in our thinking and the delivery of our services. It is what we meant at the outset by a paradigm shift.

The third column of Table 1 describes access materials, which involved a combination of established practices as well as practices that required new organisational efforts. We were comfortable in creating written materials and pictures, and working with flipcharts to support the communication of those we worked with in service-delivery contexts. But we also needed to create materials to make other aspects of our business accessible. For example, we needed to attend to the accessibility of our recruitment materials, training programmes, and administrative practices required to get the job done.

The processes described in the fourth column of Table 1 indicate yet another domain where we were able to rely somewhat on established practices, but also

TABLE 1
Roles of people with aphasia in different contexts, and examples of access materials and
practices for each

Examples of contexts	Role of people with aphasia	Examples of access materials	Examples of processes*
Choicemaking.	Service user. Choice maker. Insider view of the group.	Posters. Appointment letters. "Reports" documenting key decisions.	Careful preparation of materials and environment. Environment with room to browse. Time to browse and ask questions, see what's interesting. Staff/students/volunteers to support communication. People with aphasia as guides, story tellers and confidence supporters. One-to-one interviews to review and prioritise choices. Accessible letter to confirm choices and decisions.
Co-delivery of conversation groups.	Organiser. Group facilitator. Problem solver.	Photos, news clippings, pages from internet to support discussion of chosen topics. Coloured card to help participants divide into smaller groups. Pen and paper for on-line communication support. Flipchart in group rooms with topic heading.	Pre-group meeting between facilitators with aphasia and volunteer supporters. Clarification of roles of co-facilitators with aphasia and volunteers. Volunteers assigned for one-to-one support with specific group members where appropriate. Weekly problem solving meeting post-group. Group facilitation training course offered to people with aphasia on annual basis.
Trainers for courses taken by service providers.	Teacher. Expert. Demonstrator. Assessor.	Trainer job outline Recruitment. Explanation of training aims. Feedback forms. Teaching materials, e.g., videos. Good and bad examples on video. Observation checklists. Personal experiences— described and acted out. Minutes of sessions.	Time to form relationships. Time to revisit worries and concerns. Ongoing clarification about purpose of training and role of trainers with aphasia. Support and confidence building from group facilitators and group members about what trainers with aphasia have to offer. Six-session training programme. Recap session to session. Time to practise giving feedback and refine skills. Checking and documenting preferences. Probing and acting out good experiences and bad experiences to elicit detail.

(Continued)

Table 1
(*Continued*)

Examples of contexts	Role of people with aphasia	Examples of access materials	Examples of processes*
Employees.	Staff member. Advocate and conduit for suggestions by people with aphasia to staff and senior management team at Connect. Co-ordinator of involvement activity. Contributor to planning and monitoring of services. Questioner.	Accessible job description. Accessible advertising, interview letters and interview guidelines. Minutes from meetings and discussions.	Recruitment process: (support at intro meeting, support to develop portfolio, communication supporters at interview panel, applicants studied interview questions). Accessible explanation of business plans, project work (powerpoint presentations). Longer line management meetings. Written notes from all line management meetings. Meetings and documents protocol to ensure as communicatively accessible as possible.

*Things that were done.

needed to tailor them and add to them to achieve our new purposes. We found that, in order to arrive at authentic involvement, we had to do much more work around the edges of a targeted event than previously. For example, accessibility of an event often depended on whether the person had received proper preparation for that event, and whether sufficient time was given for participation during the event. Also, because inclusion in these events was often ongoing, we found that feedback and minutes reviewing what had happened were key to continuing access.

It was the dynamic interaction of the resources, processes, and people listed in Table 1, and the combination of established and newly created paradigms, that offered people with aphasia the conditions for better communication access. The result was a kind of communication access that provided a gateway for people to take part and engage with the work of an organisation on more equal terms. We are optimistic that these sorts of methods and ways of thinking, both by us and by people with aphasia, can serve as a vehicle for ongoing, authentic involvement in different provider contexts.

As Alan Hewitt points out, however, communication access is not an easy concept to grasp or act upon: "Communication access is a very slippery thing. It's everything to do with communication and involvement. It's easy to get lost cos it's so big."

In our definition, communication access is not synonymous with involvement but is a means for attaining it. We feel that working to make organisations communicatively accessible can be an important step along the way to a more inclusive society.

In this article we have described our attempts to make our organisation more inclusive. Attending to different involvement contexts at Connect, and addressing particular communication access needs in bite-size chunks has helped us increase involvement and the equality of relationships between people with and without aphasia who engage in our day-to-day business. Some aspects of what we have done have been drawn from established practices. Others have required us to shift our ideas. This has been difficult, and has involved a number of challenges both for Connect and for all services/organisations working with people with aphasia, including the following:

- Resistance to change. In order to make Connect's practice meaningful to and inclusive of people with aphasia, we have had to alter the ways we do things. Often this means abandoning our notions of what we, as therapists and facilitators, think is best for our clients. Changing practice involves changing mindset and structures in addition to introducing new activities. So we have had to give ourselves permission to spend valuable time working with people outside traditional therapy models of interaction. We have had to reconsider traditional power relations as we empower people with aphasia to assume new and different responsibilities and identities within the organisation.

- Using time differently. Running projects in an inclusive way often requires reflection on priorities and reallocation of precious time and resources. Investing time in preparation for a process or project, such as a training session or an interview, can provoke anxiety and tensions about where finite resources are best spent. However, we have learned that time spent in this way is time well spent, as it leads to stronger choices, more commitment, and a way for us to access the huge resource provided by people with aphasia.

- Need for new skills and creativity. Comfortable and familiar ways of working, for example in one-to-one sessions or in small therapeutic groups, is not always easy to transfer to more inclusive practices. In these new contexts, the focus has fallen on accomplishing an organisational task together with other people, rather than on developing an individual's skill. We have learned to evaluate processes differently, for example, by auditing the provision of communication access rather than examining a person's performance ability.

- Revising notions of competence. In each Connect project in which they have been involved, people with all degrees of aphasia have demonstrated impressive degrees of competence and creativity. Those with severe aphasia have been able to contribute significantly, if given proper support. The explicit demonstration of competence in these new roles has been critical in opening the eyes of people with and without aphasia to new possibilities. But in many cases, people with aphasia took time to combat their own feelings of incompetence and to develop the confidence to adjust to new, more equal roles.

Responding to such challenges within time and resource-poor services requires more than just making a few documents accessible. Transforming ways of working requires ongoing attention to communication, participation and evolving staff–client relationships (Stacey et al., 2000). In addition to attending to the processes and practicalities of communication access outlined in Table 1, we believe that there are other practical steps that service-provider organisations can take to engage with and develop their relationships with people with aphasia. Some examples from our own practice include:

- Time and opportunity for all staff in the service to debate and discuss organisational values and the way these are enacted (or not) within organisational practice—e.g., dedicated staff meetings and service development meetings focus on values and regularly revisit these.

- Mandatory training for all staff in Disability Equality and Communication Access—e.g., how to make documents and processes communicatively accessible.
- Opportunity for service users to engage in the monitoring and evaluation of organisational practice, values, and staff attitudes—e.g., training a small team of people with aphasia to be involved in 360° appraisal, performance reviews that explicitly reference staff challenges and achievements in attending to service values.

CONCLUSION: WHY WE FEEL IT'S BEEN WORTH IT

The emphasis on inclusion has transformed Connect's practices and yielded a number of expected and unexpected advantages. First, people with aphasia have provided a previously untapped resource at Connect, enabling us to extend our capacity and range of services.

Second, evidence from an independent evaluation suggests that working in this way has improved the health outcomes of people with complex and long-term needs (van der Gaag et al., 2005). Becoming involved in different aspects of Connect's work and activities has helped to prevent withdrawal and depression for many of our volunteers with aphasia. Many have reported benefits such as improved communication skills and confidence through becoming engaged and doing "something real".

Third, trying to work inclusively appears to have made Connect's activities more transparent and relevant for those with aphasia, for the service providers who attend our courses, and for our staff (van der Gaag & Mowles, 2005).

Fourth, working inclusively has allowed us to explore meaningful compliance with governmental mandates on user involvement. Connect clients not only manage their own aphasia, but also profoundly influence the organisation that provides services to others with aphasia.

Perhaps the most compelling reason that these efforts have been worth the time and effort invested is that we are now thinking about aphasia in terms of communication access, and are able to identify what this means. This framework has allowed us to think beyond our organisation and our particular clients, and to configure what needs to be done in order to make organisations and society more inclusive.

REFERENCES

Beukelman, D., & Mirenda, P. (1992). *Augmentative and alternative communication: Management of severe communication disorders in children and adults*. Baltimore: Paul H. Brookes.

Byng, S., & Duchan, J. (2005). Social model philosophies and principles: Their applications to therapies for aphasia. *Aphasiology, 19*, 906–922.

Chapman, R. (1981). Exploring children's communicative intents. In J. Miller (Ed.), *Assessing language production in children* (pp. 111–136). Baltimore: University Park Press.

Davis, G. (1980). A critical look at PACE therapy. In R. H. Brookshire (Ed.), *Clinical aphasiology: Conference proceedings* (pp. 248–257). Minneapolis, MN: BRK Publishers.

Department of Health (2001). *The expert patient – A new approach to chronic disease management in the 21st century*. Retrieved 5 September 2005 from www.dh.gov.uk

Department of Health (2003). *Building on the best: Choice, responsiveness and equity in the National Health Service*. Retrieved 5 September 2005 from www.dh.gov.uk

Department of Health (2005). *The National Service framework for long-term conditions*. Retrieved 5 September 2005 from www.dh.gov.uk

Hewitt, A., & Byng, S. (2003). From doing to being: From participation to engagement. In S. Parr, J. Duchan, & C. Pound (Eds.), *Aphasia inside out*. Buckingham, UK: Open University Press.

Holland, A. L. (1980) *CADL: A test of functional communication for aphasic adults*. Baltimore: University Park Press.

Kagan, A. (1998). Supported conversation for adults with aphasia: Methods and resources for training conversation partners. *Aphasiology, 12*, 816–830.

Light, J., Dattilo, J., English, J., Guitierrez, L., & Hartz, J. (1992). Instructing facilitators to support the communication of people who use augmentative communication systems. *Journal of Speech and Hearing Research, 35*, 865–875.

LPAA Project Group (2001). Life participation approaches to aphasia. In R. Chapey (Ed.), *Language intervention strategies in aphasia and related neurogenic communication disorders* (4th ed.). Philadelphia, PA: Lippincott, Williams & Wilkins.

Lyon, J. (1989). Communicative partners: Their value in re-establishing communication with aphasic adults. In T. Prescott (Ed.), *Clinical aphasiology conference proceedings*. San Diego, CA: College Hill Press.

Lyon, J., Cariski, D., Keisler, L., Rosenbek, J., Levine, R., & Kupula, J. et al. (1997). Communication partners: Enhancing participation in life and communication for adults with aphasia in natural settings. *Aphasiology, 11*(7), 693–708.

Lindsay, J., Penman, T., & Pound, C. (2000). *Partnerships in practice*. Presentation at International Aphasia Rehabilitation Conference, Rotterdam.

Manolson, A. (1992). *It takes two to talk*. Toronto, Canada: A Hanen Center Publication.

National Institute on Disability and Rehabilitation Research, United States Department of Education (2005). *Participatory action research*. Retrieved 19 June 2005 from http://www.ed.gov/searchResults.jhtml.

Pound, C., & Hewitt, A. (2004). Communication barriers; Building access and identity. In S. French & J. Swain (Eds.), *Disabling barriers: Enabling environments* (pp. 161–168). London: Sage Publications.

Prutting, C. (1982). Pragmatics as social competence. *Journal of Speech and Hearing Disorders, 47*, 123–134.

Stacey, R. D., Griffin, D., & Shaw, P. (2000). *Complexity and management – fad or radical challenge to systems thinking*. London: Routledge.

Swain, J., Clark, J., Parry, K., French, S., & Reynolds, F. (2004). *Enabling relationships in health and social care: A guide for therapists*. London: Butterworth Heinemann.

van der Gaag, A., & Mowles, C. (2005). Values in professional practice. In C. Anderson & A. van der Gaag (Eds.), *Speech and language therapy: Issues in professional practice* (pp. 10–26). London: Whurr.

van der Gaag, A., Smith, L., Davis, S., Moss, B., Cornelius, V., & Laing, S. et al. (2005). Therapy and support services for people with long-term stroke and aphasia and their relatives: A six-month follow up study. *Clinical Rehabilitation, 19*(4), 372–380.

APHASIOLOGY, 2007, 21 (1), 39–66

Ψ Psychology Press
Taylor & Francis Group

Communicative access and decision making for people with aphasia: Implementing sustainable healthcare systems change

Nina N. Simmons-Mackie

Aphasia Institute, Toronto, Canada, and Southeastern Louisiana University, Hammond, LA, USA

Aura Kagan and Charlene O'Neill Christie

Aphasia Institute, Toronto, Canada

Maria Huijbregts

Baycrest, Toronto, Canada

Sara McEwen

Toronto, Canada

Jacqueline Willems

University Health Network, Toronto Western Hospital, Canada

Background: Communicative access to information and decision making in health care appears limited for people with aphasia in spite of research demonstrating that communicative participation can be enhanced with skilled communication partners and appropriate resources. In order to address this concern, a project was designed to target the "systems" level of health care via a multi-faceted, team-based intervention called the Communicate Access Improvement Project (CAIP).

Aims: This project aimed to improve communicative access to information and decision making for people with aphasia within three healthcare systems (i.e., acute care, rehabilitation, long-term care) by increasing teams members' knowledge of and skill in providing communicative supports and by facilitating the implementation of facility-specific communicative access goals.

Methods & Procedures: Three teams representing diverse disciplines participated in the project that included a 2-day training session for each team, development of institution-specific communicative access improvement goals and materials, and on-site follow-up and support from a project speech-language pathologist. In order to determine the outcomes of team training and follow-up, qualitative research methods were employed including observation, focus groups, and open-ended interviews with team members. Qualitative data were collected before and after the 2-day skills training and after a 4-month follow-up period. Using qualitative thematic analysis the qualitative data were analysed in order to evaluate the training process, to estimate the impact of training on

Address correspondence to: Nina Simmons-Mackie PhD, 131 Orchard Row, Abita Springs, LA 70420, USA. E-mail: nmackie@selu.edu

The authors would like to acknowledge funding from the Ontario Stroke Strategy as well as the organisations that participated from the Toronto West Stroke Network.

http://www.psypress.com/aphasiology   DOI: 10.1080/02687030600798287

team knowledge, attitude, and practice, and to identify trends, themes, emerging patterns, and primary issues associated with communicative access (Spradley, 1980). *Outcomes & Results*: After the 2-day training, all teams demonstrated increased knowledge of methods of supporting communicative access, and improved understanding of access and inclusion for aphasia. After follow-up, the rehabilitation and long-term care teams achieved communicative access improvement goals and identified examples of systems changes and increased participation of people with aphasia within their programmes. They also perceived changes in team member values that supported communicative access. The acute care team reported less success in implementing goals for systems change after the 4-month follow-up. Barriers to and facilitators of sustainable system change were identified.

Conclusions: Targeting systems-level change appeared to be a useful approach to improving access to healthcare information and decision making for people with aphasia. The project provided insights into factors that facilitated or impeded communicative access in each healthcare setting and provided valuable information for future interventions designed to improve communicative access for people with aphasia.

Communicative access to participation in daily life is often taken for granted. Yet many people with aphasia face significant barriers to communicative access (Kagan & LeBlanc, 2002; LeDorze, Julien, Brassard, Durocher, & Boivin, 1994; Le Dorze et al., 2000; Parr, 2004; Parr, Byng, & Gilpin, 1997). For example, people with aphasia might be unable to join in peer conversation, to make choices about their living situations, or to obtain information about their health conditions. When communicative access is reduced due to a communication disability such as aphasia, there can be a dramatic impact on life participation and satisfaction (Cruice, Worrall, Hickson, & Murison, 2003; Parr et al., 1997; Ross & Wertz, 2003).

In recognition of the significance of the issue of "accessibility", government and accreditation bodies around the world have developed guidelines, mandates, and laws to foster equal access for individuals with disabilities. For example, in Ontario, Canada, the Ontarians with Disabilities Act (ODA, 2001, Preamble p. 1) states that "The people of Ontario support the right of persons of all ages with disabilities to enjoy equal opportunity and to participate fully in the life of the province." The United States government has mandated via the Americans with Disabilities Act (1990) that all citizens should have full and equal access to information, decision making, services, and activities, and when necessary appropriate aids or services should be provided to promote access. Similarly, many healthcare accreditation agencies stipulate that patients must have informed participation in decisions regarding their health care and substantive input into development of goals (e.g., Commission on Accreditation of Rehabilitation Facilities, 2005; Joint Commission on Accreditation of Healthcare Organisations, 2005). In fact, in the realm of health care "it is taken as given that communication and understanding between provider and patient are essential to the successful provision of health care" (Downing & Roat, 2002, p. 3). Without communication between the provider and the patient, health care is impeded. For example, "patients are more likely to take medication effectively if they have been involved in discussions about treatment options, and understand and support the decision about what is prescribed" (Drew, Chatwin, & Collins, 2001, p. 58). In spite of the growing recognition that communication is essential in healthcare delivery, studies describe diminished communicative access in health care in a variety of populations including individuals with aphasia (e.g., Alborz, McNally, & Glendinning, 2005; Alejandro, 2000; Byng, Farrelly, Fitzgerald,

Parr, & Ross, 2003; Downing & Roat, 2002. Law, Bunning, Byng, Farrelly, & Heyman, 2005). In addition, a growing literature provides strategies for enhancing communicative access and decision making in health care for various populations (e.g., Byng et al., 2003; Farrell, 1997; Kagan & LeBlanc, 2002; Kagan, Winckel, & Shumway, 1996). However, it has been our experience in North America that *communicative* access has not been put into practice in the same way as *physical* access. Whereas the latter has improved in recent times, communicative access is often narrowly defined in terms of technology for hearing-impaired people rather than defined in terms of broader issues including language barriers. We define communicative access more extensively in terms of participation in communicative events, giving and getting information, and making informed decisions. For people with restrictions in communication abilities, communicative access might, and often does, require accommodations or adaptations.

Communicative access appears limited in spite of research that has demonstrated that communicative participation for people with aphasia can be enhanced by providing skilled communication partners and appropriate communication resources (e.g., Généreux, Julien, Larfeuil, Lavoie, Soucy, & Le Dorze, 2004; Hickey, Bourgeois, & Olswang, 2004; Kagan, Black, Duchan, Simmons-Mackie, & Square, 2001; Lyon, 1998; Lyon et al., 1997; Rayner & Marshall, 2003; Rose, Worrall, & McKenna, 2003; Simmon-Mackie, Kearns, & Potechin, 1987/2005). For example, Kagan et al. (2001) demonstrated that people with aphasia participate more effectively in conversations with a trained partner. Kagan (2000) has trained a variety of disciplines such as chaplains, social workers, and various healthcare providers in methods for supporting communication with people with aphasia. Hickey, Bourgeois, and Olswang (2004) report on the training of volunteers as communicative partners for people with aphasia in nursing homes. Legg, Young, and Bryer (2005) trained medical students to interview patients with aphasia using supported conversation methods adapted from Kagan et al. 2001. Rose et al. (2003) found that "aphasia-friendly" materials assisted people with aphasia in comprehending health information. These studies confirm the notion that appropriate resources can help support successful communication, that non-aphasic individuals can be trained to support communication in aphasia, and that people with aphasia participate more effectively in conversation with trained partners.

Although significant changes in communicative participation of people with aphasia have been observed at the level of *individual dyads*, the ultimate outcome goal is improved communicative access and participation in the larger realm of *society or systems*. Without support from systems and social institutions, long-term sustainable changes in communicative access are unlikely. If change at the level of society and systems is the ultimate outcome, it makes sense to "begin at the end" and direct intervention efforts to this level (Kagan, Simmons-Mackie, & Threats, 2003). There is little information about intervention and outcome related to improved communicative access within the larger realm of society or systems. Therefore, consistent with our ongoing focus on communicative participation in aphasia, we were interested in exploring communicative access and participation at the "systems" level. We chose to focus on sustainable systems change within the healthcare system since this is a familiar setting for people with aphasia. Within healthcare settings, people with aphasia are barraged with information and choices ranging from daily concerns such as menu choices or scheduling options to serious issues such as whether to enrol in an experimental drug protocol, have major surgery, or participate in discussions about living situations or end-of-life decisions.

The investigation aimed to discover the outcome of team training and system change across three healthcare facilities. Three healthcare teams received training to support communicative access to information and decision making for people with aphasia and to facilitate increased participation within programmes. Although the project focused explicitly on training healthcare teams, the Communicative Access Improvement Project (CAIP) was designed to ultimately affect participation of people with aphasia in their own health care (see model in Figure 1). We hypothesised that:

1. teams would increase their understanding of aphasia, and their knowledge of and skill in providing communicative access in aphasia;
2. teams would identify specific "do-able" changes that could be made within their facilities in order to increase communicative access for people with aphasia;
3. teams would implement selected changes within their facilities; and
4. teams would perceive that these changes improved communicative access for people with aphasia.

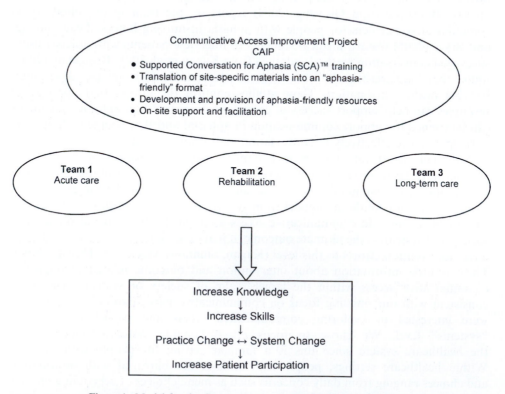

Figure 1. Model for the Communicative Access Improvement Project.

METHOD

Participants

In order to investigate this training programme and its outcomes, qualitative research methods were employed, with each healthcare facility considered a "case". The three facilities that participated in the project were selected to represent different levels of health care including acute care, rehabilitation, and long-term care (i.e., nursing home). All three facilities were large independent organisations that were considered representative of this level of care located within a large urban area in one Canadian province. The facilities were not related; that is, these were not different programmes within one system. The acute care facility was a large tertiary medical centre. The rehabilitation centre was a free-standing facility offering comprehensive rehabilitation services. The long-term care facility was a large, not-for-profit residential programme accepting residents with a variety of diagnoses. A manager associated with stroke care was identified within each facility. This manager selected a team to participate in the project, with a requirement that the manager him/herself participate in training and goal setting. In so doing, we hoped to enhance administrative buy-in to team decisions. Team members were required to work in a setting with individuals with stroke or aphasia. The rehabilitation and acute care facilities had designated "stroke teams" that were responsible for managing individuals post-stroke; participants represented members of these teams. The long-term care facility did not have teams designated for particular populations; rather, the manager selected team members from all staff within the facility. Each participating team represented a variety of disciplines (see Table 1). These ranged from non-clinical staff, such as housekeeping, to team leaders, such as managers and clinical educators. Variation in team composition reflected the different culture and practices of each facility. Teams also varied in their experience in health care and working with aphasia. In Table 2 the mean number of years of experience for team members, calculated based on self-report, is reported for total time practising in the profession and time practising in an environment where individuals with aphasia were encountered. On average, rehabilitation team members were most experienced, while acute care team members were least experienced.

TABLE 1
Team member participants listed by discipline

Acute care: 11 team members	Rehabilitation: 15 team members	Long-term care: 11 team members
2 Clinical Nurse Specialists	4 Speech Language Pathologists	1 Nurse
1 Speech Language Pathologist	3 Occupational Therapists	2 Practical Nurses
2 Occupational Therapists	4 Physiotherapists	1 Physiotherapy Assistant
2 Physiotherapists	1 Social Worker	1 Social Worker
1 Physiotherapy Assistant	1 Community Resource Worker	1 Clinical Educator (Nurse)
2 Social Workers	1 Stroke Manager	1 Health Care Aid
1 Team Manager	1 Stroke Coordinator	1 Housekeeper
		1 Food Services Worker
		2 Recreation specialists

TABLE 2
Team members' years of experience

	Acute	Rehabilitation	Long-term care	Total
Mean yrs experience (SD)	6.2 (5.6)	15.1 (8.7)	15.0 (6.8)	12.2 (8.0)
Mean yrs aphasia experience (SD)	2.6 (1.4)	10.7 (7.4)	9.8 (8.6)	8.0 (7.4)

Procedures

Intervention was delivered in two parts: (1) a 2-day training and (2) post-training support and follow-up. The post-training support and follow-up was included as part of the intervention in keeping with a "beginning with the end" philosophy. That is, we devised training to focus on our end goal of sustainable change in communicative access for people with aphasia in the participating facilities. Based on past experience and strong evidence from a recent systematic review (Thomson-O'Brien, Freemantle, Oxman, Wolf, Davis, & Herrin, 2004), we believed that the 2-day training alone might not effect sustainable systems change.

Two-day training. Each team participated as a group in a 2-day programme based on Supported Conversation for Aphasia™ (SCA) training methods (Kagan, 1998). Training included:

1. Information about aphasia.
2. Hands-on experience in using Supported Conversation, focusing on access to information and decision making for people with aphasia.
3. Brainstorming about access issues within their facilities.
4. Selection of facility-specific goals designed to enhance communicative access.

Post-training support and follow-up. Following training, teams participated in a 4-month follow-up phase. During this time teams worked at their facilities, and continued to identify communicative access goals and to implement their goals with the following assistance:

1. Project staff assisted teams in developing and producing individualised support resources.
2. A project speech-language pathologist (SLP) provided periodic on-site support including assistance with ongoing problem-solving and implementation issues.

Each team was free to define the amount of support needed from the project SLP during this follow-up phase. By allowing the teams flexibility in self-directing their follow-up, we hoped that sustainable and stable change would be more likely (Law, Polatajko, Pollock, Carswell, Baptiste, & McColl, 1994; Thomson-O'Brien et al., 2004). The project SLP's support included on-site problem solving, attending team meetings, and providing material resources. In addition, the project SLP periodically initiated telephone contact with managers or team members in order to discuss progress and offer assistance.

Data collection

Qualitative data were collected before training, after training, and after the 4-month follow-up. This consisted of observation, interviews, and focus groups. An *observation checklist* involved on-site focused observation within each programme for approximately 2 hours. The original purpose of this observation was to identify communicative strategies and resources used by staff. Once initial observations were completed, however, the observations did not provide detail sufficient to reliably describe interactive strategies used with people with aphasia. Therefore, the observation data were used primarily to gain familiarity with programmes, verify staff descriptions of general procedures, and discover physical characteristics of the facilities. The data that ultimately provided the primary findings of this project were obtained from interviews and focus groups. Individual *interviews* were completed with managers and speech-language pathologists. The same individuals were interviewed on each occasion. In addition, focused interviews were administered individually to specific team members when clarification of an issue was needed. *Focus groups* consisted of open discussions with each team, with a facilitator guiding the topic in key areas. All team members participated in the focus groups at each stage of the project with a few exceptions. For the rehabilitation team, three team members were replaced during the final focus group by new participants who had been participating as team members. One acute care team member failed to attend the final focus group; all other members attended all focus groups. For long-term care, four team members were absent from the final focus group. The managers and investigators felt that sufficient continuity of focus group participants was retained in order to represent the perspectives of teams. Different individuals conducted interviews and focus groups and different individuals conducted focus groups for training versus follow-up. The project SLP conducted interviews. Focus groups were conducted by one of the investigators and a project consultant. While the interviewer and facilitators made every effort to encourage open and honest discussion and different interviewer/facilitators were involved in data collection sessions, the involvement of a study investigator and the project SLP in data collection could have affected participants' willingness to freely express opinions and criticisms of the programme.

The interviews and focus groups were designed to target essentially the same information (see sample questions in Appendix A). The two forms of data collection allowed the researchers to triangulate data in order to help to verify findings. In addition, we felt that individual interviews with a familiar interviewer (the project SLP) might provide a context for sharing of information that might not emerge in a group setting. The interviews and focus group questions were "open-ended" in order to collect perspectives of the participants and to avoid biasing informants as much as possible (Spradley, 1979; Westby, 1990). While interviewers and focus group facilitators were provided with sample questions and topics to target, they were free to follow up on topics introduced by participants or pose questions that evolved out of discussions. Specifically, we wished to gather information about the knowledge and perspectives of participants regarding access to information and decision making by people with aphasia in their programmes. Data from interviews and focus groups were used to evaluate the training process, and to estimate the impact of training on team knowledge, attitude, and practice. In addition interviews and focus groups provided data on team members' perceptions related to access to information and decision making by people with aphasia. Interviews and focus groups were audio recorded and orthographically transcribed.

In addition to the qualitative data, a very short questionnaire was completed by the participants prior to the training and after the final focus group. The questionnaire was designed to evaluate knowledge of aphasia and supported communication, and the final questionnaire provided an opportunity for participants to give written feedback regarding the experience. The results of the questionnaire were consistent with the qualitative results reported here. These data are not included in this analysis, and will be reported elsewhere in the future (McEwen, Kagan, Simmons-Mackie, O'Neill-Christie, Huijbregts, & Willems, 2006).

Data analysis

The interview and focus group data were analysed using qualitative thematic analysis (Spradley, 1980). While data from each data source were catalogued separately in order to identify differences and similarities across facilities or data collection sources, all of the data were merged in the interpretive analysis in order to arrive at and verify overarching categories and themes. The reported findings include both focus group and interview data. The investigators who analysed the data did not participate in data collection or training. While vested interests might have biased qualitative data analysis, standards of data analysis consistent with qualitative research were maintained. At all stages, the researchers made a conscious effort to remain reflective and disciplined, and every attempt was made to understand the situation without pre-existing expectations. This allowed the issues and common threads to emerge from the data (Mertens, 1997). Analysis consisted of cyclically reviewing the large body of transcribed data to identify "semantic categories" (see Table 3 for a listing of major categories emerging after training). Categories consisted of words or phrases that formed natural groupings. For example, participants often mentioned "people" responsible for communicating with individuals with aphasia. Therefore, a category "who communicates" was identified.

TABLE 3
Categories derived from pre- and post-training interviews and focus groups

Category	Brief description of category
Ways of communicating	Includes mentions of resources, materials, and strategies that people use to communicate
Who communicates	Includes who is responsible for communication and mentions of communication partners
Barriers/facilitators	Includes things identified that help or hinder communication, access, or participation
Changes	Explicit mention of some change observed or reported in persons with aphasia, caregivers, staff, or procedures
Knowledge of aphasia	Refers to knowledge of the diagnosis and its characteristics (not knowledge of "support" or ways to communicate)
Participation	Includes mention of any aspect of participation or decision making.
Psychosocial/behaviour issues	Includes mention of feelings (e.g., sad) or "actions" such as crying or kicking someone.
Access to information	Refers to references to information given to the person with aphasia and/ or their reception of information

Next, subcategories and contrastive categories within the umbrella categories were identified. Finally, each line of transcript data was colour coded to identify occurrence of categories and subcategories within the data set. Occurrence rates and patterns within and across categories pre-training, post-training, and at follow-up were analysed to identify trends, themes, emerging patterns, and primary issues. These contributed to an understanding of participants' knowledge and experiences.

Methods used to ensure the authenticity of the findings included comparing information gathered from different sources, finding multiple examples to verify the existence of a finding, looking for disconfirming evidence that refuted a finding, and having the project speech-language pathologist review results and confirm that the findings were consistent with her experiences and observations. In addition, a second investigator "audited" the analysis in order to ensure agreement on categories and subcategories. This involved verifying the categories to determine if they were consistent with the data, and cycling through the data to identify specific examples to verify or refute the category choices.

FINDINGS

Analysis of the qualitative data revealed patterns of responding both across teams and at specific times during the project. Outcomes discovered at the end of the 2-day training were similar across the three teams. However, at the end of the 4-month follow-up differences in outcomes emerged across the teams. In general, discussions before and after the 2-day training focused explicitly on how to communicate with people with aphasia. In other words, in the pre- and post-training discussions the team members talked about "concrete" elements of communication (e.g., pictographs, pen/paper, strategies, who communicates). By contrast, the overall concentration of the final focus group discussions (after the 4-month follow-up) shifted towards the process of training, implementing goals, and internal states or feelings (e.g., awareness, confidence). Because of the differences in the orientations of teams at these two points in time, the findings will be presented in two parts: (1) before and after the 2-day training, and (2) after the 4-month follow-up.

Findings before and after the 2-day training

Analysis of qualitative data collected immediately after the 2-day training revealed: (1) increased team knowledge of ways to facilitate and support communication in aphasia, (2) altered team conceptions of communicative access and participation, (3) changes in conceptions of who should accept responsibility for communication, (4) increased team insight into practices affecting access and participation within each facility, and (5) identification of potential communicative access improvement goals to implement within each facility. Each of these findings will be discussed in detail below.

Knowledge of ways to support communication in aphasia

Within the qualitative data a category was identified and labelled "ways of communicating". This category included "strategies" that were used to facilitate communication and "resources" or materials that were used to support communication. Since training included explicit information on supporting communication, it was not surprising that marked differences emerged between pre-training and post-training descriptions of the strategies and resources used with people with aphasia. After training, team members mentioned a greater number and variety of strategies and resources, and the supports mentioned were more appropriate. The following are representative examples to demonstrate "pre-training" resources used to get or give information to people with aphasia.

> *"I would have him sit and read it 3 or 4 times and then come back in an hour."*
> *"get something like an alphabet board"*
> *[to get information] "have them write"*

Contrast the pre-training examples with representative post-training examples of methods used to facilitate communication:

> *[to get personal information] "everyone with aphasia could have a booklet at their bedside.*
> *… include their life history, personal needs, life directives, who are they and so forth."*
> *[to discuss goals] "have all the key goals and use some pictures"*
> *[regarding signage] "… for example, a sign says this way to OT [Occupational Therapy]*
> *but what if there was a little picture to show that it was OT"*

In general, references to specific resources moved from vague or inappropriate methods (e.g., writing instead of speaking, alphabet boards) to creative applications that integrated resources into specific aspects of programmes (e.g., pictographs, individualised communication booklets). Also, the number of different strategies reported to enhance communication doubled in post-training discussions (from 25 to 52). Prior to training there were reports that team members preferred to "terminate" interactions if a person with aphasia had trouble communicating, or that decisions were made for the person with aphasia without asking him/her. After training, participants reported creative methods of modifying their own communication and said that they would plan ahead to ensure that communication was maximised. For example, in discussing how case conferences could be adapted, participants noted the following after training:

> *"prepare ahead … make it easier for them to answer questions by providing some choices"*
> *"prepare for the conference … go to them before the conference and get to know what they*
> *want to talk about."*

Conceptions of "communicative access" and "participation"

A second finding after training was that teams demonstrated qualitative changes in their understanding of the concepts of "communicative access" and "participation", and began to expand their ideas of the contexts where access to information and decision making was possible. Prior to training, teams either voiced that they did not know what was meant by communicative access or else defined it in terms of "getting the same opportunities as" other patients. In other words, uniform or equal treatment was considered the same as providing access, as evidenced in the following excerpts from pre-training transcripts:

> *"… they have access because we use the same approach as used with people without*
> *aphasia"*

"... everyone is treated the same"
"Aphasic residents get to participate in all activities"
"[They participate]... monthly floor meetings are attended by all ..."
"have residents follow the crowd—just do what the others are doing ... play games that don't require mental power"

After training, participants seemed to understand that in order to have *equal* access to information, people with aphasia required *different* approaches, and that adaptations are needed to enhance understanding and decision making. Furthermore, they redefined participation as genuine "involvement" rather than simply passive presence.

"Involve the client more ... provide pictures and ask questions directly to the client"
"An indicator of success is if the client is involved ... and expressing wishes and feelings and needs."

Responsibility for ensuring communicative access

Another area of change exposed via the qualitative analysis involved the category of "who is responsible for communication". Prior to training, team members often referred to specific people who communicated with patients with aphasia or who were responsible for ensuring communicative access to information and decision making. A theme that pervaded the pre-training discussions of "who communicates" was "handing over" communication to someone else, usually a family member or the speech-language pathologist (SLP).

"The SLP is contacted if a person is having difficulty communicating."
"... I would use the SLP. She would help me with patients with aphasia ..."
"Often information is given to the wife, or not even provided at all."
"The information is given to the family"
"... often wait until the family arrives."

Although prior to training, the speech-language pathologist and the family were overwhelmingly the most frequently identified "responsible" parties, after training, team members changed their conceptions of who is responsible for ensuring communicative access from "someone else" to "all of us". Teams clearly recognised after training that true access means that everyone needs to be able to support communication whenever and wherever the need arises.

"all of us [are responsible]"
"... all our staff members, all of our support staff, receptionist. Education and training for everyone right from maintenance workers to cafeteria staff."
"[the ideal is]... cafeteria is aphasia friendly, receptionist has them [resources]"

On the long-term care team, all staff expressed a sense of responsibility for supporting communication including those from non-clinical backgrounds. For example the housekeeper said:

"I always ask residents when is the best time to clean their room—I couldn't do this with aphasic residents. But I could show them a clock and [try to let them have a choice]."

Insight into practices potentially affecting access and participation

After the 2-day training, the teams identified relevant information and situations within their programmes that should be accessible to people with aphasia, and speculated on possible barriers and facilitators of access. For example, teams felt that people with aphasia should understand programme policies and rules, have access to forms such as consents for treatment, and should have access to information and choices regarding goals, programme activities, menus, and patient education. Although some of these situations were identified prior to training, there were many more specific suggestions for facilitating participation after training.

Identification of facility-specific communicative access goals

At the end of the 2-day training, teams were asked to generate potential goals that would help make their facility more communicatively accessible. This brainstorming discussion focused not only on identifying what might be done, but also how goals might be implemented and how changes would be sustained. The list of goals generated by each team after training was extensive and creative (see Appendix B for one example). After identifying potential goals, each team discussed the feasibility and sustainability of potential changes and decided what goals they could actually implement within the 4-month follow-up. For example, the acute care team planned to implement an "aphasia advocacy team" including a protocol for the team, approval by hospital committee, a weekly meeting to address issues of clients with aphasia, and an "aphasia alert" paging system to provide a team member when needed. The rehabilitation team planned to identify a trainer(s) who would be responsible for ensuring ongoing training in methods of providing communicative access to people with aphasia within their facility. Thus, new staff and additional team members could be trained to ensure sustainable change. The long-term care team identified the need to revise admission procedures to be more "aphasia friendly" including developing an aphasia friendly intake sheet, working with people with aphasia at admission to ensure input into diet and activities, and supplementing admissions packets with pictographic resources.

Findings after 4-month support and follow-up

At the completion of the 2-day training, all teams expressed enthusiasm and commitment to make changes within their systems. Each team embarked on the support and follow-up phase of the project with plans for improving communicative access within their facilities. Not all goals listed by the teams were targeted during the follow-up phase. Teams discussed the feasibility of implementing various goals on their lists in order to identify one or more "do-able" goals to be completed during the 4-month follow-up. The project SLP was directly involved in choice of goals. Then each team defined the parameters of their chosen goals, planned implementation, and identified needed resources with the help of the project SLP as needed.

As the follow-up phase progressed, differences across teams became apparent. For example, the long-term care team met every other week to work on their goals and share success stories. The rehabilitation team held regular meetings approximately every 3 weeks. The acute care team was unable to meet for some time

TABLE 4
Positive and negative statements

Setting	Positives	Negatives	Total # evaluative comments
Acute	29% (19)	71% (46)	65
Rehabilitation	88% (43)	12% (6)	49
Long-term care	93% (54)	07% (4)	58

Proportion (and number) of positive and negative statements relative to total number of "evaluative" statements for each team in the final focus group transcripts.

following training due to illness of the team manager and scheduling of team meetings was difficult to coordinate.

The following sections will present an overall analysis of team perceptions in order to capture the different orientations of the acute care, rehabilitation, and long-term care teams, as well as specific findings relative to team members' (1) success in identification of facility-specific goals, (2) application of knowledge and skill to daily practice in supporting communicative access for people with aphasia, (3) implementation of identified facility-specific goals, (4) identification of barriers and facilitators to communicative access, and (5) other gains after follow-up.

Overall perceptions regarding training and outcomes

Overall, the rehabilitation and long-term care teams reported markedly positive opinions about the training, the projects, and the outcomes after the follow-up phase. Both teams expressed that the project had been successful and both expressed a strong desire to continue using techniques and working on applications after follow-up. Both teams related many examples of changed procedures, thinking, and roles. The acute care team was not as positive about the training, the projects, and the outcomes after the follow-up phase. They offered opinions and observations about why the project was not entirely successful in the acute care setting. In order to capture the markedly different orientation of these final group discussions, an analysis of affective "tone" markers within the discourse was undertaken. This involved a count of all words within the talk of team members representing either a positive (e.g., "very helpful", "so rewarding") or negative (e.g., "very challenging", "disappointing") condition or evaluation. Table 4 presents this analysis of "tone markers". These data represent the proportion of positive/negative words or phrases to the total number of evaluative statements for each team in final focus group transcriptions. Analysis was undertaken to ensure that no facility was misrepresented in these data due to time spent in interviews and that evaluative comments were distributed across participants. Note that there is a higher proportion of positive statements among rehabilitation and long-term care participants, but a higher proportion of negative statements among the acute care participants.

Interestingly, these statements also differed in the "degree" of positive versus negative valence. The following are representative examples of "positive" statements in the rehabilitation and long-term care discussions:

"I found it very rewarding"
"I definitely think it has improved ..."
"We are definitely very happy"

"It really is phenomenal"

Positive statements in the acute care discussion were often "qualified" or keyed downward in tone, as the following positive evaluative statements in the acute care discussions indicate:

"I see a value ... [but] I think it is a time issue."
"I think we have made increments ..."
"... this was a good start"

In addition to the "affective" evaluation of the project by team members, specific outcome categories were identified in the final focus group/interview data. The following is a discussion of these follow-up phase categories.

Identification of facility-specific goals

In the immediate post-training period, all three teams successfully identified and defined several facility-specific goals to achieve during follow-up. Long-term care and rehabilitation teams continued to address their chosen goals during follow-up. After the first month of follow-up the acute care team revised their goals due to concerns about the broad scope of projects, workload issues and difficulty getting physician involvement.

Application of knowledge and skill to daily practices

All three teams reported increased knowledge and skill in supported communication for people with aphasia. However, facilities differed in their reported implementation of ongoing communicative supports within their daily work. The long-term care team described huge changes in their daily practices. Team members related exciting stories about patients with aphasia starting to participate in activities, and "noncompliant" or "difficult" patients who changed once communication was established (see Appendix C for examples). The rehabilitation team also reported expanded knowledge and successful applications of skills to daily practice. Although the actual resources and strategies discussed by the rehabilitation and long-term care teams were essentially the same as those reported in the "post-training" interviews (e.g., pictographs, gestures, drawing, pen/paper, etc.), team members reported *ongoing use* of the supports, and reported that these ways of communicating were actually working to enhance participation and access to information in their settings. Examples of successful applications were provided such as:

"We used an aphasia friendly consent form and I found out the gentleman would like to play chess ...[ ]... I found it very rewarding"
"it enables us and the patient to communicate more complex information"
"I used the picture that asks the patient what you could do before stroke and what you do after stroke. I find it is very powerful because he was able to point to pictures of what he does and then after he only points to sleeping. It was really powerful to let me know that he is really limited and for him to be able to tell me all those ... and then nothing"

Also, rehabilitation and long-term care teams reported a dramatic shift towards sharing responsibility across all staff for communicating with people with aphasia.

"I said in my first interview that anything to do with communication was a speech path thing and I think everybody now feels comfortable and skilled to deal with it on their own"

"In the past I would turn to the family to get the answer but now I go directly to the person and use the tool."

"Before this project if we had a person with aphasia we tend to approach SLP as a key contact, but I think what we learned from, I believe at least for myself, I feel more confident to try to get information versus wait for them to get involved. So I think that is a big change … a good change."

During the final focus groups and interviews rehabilitation and long-term care team members gave examples of events or situations where people with aphasia were now actually participating. They also reported that both staff and patients felt more successful and involved. Clearly these two programmes perceived that they had been successful in applying their learned skills to enhance the participation and access of people with aphasia.

"where residents were isolated not participating in programs for six months, [they] became curious and then were beginning to participate in programs and activities on the unit.'

"they are able to participate much more and be actively involved in their own rehab where before it was more through the family. …[ ]… It's kind of empowering for them."

"It has also given us a way to provide our clients with copies of their goals in a more aphasia friendly format using pictures versus before it was just all words."

The acute care team reported increased awareness of communicative access and a new common knowledge base. However, only modest applications of communicative supports within individual team members' practices were reported. In fact, discussions of strategies and resources elicited some negative comments from acute care team members as follows:

"They are too time consuming before people really know what you are going to do. … You don't actually need all the materials"

"The materials are great but they can be a distraction. It becomes this thing that people think will solve the problem of almost anybody who comes in but we have discovered that is not the case."

Implementation of facility-specific goals

The three teams showed different outcomes related to actual implementation of facility-specific goals. The long-term care team succeeded in (1) establishing and maintaining an "aphasia team" responsible for ensuring communicative access, (2) training volunteers who participate in a communicatively accessible visiting programme for residents with aphasia, (3) developing a pictographic informed consent resource and training a volunteer to use this, (4) developing accessible pictographic resources for a variety of activities, and (5) improving participation in case conferences and goal setting for people with aphasia.

The rehabilitation team succeeded in (1) training volunteers to assist with participation and access, (2) implementing pictographic resources and strategies for goal setting and informed consent, (3) developing an aphasia-friendly tool for the receptionist, and (4) scheduling training for the receptionist and front office staff.

Realisation of these goals in rehabilitation and long-term care were reflected in positive statements about programmatic changes:

"I got his consent which was more important to me than anything. He was able to give it himself."
"We have the care conference information now so that they can really take part after they've arrived ..."
"With the pictorial ... it is able to get patients involved in participating in the discussion."

Overall, the rehabilitation and long-term care teams were overwhelmingly positive in their descriptions of the outcome of their communicative access improvement projects, and indicated plans to continue expanding their goals and improving access within their settings.

The acute care team did not implement their planned goals as hoped. During much of their final focus group, they gave reasons why the project was not a success or might not have been appropriate for their healthcare setting. Team members expressed "frustration" with unrealistic expectations for improving communicative access and participation in their setting. Following are examples of assessments of outcome by acute care team members:

"I don't know but I don't think anyone took advantage of this service [Aphasia Team]"
"What was frustrating was that maybe the expectations were set in a way that we would revise them."
"And you wonder with all the personnel going into this ... I mean we want to get enough bang for the buck and so far it seems that there is an awful lot of staff, an awful lot of personnel and an awful lot of time that would potentially be invested and the return has not been great."
"I don't know if this is the best focus for acute"

Acute care team members felt that they gained knowledge and skills from the project, and this knowledge enhanced their ability to communicate with one another regarding access issues. However, their planned "aphasia team" was not considered a success. Despite disappointment that goals were not realised, the acute care team planned future training of staff in supported communication.

Identification of barriers to sustainable system change

The fourth finding at follow-up relates to the identification of the perceived barriers to systems changes. While rehabilitation and long-term care team members did identify potential barriers to achieving communicatively accessible programmes, the vast majority of barriers were described by the acute care team. Barriers related to the following general categories: (1) staffing issues, (2) organisational/programme issues, (3) lack of success, and (4) attitudes and beliefs.

Staffing issues. Acute care team members noted that a major barrier to achieving the goal of an accessible programme was ongoing staff turnover (not only related to hiring, but also rotations of teams and residents) and constant "traffic" of new people on their units. While this barrier was also identified for the rehabilitation and long-term care teams, it subjectively appeared that the factor was more "damaging" to the continuity of programming in acute care.

Organisational/setting issues. Acute care team members frequently discussed the unique characteristics of their setting. These perceived differences in the acute care setting were most often sited as the reasons for difficulty with the project. These setting issues included: (1) difficulty communicating with team members, (2) lack of appropriate patients and short lengths of stay, (3) programme culture of a "medical model", and (4) limited time and rapid pace of work. The following is a brief discussion of each of these barriers related to the acute care setting.

- *Difficulty communicating with team members.* Acute care team members reported little time for face-to-face interaction. Time, physical proximity, number of people and styles of communication appeared to affect the "spread" of knowledge and the buy-in of staff in acute care. For example, compare the following comments regarding informing physicians by the acute care and the rehabilitation team:

  Acute: *"Staff physicians were informed a couple of weeks ago by email"*
  Acute: *"I don't know, has any medical team taken advantage of our services—you certainly had a nice note in the chart advertising your service"*[1]
  Rehabilitation: *"… one other thing is that [team member] met with Dr [X] with that booklet 'Talking to your doctor' and I think she went through it and he thought it was useful and he is going to try using it. So he is kind of on board with it too."*

- *Lack of appropriate patients and short lengths of stay.* Acute care team members noted that patients in their setting were often ill, and severely involved and focused on their own illness, grief, and shock. Patients were in and out before team members were able to establish a relationship. Team members felt that they were "not ready" for communicative access. Thus, the goals of the project were perceived to be inconsistent with their population. In addition (and perhaps more importantly), the perceived lack of appropriate candidates for communicative supports resulted in lack of opportunity to practise implementing supports for patients. Thus, there was little opportunity for staff to expand skills or experience success.

  "The number of patients to actually work with were not that great so you end up with a diminishing return. People had the education and the experience and then in the end not a great number of patients to keep skills up with."

- *Programme culture and goals of a "medical model".* Team members noted that in acute care, medical care is the goal and the medical model predominates; therefore, communicative access is not a priority.

  "Like the decision about where you are going to go. That is a major decision but it is not really up to the patient—like they can't say I want to go here."

---

[1] The speaker is addressing the rest of the team in the first utterance (asking if their aphasia team services had been utilised). She then shifts to address a particular team member who had posted a "notice" offering the aphasia team service in a specific medical chart. The shift from "our service" to "your service" likely reflects the speaker's shift from referring to the team services (including herself) to referring specifically to her colleague's offer of her own aphasia team services (your service).

- *Limited time and rapid pace of work.* Team members noted that the pressures in acute care differ from later stages of care with an emphasis on quickly assessing, stabilising, and moving patients out. Thus, time was perceived as a major barrier to achieving communicative access.

Lack of success/unrealistic expectations. Another barrier to accomplishing goals in acute care was the lack of motivating experiences and successes. Team members noted that supported communication does not have "concrete" results like other types of care.

> *"one of the models we thought of was the Tracheostomy Rounds model, but their outcomes are more obvious and you are more aware that you have succeeded—like the patient is still alive, the tracheostomy tube came out."*

Team members reported that the aphasia advocacy team was not used by physicians, and that using supported communication proved difficult. It appeared that this early lack of success undermined the motivation of the team and became self-perpetuating. Team members related that their original expectations were not realistic. They felt that the training might have been misleading in that it was based on individuals who were long post-onset and had experience with supported conversation.

> *"We have the materials and resources so that if there is the 'perfect' aphasic patient that we can use the materials on, great, we will go forward with it. However, if we don't why are we trying to kill ourselves with trying to use these materials and to do this with someone when it just isn't going to work."*
> *"Those patients at the Aphasia Institute seemed completely different. Like they were the perfect subjects. Like they were the ideal aphasic patient that you could use this stuff on."*

Attitudes, beliefs and biases. The acute care team did not appear to "buy-in" to the approach during the follow-up phase of the project. It is not entirely clear if this lack of buy-in was related to lack of leadership, obstacles inherent in acute care (as articulated by the team members), the undermining effects of failure and frustration, and/or a possible bias against the approach by one or more team members (e.g., *"Early on we suspected it might not be a good fit"*). For whatever reason, it appears that this team lost the level of commitment that they expressed immediately after the 2-day training.

Identification of facilitators of sustainable system change

Long-term care and rehabilitation team members described a variety of "facilitators" that they felt enabled success of the project within their programmes. These included (1) the overall design of training and follow-up, (2) experiences of success, and (3) aspects of their own organisations or programmes.

Design of training and follow-up. Aspects of the training and follow-up that participants reported as facilitators of system change included the intensive 2-day training, the chance to put training into practice via concrete goals, guidance, and support of the project SLP, the feeling of ownership generated via facility-specific training and implementation, the focus on "teams" (e.g., team identity, team building), and the inclusion of multiple disciplines in the project. Team members reported that they were able to learn from each other, share successes, and promote creative problem solving.

Experiences of success. Success helped teams maintain momentum and enthusiasm and created a positive cycle. Each positive result elicited positive feedback from staff, families, and patients, creating motivation for additional change. The reader will recall that the lack of success was reported as a barrier to system change by acute care team members.

Organisational/programme issues. Positive organisational factors included having a pool of patients to apply what had been learned, having organisational and managerial support (e.g., time to meet, approval of projects, positive feedback), and opportunities to meet and work as a team.

Other gains identified at follow-up by rehabilitation and long-term care

Values. An important change that was evident throughout the rehabilitation and long-term care final discussions was a pervasive shift in their feelings about communicative access and their values as a team. They made frequent comments about increased awareness of communicative access, empathy, increased confidence, and motivation to persevere in providing access.

> "… more awareness, more understanding, more empathy."
> "it's having that awareness and always having that orientation for me is something that I didn't have and that is always there now."

Related to this shift in awareness was increased insight into their own knowledge and practices. Prior to the training several team members believed that they were doing a good job providing communicative access. After the training they were able to "retrospectively" recognise their own limitations. This is an important insight relative to staff potentially "not recognising" that they or their programmes need improvements.

> "I guess I always thought I was a good active listener, so that in my perception I thought I was doing a reasonable job, but I think my horizons were a little limited and now that I have more tools to work with it has just opened up more."
> "I think it made me much more sensitive. When I reflect back on the test [pre-post questionnaires] we did the other day, I think I overrated myself in the beginning better than I thought I was, and when I took that course it really opened my eyes that I had things to learn and a lot of strategies to learn about."

These insights were reflected in a general shift in values. Immediately after training, teams demonstrated a change in their definitions of communicative access (i.e., a new understanding of access). In final focus groups and interviews, participants appeared to have assimilated this new definition into a shift in values. This shift in values appeared to be a change in the "culture" of the long-term care and rehabilitation programmes to embrace communicative access and participation as an inherent aspect of their work. While teams bought-in to communicative access after the training, the final focus groups for these two programmes evidenced, through discourse and word choice, a deeper belief in the importance of suffusing their programme with accessibility values and practices.

"It has had a major impact on the culture of the stroke programme."
"… because this has become part of our approach with providing care to our resident population."
"now certain things are popping up in my mind like a scale that we can use for a certain test—'oh I need to make that more aphasia friendly'."
"It's an awareness that the team has that informs, that will inform everything that we do as a team from now on."

Because of the projects and the shift in values, the rehabilitation and long-term care teams and their organisations accepted alterations in the way business was conducted. For example, "time" was reassessed as it applied to performing the job, as the following quotes indicate:

"Now is almost like we have to give the time to these people otherwise it is like discrimination. And so that came out by being part of that process."
"Now I think we are allowing ourselves more time and really make an emphasis on the conversation. That is a change."

Generalisation of results. Findings suggested that the training and follow-up generalised to affect professional identity, job satisfaction, and patient populations other than people with aphasia. For example, rehabilitation and long-term care team members appeared to feel that the project enhanced their identities as specialists. Some staff also reported that their jobs became less stressful or that they were less fearful of interacting with people with aphasia.

"I had a man on my unit … I would avoid him because I was feeling uncomfortable …[ ]… shortly after that [training] we were working quite well together."
"[re. a volunteer]… I didn't really see her interacting with our residents with aphasia. But after that I had a conversation with her and she told me she feels more comfortable talking with this gentleman using the implements."
"And it made my job way less stressful"
"… one of my colleagues actually said like every day is a wonderful day … it just made things so much easier for everything she's doing …"
"probably some time-saving there." [referring to each team member doing own communicating with patients with aphasia]

Staff also reported that their knowledge and practices related to communicative access for aphasia generalised to other patient populations who have difficulties in communicating.

"… not only with aphasia regarding strokes but also with our residents with dementia and other diagnoses"
"This method that we use is not only helpful for residents that have aphasia but also for people that cannot speak English"

Thus, changes in rehabilitation and long-term care extended beyond the outcomes anticipated by the project staff.

DISCUSSION

Findings suggest that the Communicative Access Improvement Project had a positive outcome in terms of team knowledge of alternative communication methods and team identification of appropriate resources and strategies for particular situations. There were clear changes in the way participants described communicative access and decision making before and after training, and in their recognition of shared responsibility for promoting access. In addition, marked changes at the "systems" level were reported for two of the participating healthcare teams and some change in the third team. The most positive response came from the long-term care team. The staff of this facility repeatedly related stories and descriptions of exciting changes occurring in their programme. Positive systems changes also occurred within rehabilitation. Outcomes in these two facilities included reported implementation of skills and knowledge within daily practices, changes in programme functions to support communicative access, and suffusing of accessibility values into programme culture and operations. In contrast, pervasive systems-level changes were not apparent in acute care. While disappointing, this confirmed the notion that increased knowledge does not necessarily translate into sustainable practices or organisational changes.

These three cases suggest that a systems-level intervention might indeed be a useful approach to improving communicative access. Of particular interest was the dynamic nature of the process. In other words the outcomes constituted more than differences in pre/post knowledge of static course content. Rather, the teams became engaged in formulating their own goals for changing individual systems, and each team outlined a variety of strategies to achieve goals within their institutions. It is interesting that all teams concluded training with an equal amount of enthusiasm and agreement that change was needed in their environment. As teams returned to their work environments, however, and the day-to-day pressures became a reality, the teams responded differently to implementation of goals. These differences provide insights into variables that influence systems change.

One variable of interest related to definitions of communicative access. Clearly teams lacked a full appreciation of communicative access prior to training, and understanding of communicative access was enhanced with training. However, as we studied our data we (the investigators) found that we needed to consider the varied aspects of communicative access. For example, during follow-up, acute care team members noted that communicative access and decision making are not possible during acute medical care. They tended to equate "access" concretely with independent decision making or use of pictographic resources. Perhaps team members failed to understand the subtleties of access and inclusion, or perhaps we presented an overly concrete conception of access. During acute health care it would seem important to maximal recovery for patients to understand what is happening to them and feel included in the process. Embracing the values of communicative access in acute care settings might mean using communicative styles and strategies that engage patients in the process and reduce anxiety. Thus, future projects should consider the multiple levels of communicative access, inclusion, and participation, and ensure that participants grasp the underlying values of communicative inclusion for all people.

Issues of leadership, institutional culture, and work environment played important roles in promoting both successful and unsuccessful outcomes. For example, teams felt that their ability to self-select goals and self-direct implementation was critical to achieving sustainable change. This mirrors evidence from the rehabilitation literature suggesting that clients who define their own goals demonstrate improved outcomes and satisfaction (Law et al., 1994). Thus, sustainable change appeared to require the active involvement of team members in the process, including training that was tailored to individual teams, facilitating team problem solving and creativity, and providing on-site, individualised support. In addition, the inclusion of managers appeared to facilitate the process of system change. In the long-term care team, upper administration with decision-making power attended every meeting with frontline staff. Decisions made by the team were supported and quickly implemented. In rehabilitation, the manager facilitated the team projects and was able to make some decisions, but at times the team had to wait for approval of projects. It is possible that such delays could diminish momentum, even when approval is forthcoming. The acute care team lacked leadership (due to illness) resulting in difficulties in moving forward, irregular meetings, and disagreements about how to implement projects. A manager not only facilitates implementation of organisational goals—a skilled manager can often overcome conflicts, attitudinal biases, and lagging motivation. When organisations foster leadership and support "bottom-up" initiatives, then changes in practice are most likely to occur (Rappolt, Pearce, McEwen, & Polatajko, 2005; Skinner, 2002). Thus, it is probable that leadership influences system-wide outcomes.

Another variable affecting outcomes appeared to be the culture of the facilities. Rappolt et al. (2005) studied healthcare practices in a post-stroke population and found that organisational characteristics were key determinants of practice change. Organisations that showed the most change in their practices were those that valued educational programmes, demonstrated strong teamwork, and were committed to "best practices". The long-term care and rehabilitation teams demonstrated a strong team ethic and teams appeared to work closely together to achieve their goals. The acute care team expressed differences of opinion and less agreement during the follow-up phase of the project. It is likely that the culture of each team influenced outcomes. Additionally, the teams differed in their knowledge and experience. The acute care and rehabilitation teams projected an image of "expertise" related to rehabilitation and aphasia from the beginning. They used more professional "jargon" and seemed more informed about aphasia than the long-term care team. These teams, particularly the acute care team, seemed to operate within a "medical model". Team composition also reflected differences in the cultures of these facilities. In terms of knowledge and expertise, the long-term care team was the least knowledgeable and educated about aphasia and communicative access. It is probable that once new skills were acquired, this created more opportunity for positive new experiences in long-term care. Also, although they had the most to learn, the newly acquired knowledge of long-term care team members did not have to "fit into" an existing belief system or existing conceptions of their own roles. In effect, the long-term care team was starting with a "clean slate". Their new experiences did not conflict with prior practices and this probably contributed to the overwhelmingly positive outcomes in the long-term care setting. Also, long-term care and rehabilitation team members reported considerably more years of experience than acute care team members.

Perhaps the professional maturity of teams influenced their ability to understand and adapt to changes in practice and culture.

Finally, the work environment undoubtedly affected outcomes. The pressures on staff and pace of work varied across facilities with the fastest-paced, highest-pressure environment being acute care. While other teams reported time pressures, the long-term care and rehabilitation teams and administrators allocated time for meeting, planning, and implementing change. Thus, the commitment of time was an important factor. The team reporting the least amount of time made the fewest changes—the team who spent the most amount of time made the most change. In addition, the work environment affected team members' opportunity to use communicative supports to form meaningful relationships with clients. Environments with longer lengths of stay and ongoing interactions and relationships between staff and patients (i.e., long-term care, rehabilitation) created contexts in which investment in communicative access was rewarded.

Clinical implications

Based on our experiences with the Communicative Access Improvement Project we would recommend that others pursue similar approaches to change at the systems level. In recognition of factors that influenced outcomes, future approaches to improving communicative access at the systems level should take into account issues of leadership, institutional culture, and placement of facilities on the continuum of health care. The barriers and facilitators described by the team participants provide valuable information for future projects. For example, specific methods of eliminating barriers such as those identified by the acute care team must be identified and addressed in the training package. While we attempted to individualise the training to each team, perhaps future efforts might focus on designing training for particular healthcare settings and including examples that are drawn from the targeted level of care. By designing facility-specific training, it is possible that teams would generalise training more easily to their own settings (Skinner, 2002). Additionally, as we (and others) gain experience in working with various healthcare teams, we hope to identify improved methods of marrying our knowledge to various settings. Also training should not only include explicit discussion of resources and strategies for facilitating communicative access, but also foreground the philosophy of communicative access and promote discussion of the "communication for all" philosophy as it might be realised within individual programmes.

Based on subjective impressions and experiences, we felt that focusing training on teams and encouraging teams to take charge of their own projects were factors in the sustainability of changes. However, when team function is not within the control of project personnel, unforeseen circumstances (e.g., illness of a manager) can have significant effects on outcomes. Future efforts might include identifying "minimum criteria" for a facility to be included in a project such as this. For example, one "minimum criterion" might be that an "alternate" leader be identified to ensure that the project continues to be viable. Additionally, more intense intervention by the project SLP might be required when projects appear to be floundering. For example, the project SLP suggested post hoc that she might have encouraged the acute care team to "think small" in order to avoid overextending their efforts.

Limitations of the study and future research directions

The outcomes of this project were interesting and informative. This project serves as a demonstration of the potential for systems intervention and also raises issues relevant to future clinical and research efforts. However, qualitative and interpretive findings should not be construed as experimental evidence of effectiveness of the project. Rather our purpose was to explore the process of systems change in order to better understand issues related to communicative access. Future research might be directed at more controlled effectiveness studies of systems change in health care. In addition, our data represented perceptions of team members regarding changes in their own practices, as well as changes they perceived in communicative participation of people with aphasia. Future research might involve interviews of people with aphasia in order to better understand their perceptions of communicative access before and after an intervention such as the Communicative Access Improvement Project. Additionally, observational data could be collected to determine objective evidence of change in communicative access. For example, data might be collected during all informed consent procedures on a particular hospital unit to document specific behaviours and resources, or to score levels of success in providing access to information or decisions (assuming that institutional clearance can be obtained for such research). Finally, the Communicative Access Improvement Project involved three healthcare facilities and was limited to the Canadian healthcare system. Future research might expand the number of facilities and levels of care studied, as well as investigating similar projects in other healthcare systems.

CONCLUSION

In conclusion, the Communicative Access Improvement Project provided information on improving communicative access to information and decision making for people with aphasia, and enhanced our understanding of the process of systems change. Thus, "beginning at the end" by targeting systems-level change appeared to be a useful approach to improving participation of people with aphasia. The 2-day training changed attitudes, increased knowledge of supported communication, and allowed teams to generate concrete goals for systems change. On-site follow-up increased the likelihood of sustainable systems change. Finally, soliciting perspectives of the team members regarding the training, their experiences, and the outcomes, provided valuable insights into factors that facilitated or impeded communicative access in each healthcare setting. Armed with insights gained from this project, we hope that future projects will continue to expand communicative access for people with aphasia within health care and other realms of society.

REFERENCES

Alborz, A., McNally, R., & Glendinning, C. (2005). Access to health care for people with learning disabilities in the UK: Mapping the issues and reviewing the evidence. *Journal of Health Services Research and Policy, 10*(3), 173–182.

Alejandro, B. (2000). Access to health service delivery for Hispanics: A communication issue. *Journal of Multicultural Nursing and Health, Summer, 6*(2), 7–17.

Byng, S., Farrelly, S., Fitzgerald, L., Parr, S., & Ross, S. (2003). *Having a say: Involving people with communication difficulties in decisions about their health care.* Research report from URL http://www.healthinpartnership.org/studies/byng.html [retrieved on 14 August 2005].

Commission on Accreditation of Rehabilitation Facilities. (2005). *Standards for medical rehabilitation* [Web Page]. URL http://www.carf.org/providers.aspx [retrieved 2 February 2005].

Cruice, M., Worrall, L., Hickson, L., & Murison, R. (2003). Finding a focus for quality of life in aphasia: Social and emotional health, and psychological well-being. *Aphasiology*, *17*(4), 333–354.

Downing, B., & Roat, C. (2002). Models for the provision of language access in health care settings. *The National Council on Interpreting in Health Care Series Papers*. URL http://www.ncihc.org [retrieved 12 August 2005].

Drew, P., Chatwin, J., & Collins, S. (2001). Conversation analysis: A method for research into interactions between patients and health-care professionals. *Health Expectations*, *4*(1), 58–70.

Farrell, C. (1997). *Health care partnerships; Debates and strategies for increasing patient involvement in health care and health services*, London: King's Fund.

Généreux, S., Julien, M., Larfeuil, C., Lavoie, V., Soucy, O., & Le Dorze, G. (2004). Using communication plans to facilitate interactions with communication-impaired persons residing in long-term care institutions. *Aphasiology*, *18*(12), 1161–1175.

Hickey, E., Bourgeois, M., & Olswang, L. (2004). Effects of training volunteers to converse with nursing home residents with aphasia. *Aphasiology*, *18*(5–7), 625–637.

Joint Commission on Accreditation of Healthcare Organisations. (2005). *Comprehensive accreditation manual for hospitals: The official handbook (CAMH)* [Web Page]. URL www.JCAHO.org [retrieved 2 February 05].

Kagan, A. (1998). Supported conversation for adults with aphasia: Methods and resources for training conversation partners. *Aphasiology*, *12*(9), 816–830.

Kagan, A. (2000, November 19). *Increasing access to medical services for people with aphasia.* Presentation at the American Speech-Language-Hearing Association Annual Convention, Washington, DC.

Kagan, A., Black, S., Duchan, J., Simmons-Mackie, N., & Square, P. (2001). Training volunteers as conversation partners using "supported conversation for adults with aphasia" (SCA): A controlled trial. *Journal of Speech, Language and Hearing Research*, *44*(3), 624–638.

Kagan, A., & LeBlanc, K. (2002). Motivating for infrastructure change: Toward a communicatively accessible, participation-based stroke care system for all those affected by aphasia. *Journal of Communication Disorders*, *35*(2), 153–169.

Kagan, A., Simmons-Mackie, N., & Threats, T. (2003, November 13). *Beginning at the end: Participation-based outcome evaluation in aphasia.* Presentation at the American Speech-Language-Hearing Association Annual Convention, Chicago, Illinois.

Kagan, A., Winckel, J., & Shumway, E. (1996). *Pictographic communication resources.* North York, Canada: Aphasia Institute.

Law, J., Bunning, K., Byng, S., Farrelly, S., & Heyman, B. (2005). Making sense in primary care: Leveling the playing field for people with communication difficulties. *Disability & Society*, *20*(2), 169–184.

Law, M., Polatajko, H., Pollock, N., Carswell, A., Baptiste, S., & McColl, M. (1994). The Canadian Occupational Performance Measure: Results of pilot testing. *Canadian Journal of Occupational Therapy*, *61*, 191–197.

Le Dorze, G., Julien, M., Brassard, C., Durocher, J., & Boivin, G. (1994). An analysis of the communication of adult residents of a long-term care hospital as perceived by their caregivers. *European Journal of Disorders of Communication*, *29*, 241–267.

Le Dorze, G., Julien, M., Généreux, S., Larfeuil, C., Navennec, C., & Laporte, D. et al. (2000). The development of a precedure for the evaluation of communication occurring between residents in long-term care and their caregivers. *Aphasiology*, *14*(1), 17–51.

Legg, C., Young, L., & Bryer, A. (2005). Training sixth-year medical students in the use of supported conversation techniques in obtaining case history information from adults with aphasia. *Aphasiology*, *19*, 559–576.

Lyon, J. G. (1998). Treating real-life functionality in a couple coping with severe aphasia. In N. Helm-Estabrooks & A. Holland (Eds.), *Approaches to the treatment of aphasia* (pp. 203–239). San Diego, CA: Singular.

Lyon, J. G., Cariski, D., Keisler, L., Rosenbek, J., Levine, R., & Kumpula, J. et al. (1997). Communication partners: Enhancing participation in life and communication for adults with aphasia in natural settings. *Aphasiology*, *11*(7), 693–708.

McEwen, S., Kagan, A., Simmons-Mackie, N., O'Neill-Christie, C., Huijbregts, M., & Willems, J. (2006). *A systems approach to improve knowledge translation in three health care contexts.* Work in progress.

Mertens, D. (1997). *Research methods in education and psychology: Integrating diversity with qualitative and quantitative approaches.* Thousand Oaks, CA: Sage Publications.

Ontarians with Disabilities Act (ODA). (2001). *Accessibility Ontario: Ontarians with Disabilities Act, Preamble*. Retrieved 22 April 2005 from http://www.gov.on.ca/citizenship/accessibility/english/act2001.htm

Parr, S. (2004). *Living with severe aphasia: The experience of communication impairment after stroke*. Brighton, UK: Pavilion Publishing.

Parr, S., Byng, S., & Gilpin, S. (1997). *Talking about aphasia*. Buckingham, UK: Open University Press.

Rappolt, S., Pearce, K., McEwen, S., & Polatajko, H. (2005). Exploring organisational characteristics associated with practice changes following a mentored online educational module. *The Journal of Continuing Education in the Health Professions, 25*, 116–124.

Rayner, H., & Marshall, J. (2003). Training volunteers as conversation partners for people with aphasia. *International Journal of Language and Communication Disorders, 38*(2), 149–164.

Rose, T., Worrall, L., & McKenna, K. (2003). The effectiveness of aphasia-friendly principles for printed health education materials for people with aphasia following stroke. *Aphasiology, 17*(10), 947–963.

Ross, K., & Wertz, R. (2003). Quality of life with and without aphasia. *Aphasiology, 17*(4), 355–364.

Simmon-Mackie, N., Kearns, K., & Potechin, G. (2005). Treatment of aphasia through family member training. *Aphasiology, 19*(6), 583–593 (originally published in 1987).

Skinner, H. (2002). *Promoting health through organisational change*. San Francisco: Benjamin Cummings.

Spradley, J. P. (1979). *The ethnographic interview*. New York: Holt, Rinehart & Winston.

Spradley, J. P. (1980). *Participant observation*. New York: Holt, Rinehart & Winston.

Thomson-O'Brien, M., Freemantle, N., Oxman, A. D., Wolf, F., Davis, D., & Herrin, J. (2004). *Continuing education meetings and workshops: Effects on professional practice and health care outcomes (Cochrane Review). The Cochrane Library, Issue 4*. Chichester, UK: John Wiley & Sons, Ltd.

US Government. (1990). *Americans with Disabilities Act*. Public Law 336 of the 101st US Congress.

Westby, C. (1990). Ethnographic interviewing: Asking the right questions to the right people in the right ways. *Journal of Childhood Communication Disorders, 13*(1), 101–111.

APPENDIX A

Examples of questions used in interviews and focus groups

❖ Facilitator/Interviewer describes a brief scenario such as *"a patient on your unit is crying, frustrated and upset. You do not know what is the problem."* What would you do in this situation?

❖ Describe situations in your program in which patients need to give or get information.

❖ Describe situations in your program in which patients make decisions.

❖ Tell me about sharing of information between staff and people with aphasia in your facility.

❖ Do people with aphasia have the same access to information as other people in your facility?

➢ Tell me about communicative access or access to information by people with aphasia in your program/facility.

➢ Think of a person with aphasia coming into your facility. How would they get information in your facility?

➢ Is this the same or different than before the project? ("Post" question only)

❖ Tell me about people with aphasia and decision making in your facility? Describe/give examples.

➢ Think of a person with aphasia in your facility. How would they participate in decisions in your facility?

➢ Is this the same or different than before the project? ("Post" question only)

❖ You have participated in training and/or in implementing this project. Can you share some of your thoughts about the experience? ("Post" question only)

❖ What advice would you have for another team, starting up a similar project to improve communicative access? ("Post" question only)

APPENDIX B

Goals generated by one team immediately after 2-day training

Project #	Goal	Examples of how goal could be implemented
1	Aphasia-friendly signage	• Add pictographs to signs
2	Aphasia-friendly resources	• Develop program-specific resources • Insure that support resources are readily available in all areas (e.g., therapy)
3	Improve initial contacts	• Train receptionist • Targeted resources available at front door & at reception • Train person who books transportation
4	Aphasia-friendly cafeteria	• Train staff • Improve signage
5	Improve goal-setting process	• Use written goals with key words & pictographs • Modify frequency and manner of talking about goals • Have a "goal coordinator" review goals with patient
6	Improve discharge process	• Develop adapted info about community programs, day programs, etc. • Develop a large (aphasia-friendly) binder with tabs/topics related to discharge issues
7	Improve stroke education program	• Trained facilitator prepares ahead & supports participation • Improve process of asking questions – compile list of FAQs* and add pictographs • Overheads with pictographs, drawing, etc. to support presentation • Consider a stroke education group just for aphasic patients
8	Improve Family Conferences	• Meet with patient ahead of time to identify key issues • Prepare ahead • Use a flip chart with key points • Structure the conference • Use pictographic and other supports • Provide "handout" for PWA* to take away • Allow more time for conferences of PWA
9	Improve team communication	• Entire team responsible for insuring own skill as a communication partner • SLP* works with PWA to build skills in using supports and participating
10	Resource teams	• Develop team as a "resource" to others to promote communicative access throughout facility • Provides consultation to other teams regarding communicating with PWA
11	Promote participation in focus groups	• Provide a means for PWA to participate in facility focus groups
12	Staff training	• Train all staff in supported communication • SLP uses modules from AI* for ongoing staff training • Include in new staff orientation • Add information for ESL* speakers

   * FAQs = Frequently asked questions; PWA = Person with aphasia; SLP = Speech-language pathologist; AI = Aphasia Institute; ESL = English as a second language.

APPENDIX C

Anecdotes provided by long-term care team

1. The team had mentioned a resident with severe aphasia during the training discussions. He was described as very introverted, never attended events, came to the dining room to eat and then returned to his room. He had no family. After training one of the team members spent ½ hour using her newly learned communicative support skills with this man and learned more about him than anyone had ever known before. After the "conversation", the resident agreed to attend one of the afternoon activities. The other residents and staff were so surprised to see him at the activity that he received a huge applause. Other staff began using supported communication with him and now he is regularly attending social events and spending less time alone. His personality has shown a noticeable difference with marked increases in greetings, smiling and engaging with others.

2. A resident on the unit was known to speak Portuguese. Staff communicated with him via a Portuguese translator, but the resident was "difficult" and had serious "behaviour problems" (kicking and biting). After training one of the nurses noticed that in admit notes the man was labelled aphasic as well as Portuguese. She decided to use some of the communicative support strategies and to her surprise he was able to communicate even though she was speaking in English. The staff began to use supports and the man's personality changed markedly. He was no longer "difficult", his care required far less time, he became more independent, he had fewer episodes of incontinence. Staff report that he now participates more in activities, gestures, initiates writing and drawing, and is making efforts to talk. The staff noted not only that he appears happier, but also that his care is far less time consuming. They have eliminated the translator and administration is very impressed with the cost savings.

APHASIOLOGY, 2007, 21 (1), 67–80

Ψ Psychology Press
Taylor & Francis Group

Access for persons with neurogenic communication disorders: Influences of Personal and Environmental Factors of the ICF

Travis Threats

Saint Louis University, St. Louis, MO, USA

Background: Access for persons with acquired communication disorders is an important area that has been evaluated and discussed using many different theoretical frameworks. Clinicians and researchers need practical frameworks and more direction to guide specific assessments of the issues influencing access.

Aim: This article discusses the issue of access through the framework of the Personal and Environmental Factors of the World Health Organisation's *International Classification of Functioning, Disability, and Health* (ICF).

Main Contribution: The ICF's Personal and Environmental Factors are discussed in relationship to access and their interactions with each other. A fuller understanding of the complexities of access issues can be achieved though the ICF framework and this article uses clinical examples to demonstrate this complexity. The clinician's role in promoting or hindering access for their clients is discussed. Lastly, the challenge of evidence-based practice and research with access issues is addressed.

Conclusions: The Personal and Environmental Factors of the ICF can be used to help elucidate the different aspects and complexity of access issues with persons with acquired aphasia. These areas need further research in order to advance intervention towards improving the lives of this population.

In looking at the quality of life for persons with acquired neurogenic communication disorders, there has been increasing attention to their ability to take advantage of the world and resources that persons without disabilities often take for granted. When looking at persons with acquired neurogenic communication disorders, the barriers to access may not always be apparent. A father in a wheelchair may have trouble getting up to his daughter's wedding in a building without a ramp, but once he does get in he can socialise and interact with family and guests without difficulty. Another father with aphasia may be able to walk up the steps but not be able to "access" the family and guests because of a communication disorder. This is not a professional stretch of the word access, as it is defined as "a means of approaching, entering, exiting, communicating with, or making use of" (*American Heritage Dictionary of the English Language*, 2000). Thus "communicating with" is as much within the meaning of the word "access" as the physical ability to enter a room. It is this "communicating with" aspect of access that is the subject of this paper—specifically personal and environmental factors that may influence this access.

Address correspondence to: Travis T. Threats PhD, Associate Professor and Chair, Department of Communication Disorders and Sciences, 3750 Lindell Blvd., Saint Louis University, St. Louis, MO, USA. E-mail: threatst@slu.edu

© 2007 Psychology Press, an imprint of the Taylor & Francis Group, an informa business
http://www.psypress.com/aphasiology   DOI: 10.1080/02687030600798303

Persons with neurogenic communication disorders have to have someone to talk to in order to be successful communicators. Other factors such as their personality traits may also influence how they interact with their environment. Despite the fact that every clinician knows how important the characteristics of the person and his or her environment are in the therapeutic intervention, there have been limited tools that could capture this essential relationship. Traditional methods of assessment target only the speech and language characteristics of persons with neurogenic communication disorders. The demand for a more holistic approach to assessment was a driving force behind the World Health Organisation's development of the 2001 *International Classification of Functioning, Disability, and Health* (ICF) (WHO, 2001).

The ICF consists of two broad domains: Functioning and Contextual Factors. Under Functioning, the ICF has the components of Body Structure, Body Function, and Activity/Participation. Contextual Factors consist of Environmental Factors and Personal Factors. Since its publication, the ICF has been discussed in relationship to persons with neurogenic communication disorders by several authors. Because of the complexity of the ICF, these articles and presentations have often touched on all of the different components of the ICF, with special attention often given to relationship among Body Function, Activity/Participation, and Environmental Factors.

Personal Factors have been discussed the least of the ICF components, most likely because Personal Factors are not coded in the ICF. Duchan (2004) has stated that by having Personal Factors in the framework, but not having them part of the coding of the classification system, this assigns it second-class status. However, the reason the WHO did not develop a classification system for Personal Factors was that the wide international variation made it impossible at that time. It should be noted that the WHO did include in the ICF that one of its future goals was the further development of the Personal Factors component.

This article focuses on a few specific aspects of both Environmental and Personal Factors, as they relate to access issues that are not often discussed by clinicians and researchers in communication disorders. Also evaluated is the relationship and interaction between Environmental Factors and Personal Factors. In aphasia therapy one can provide exemplary individual therapy, but that does not mean that these persons have anyone to talk with in their actual environments. The person also has to want to interact with the people in their environments. For a given person, Personal Factors, Environmental Factors, or a unique combination of both may most influence the level of desired access.

DEFINITIONS OF ENVIRONMENTAL AND PERSONAL FACTORS

Environmental factors are external to the person and can either be a positive or negative influence on the individual's interaction and performance in society. The ICF states that Environmental Factors "... make up the physical, social, and attitudinal environment in which people live and conduct their lives". Environmental factors are further defined as occurring at the individual or the societal level. Individual-level factors are defined (WHO, 2001, pp. 16–17) as:

> ... the immediate environment of the individual, including settings such as home, workplace, and school. Included at this level are the physical and material features of

the environment that an individual comes face to face with, as well as direct contact with others such as family, acquaintances, peers, and strangers.

The societal level factors are defined as:

> ... formal and informal social structures, services, and overarching approaches or systems in the community or society that have an impact on individuals. This level includes organisations and services related to the work environment, community activities, government agencies, communication and transportation services, and informal social networks as well as laws, regulations, formal and informal rules, attitudes, and ideologies.

Personal factors are defined (p. 17) as:

> ... particular background of an individual's life and living, and compris[ing] features of the individual that are not part of a health condition or health states. These factors may include gender, race, age, other health conditions, fitness, lifestyle, habits, upbringing, coping styles, social background, education, profession, past and current experience (past life events and concurrent events), overall behaviour pattern and character style, individual psychological assets, and other characteristics ...

Personal factors are thus those attributes within the person that have nothing to do with or are not caused by the health or disabling condition. If the health condition and disability were suddenly gone, these traits would still be there. In terms of our working with persons with acquired neurogenic communication disorders, they are what our clients had as attributes before their health condition caused their difficulties. These traits still endure, for better or worse, after the onset of their health condition and/or disability. ICF does not talk about any given trait as positive or negative, and in fact it is difficult to do so. For example, is having a highly goal-driven personality a positive or negative factor for therapy? Someone who is highly driven towards goals might be good at carryover of skills into their home environment with his or her spouse. On the other hand, a highly driven person could also pick unrealistic goals and not accept when they are not able to reach these goals, resulting in being despondent over the future.

Perhaps because Personal Factors are not coded in the ICF, there is considerable confusion, even in the literature, about how they are different from certain of the Body Function items. Part of this confusion is due to some of the Body Function items in the Mental Functions chapter. Included in this chapter are codes such as "openness to experience", "optimism", "confidence", "extraversion", and "motivation". The difference is that these characteristics are only classified as Body Function impairments when their limitation is considered pathological. For example, a person with lifelong difficulties with clinical depression might have their behaviour rated as impaired on the Body Function code "optimism". One method to distinguish the two clinically is to determine whether the personality characteristic that is seen existed before the onset of the neurogenic communication disorders. For example, if the spouse describes the person with aphasia as pessimistic and negative before the stroke, then the client's tendency to dwell mostly on failed communications is a Personal Factor. However, if the person was described as highly optimistic and outgoing and now appears unmotivated to participate in therapy, then this behaviour may be classified under Body Function. In addition, it is possible for someone to have mental health Body Function impairment, such as clinical depression, before the onset of the communication disorders that is still present or made worse post-morbidly.

ENVIRONMENTAL FACTORS AND ACCESS IN NEUROGENIC COMMUNICATION DISORDERS

Environmental factors have been extensively discussed in the disability literature within the framework of the social model of disability, with a main focus being persons with disabilities' reduced access to full participation in life and society (Oliver, 1996). In the classic medical model, the person with the disability is in deficit and their best hope for functioning lies in a health provider and/or assistive devices to make them less disabled. It is simply their problem, not society's. Even when society is called upon to help, such as charity fundraising, the emphasis is on getting the person a wheelchair or therapy, or something that would again make them less disabled. The social model represented an important step in the understanding of disability because it turned the focus from being solely on the person with the disability. The social model of disability states that it is society that limits those persons with disability and not primarily the disability itself (Tregaskis, 2002). The "cure" in the social model is for there to be collective action on the part of society to make the necessary changes, both physically and attitudinally, to fully integrate persons with disabilities into all aspects of functioning within a society.

Concerning the medical model versus the social model, the ICF strives to integrate these two opposing models, proposing a "biopsychosocial" approach. WHO states in the ICF (p. 20), "Thus, the ICF attempts to achieve a synthesis, in order to provide a coherent view of different perspectives of health from a biological, individual, and social perspective." The addition of the Environmental Factors chapter to the ICF is one way in which the ICF attempts to demonstrate that it is not purely a medical model of looking at and qualifying the person's behaviours. It is important to note that the Environment Factors chapters were spearheaded by persons in the disability rights community (Hurst, 2003). The inclusion of Personal Factors in the framework also indicates a recognition that a person is more than simply the total sum of their physical functioning. However, the fact that it is a classification system with numbers, operational definitions, and reference to using standardised norms for most behaviours puts the ICF very much in line with traditional medical thinking. Whether the "biological, individual, and social perspective" is truly integrated within the ICF, or merely put in the same book, may be subject to lively debate.

In the ICF, items listed under Environmental Factors can be either facilitators that assist a person's functioning, or barriers that hinder or limit a person's functioning. Thus, the environment is not always a negative factor, as implied in the social model. The ICF included the Environmental Factors chapters with both facilitators as well as barriers to achieve a more just society for persons with disabilities. The ICF states "The political notion that disability is as much the result of environmental barriers as it is of health conditions or impairments must be transformed, first into a research agenda, and then into valid and reliable evidence. This evidence can bring genuine social change for persons with disabilities around the world" (WHO, 2001, p. 243). Removing a barrier does not necessarily create a facilitative environment. If we only concentrate on research concerning removing barriers to access for persons with disability, then we will not pursue the equally important work on increasing facilitators.

The research agenda that the ICF refers to in order to evaluate the environment's effect on disability and functioning may be difficult to realise. Clinicians and clinical researchers are well equipped to manipulate the "environment" of a therapy session in order to effect and measure change. However, the "environment" of Environmental Factors is a particular challenge of intervention or evidence-based research. For one thing there are limited tools, if any, to reliably and validly measure many of the ICF's Environmental Factors crucial for understanding the impact of communication disorders such as the items under "Support and Relationships" (e.g., e310 Immediate family, and e330 People in positions of authority) and "Attitudes" (e.g., e450 Individual attitudes of health professions, e460 Societal attitudes). Another complicating factor is the use of the appropriate research design to study Environmental Factors and their effects on access. Rather than traditional clinical research using quantitative designs and statistics, qualitative and observational field research must be done, and greater use of these types of studies is being argued for in communication disorders (Damico & Simmons-Mackie, 2003). A third complicating factor for research is that a given factor may not always be either a barrier or a facilitator, or the extent to which it is either could vary. For example, a study seeks to ascertain the effects of family support by looking at the willingness of the spouse to adapt his or her schedule to accommodate the needs of the person with a neurogenic communication disorder. The researcher assumes that this will be a facilitator. However, what if some spouses in this study are actually upset at making these changes, which has as a negative by-product resentment towards the persons with communication disorders? So these spouses may be providing physical and societal access to all of the persons' needs, but may, because of hidden resentment, be hindering the most important access of all—access to an intimate relationship with them.

Assuming researchers could accurately measure Environmental Factors and then could even conduct qualitative or observational research to demonstrate what constitutes a barrier versus a facilitator, there would still be practical difficulties for the clinician. How does the clinician remove a barrier or increase needed facilitators for a given client? If improving access is part of the clinician's job to ensure full participation in society, then can they actually realistically achieve this goal? A second difficulty for the clinician is the application of this research in terms of how and what to measure, to prove that one has successfully intervened with these important Environmental Factors that influence access. For example, the goal of word retrieval therapy could be to decrease word retrieval latency. But what then are the goals of intervention focused on access, and how will one measure that these type of goals have been achieved?

Howe, Worrall, and Hickson (2004) wrote a review of the literature on access issues with aphasia using the ICF Environmental Factors framework. The article looked at the five domains of Environmental Factors: Support and Relationships; Attitudes; Products and Technology; Natural Environment and Human Made Changes to the Environment; and Services, Systems, and Policies. They concluded that more research needed to be done to determine which factors contributed to making an aphasia-friendly environment. Specifically, Howe et al. stated that the following should be studied in terms of their effects as either facilitators or barriers to improved access to persons with aphasia: conversational partners; written materials for persons with aphasia; systems and policy decisions and implementation; products and technology; general public knowledge concerning aphasia; and attitudes of health professionals towards persons with aphasia.

IS THE CLINICIAN A FACILITATOR OR A BARRIER?

Health professionals view themselves as the good guys when it comes to progressive attitudes towards those with disabilities. However, healthcare professionals can harbour either facilitative or barrier-producing attitudes towards persons with disabilities. For example, a clinician could view a 95-year-old client as less deserving of aggressive rehabilitation because of the client's age. In fact, in the ICF there is an Environmental Factor code specifically concerning the attitudes of healthcare professionals. The attitudes could affect how therapy goals are chosen and how intervention is implemented, including how much the clinicians work to increase their clients' access.

The concept of the clinician being a barrier is dramatically described by Reeve (2002) in the author's description of the "clinical gaze". Reeve describes it as "public stripping ... surveillance of medical experts who use the clinical gaze to identify deviance and disorder and to constitute the subject as a patient ... which leaves the recipient feeling vulnerable, exposed, humiliated and is an example of psychoemotional form of disability, as well as a form of institutional abuse" (p. 498). This sinister view of the health professional's clinical evaluation is starkly at odds with the clinicians' views of themselves as evaluating the person in order to help them. Thus, while the speech-language pathologist views the clinical evaluation as a facilitative environmental factor, obviously there are those who view this event as a barrier to full recognition of the dignity of persons with disability. To further cast the health provider as an environmental barrier position, Tregaskis (2002) states that the Union of the Physically Impaired Segregation (UPIAS) of the United Kingdom states that such professionals are dependent on the underclass disabled for their livelihood. Here, not only are we not helpful, but Tregaskis casts clinicians as parasites living off our complicity in the oppression of those with disabilities. It is implied here that perhaps we do not really want persons with disabilities to have full access and integration into society, because that would mean we would not have jobs. Reeve and Tregaskis may represent an unduly harsh view of the rehabilitation professions. Their view, and that of some who subscribe to the social model of disability, is that society, including healthcare workers, is seen as limitation or even oppression for those persons with disability. Since this model was developed to spur better environments and attitudes towards persons with disability, there may be a bias to emphasise the negative. According to Stone and Priestley (1996), disability research has an ethical responsibility to spur political action. Stone and Priestley state: "We maintain that the priorities for disability researchers must be the adoption of a social model of disablement, an overt political commitment to the development of the disabled people's movement, the use of non-exploitative research methods, and a commitment to research which is widely disseminated for use against oppression" (p. 715). Rioux (1997) states that all of disability research reflects the often unconscious bias of the researcher, whether it be medical or social models. Rioux goes on to state that what is needed is an open acknowledgement of these biases by researchers.

Despite the overt negative bias of some disability scholars, it is important not to simply dismiss their complaints. It is crucial that speech-language pathologists be self-reflective and think about whether our clients view us as facilitators to greater access in their lives, or as suggested above, just another person who diminishes their feelings of self-worth. In other words, our very presence does not automatically constitute that we are facilitators. How much time do we spend diagnosing and treating specific impairments, rather than helping the clients with the true access issues they have in their actual lives?

An example of an environmental access issue often overlooked by speech-language pathologists is the work environment (Penn & Jones, 2000). Garcia, Barrette, and Laroche (2000) surveyed speech-language pathologists, clients, and the clients' employers in regard to issues related to going back to work after the clients became aphasic. These authors found that persons with aphasia viewed themselves as carrying the burden of the reintegration process into the workplace. The employers, however, viewed themselves as part of the process of enabling persons with aphasia to successfully communicate at the job. In fact, of the groups surveyed on important aspects of work integration, only the speech-language pathologists did not mention barriers related to the specific types of communication tasks for individual clients' jobs. However, speech-language pathologists did see an important role for them concerning the attitudes of work colleagues. Thus, the speech therapists in this study recognised attitudes of fellow employees as a possible barrier, but gave limited attention to reducing the actual communication barriers their clients encounter. In this case, the clinicians were a partial environmental barrier in that they communicated to their clients, perhaps indirectly, the belief that it was primarily up to them to integrate into the workplace. Thus, their clients may not have fully advocated for themselves in that workplace. The clinicians in this study also failed to become as effective facilitators as they could have been by evaluating and intervening on the communication skills needed in the workplaces of their clients. Access to work, as Garcia et al. (2000) point out, will become increasingly difficult for persons with neurogenic communication disorders because of changes in the workplace. Service jobs with high priority on communication skills, such as the use of email, will continue to grow.

Some historical arguments against the helpfulness of clinicians should, however, be countered by the recent movements within the rehabilitation fields. In the United Kingdom, *Connect – The Communication Disability Network* has worked for inclusion of persons with communication disorders in the intervention process and also in research (Byng, Pound, & Parr, 2000). In addition, Connect's work emphasises the importance of access for person with acquired communication disorders (Parr, Pound, Byng, & Long, 1999). The Life Participation Approach to Aphasia (LPAA) (Chapey et al., 2001) of Canada and the United States has been derived from the Connect approach and is described (p. 235) as a:

> … consumer driven, service delivery approach that supports individuals with aphasia and others affected by it in achieving their immediate and longer term life goals … LPAA calls for broadening and refocusing of clinical practice and research on the consequences of aphasia … It focuses on re-engagement in life …

The LPAA philosophy goes on to state that a highly supportive environment can lessen the consequences of aphasia. Concerning Personal and Environmental factors, the LPAA states, "Intervention consists of constantly assessing, weighing, and prioritizing which personal and environmental factors should be the targets of intervention and how best to provide freer, easier, and more autonomous access to activities and social connections of choice" (p. 237).

PERSONAL FACTORS' INFLUENCE ON ACCESS

The Personal Factors component of the ICF has received the least attention of all aspects of the ICF, most likely because it is not actually coded by the classification system. However, the WHO recognised the importance of Personal Factors in influencing the ultimate outcome of disability and thus included it in the framework. This section will discuss the significant varied attributes such as race and coping strategies embodied within Personal Factors, possible influences on intervention, and interaction between Personal and Environmental Factors.

The traits listed under this component of the ICF can be split broadly into demographic information and personality traits. Demographic information includes gender, race, age, ethnicity, socioeconomic level, and nationality. These are the traits that most research uses in looking at disparities in healthcare access. In the United States, for example, there has been considerable research into access to health care for African-Americans versus Caucasian-Americans. Mayberry, Mili, and Ofili (2000) conducted a review of the health services research that demonstrated significant differences in access to medical care by race within certain disease categories.

Difference in access to medical care among groups is usually considered to be caused by environmental barriers. Williams and Rucker (2000, p. 75) state:

> Racial disparities in medical care should be understood within the context of racial inequities in societal institutions. Systematic discrimination is not the aberrant behavior of a few but is often supported by institutional policies and unconscious bias based on negative stereotypes. Effectively addressing disparities in the quality of care requires improved data systems, increased regulatory vigilance ...

This view is identical to the social model view of disability, including a government-led solution. Thus if a person with a disability is also a member of a marginalised member of a given society, then issues of environmental barriers to access become even more potentially oppressive to full participation in society.

Concerning these broader social factors of participation, the ICF (WHO, 2001, p. 7) states:

> The classification remains in the broad context of health and does not cover circumstances that are not health related, such as those brought about by socio-economic factors. For example, because of race, gender, religion, or other socio-economic characteristics people may be restricted in their execution of a task in their current environment, but these are not health related restrictions of participation as classified in ICF.

However, Reeve (2002, p. 504) states "... not all disabled people experience the same degrees of disabling barriers and discrimination: class, age, sexuality, gender, and ethnic grouping affect the consequences of impairment and hence, the social and economic experience of disability." It is understandable that the WHO would want to limit this system to health-influenced factors, but if a person is restricted in access of health, including rehabilitation services, due to race or any other attribute, then it is indeed a participation issue. Although studies along racial, ethnic, gender, and religious lines are important, they can unwittingly discourage examination of other important Personal Factors areas. There can be an assumption of homogeneity within demographic groups that does not exist, and thus the possible options for individualising intervention to increase access (Threats, 2005) can be limited.

Clinicians have to be culturally sensitive and sophisticated in our approach to clients, but ultimately we deal with individuals, not groups. Thus, while a member of a non-governmental organisation or a legislature might work for the good of a whole group, we must work for the good of the person in front of us. Culture influences, but does not dictate, the characteristics of a given person. Thus, the clinician must look at the person's culturally influenced Personal Factors, as well as other Personal Factors, to comprehensively assess a client's access needs.

The non-demographic traits included under Personal Factors can have a significant impact on access issues in those persons with neurogenic communication disorders, especially as it relates to self-advocacy. Some persons are reluctant to assert themselves even without a communication disorder. When these persons become aphasic, these traits may interfere with their ability to advocate for their needed services. Some persons' upbringings have given them a sense of can-do spirit for all endeavours, and this trait will also affect how they self-advocate.

In terms of access, Personal Factors can influence how a person responds to possible limitations secondary to disability. Reeve (2002) discusses "coming out as a disabled person" (p. 494) where the person freely admits to having a disability and still fights to be fully recognised as a contributing member of society. This is opposed to the view that only society has the problem. Reeve (2002) also states that one of the reasons that many people with disability do not always identify with political disability movements is because of this downplaying of their actual disabilities. It is also possible that political beliefs could limit identifying with such advocacy groups because their literature has definite Marxist underpinnings.

Pre-morbid views towards disability can also affect access issues. Gallois and Pittam (2002) point out that having a disability is one of the few minority groups that you can join after you reach adulthood. For a person who previously had negative views towards persons with disabilities, it can be quite devastating to now find himself or herself among those referred to as "the disabled". Preece (1995) refers to the self-advocacy as negotiating with one's environment what one really needs, and not just what others think one needs. Negative pre-morbid views of disability can negatively impact on this self-advocacy.

The emphasis on self-advocacy might strike some as another form of the medical model, in that the person must fight for themselves. However, even disability-movement-inspired government-imposed programmes about what persons with disabilities need can be paternalistic. Ultimately, people have to be helped at an individual level and those specific needs can only be articulated by the person themselves. Since a communication disorder can potentially limit this ability, the responsibility is on the speech-language pathologists to assist in the client's ability to self-advocate. In this process, the clinician needs to keep in mind that Personal Factors concerning personality traits and background influence the exchange between persons and their environments.

Included in the importance of self-advocacy is choice. Thus, a person could be given access to something but choose not to do it. This choice would not necessarily be due to negative or oppressive environment. For example, a person's workplace could be made accessible to the person returning after acquiring aphasia, but the person could decide that he or she does not want to go back to this job. The key is that the option is available, not that the person must now take it. Holding paramount Personal Factors in consideration of intervention with persons with disabilities means that they also have the right *not* to do something.

Self-advocacy is also significantly influenced by other Personal Factors including lifestyle, habits, coping styles, education, social background, past experiences, and individual psychological assets. It is tempting for the researcher or clinician to simply look up the substantial literature on each of these traits to determine how each would affect a given client's reaction to an acquired communication disorder. However, with real clients, these traits interact with each other. A higher education level could result in more financial resources, which could both result in a more aggressive approach to self-advocacy. However, this same person may be limited in achieving their goals because of their own pre-morbid maladaptive personality traits such as being overly demanding and critical of others. A person who could handle complex problems in his or her profession as a computer analyst may have difficulty in dealing with the complexities of the medical system because of past negative experiences with health care. Education and social background may or may not be predictive of personality traits needed for successful intervention and self-advocacy. Two elderly men who both were unable to complete high school and worked their entire careers as janitors might seem quite similar in terms of education, and social background, yet be quite different. One may have become a voracious reader who is active in local politics, while the other mostly watched sports on TV as his only entertainment and kept to himself. The first man may have been happily married to the same woman for many years, with six children who adore him. The other could have been married multiple times with children within and outside his marriage, and with none of his children on speaking terms because he neglected them as children. The first man may appear to be a better self-advocate because he has a stronger desire to maintain his family contacts. In addition, his supportive environment may also contribute to his self-advocacy. The second man could feel depressed that others do not seem willing to help him and thus be less willing to try to help himself.

Even pre-morbid personality traits may not be stable in the face of a major life change such as a stroke. The person who was always considered optimistic may have been viewed as such because he or she had never faced significant adversity. This person may now show aspects of his personality that were not previously evident. A person could have a spiritual change as the result of major illness that results in making positive changes in their lifestyle and outlook.

Coping styles may significantly affect how persons respond to a communication disability. In discussing communication disorders, Luterman (1991, p. 72) states: "All coping involves a stressful interaction between a person and the environment." Coping is any response to a difficulty life situation that avoids or prevents distress. Successful coping always involves the possibility of growth and always demands change. It is the people who are uncomfortable who will grow, because they are forced to derive a new set of responses to contend with a changing set of either internal or external demands. We tend to give to life what life demands of us, and when we are stressed by an external force we must find within us the strength and develop within us the resources to cope successfully. Coping is a dynamic process; it is not a stage finally won and held forever. At times it is a moment-to-moment proposition.

How persons coped with previous challenging situations may or may not be a predictor of how they react to having aphasia. Certain coping styles are maladaptive for these clients, with only some able to alter these lifelong coping strategies via therapy. In many cases the clinician may have to adapt their intervention to the coping style of their clients. For example, for those who respond to stress by withdrawing from all but their closest relatives, intervention may need to concentrate on these significant others and not try to regain the client's access to others.

The key for the clinician is to acknowledge that every client comes to the clinician with a set of traits and past experiences that will influence how he or she approaches the onset of a functional limitation. How much access the client will desire, or be willing to work for, will be influenced by these Personal Factors. How much the clinician can facilitate increased access will also be influenced by these same Personal Factors. Thus, these traits need to be taken into consideration in the final interpretation of the assessment process and in designing goals for intervention.

INTERACTION BETWEEN PERSONAL AND ENVIRONMENTAL FACTORS

For many access issues, there is an interaction between Personal and Environmental Factors that determines whether a given person with a neurogenic communication disorder is given full access to being a participatory member of society. A person's outlook on life can affect how the environment interacts with them, which in turn provides that person with more opportunities and access. Thus, the person with an optimistic positive personality may inspire others to do more to provide him or her with increased access. An environment that is accessible and supportive can help to maintain the person's pre-morbidly positive personality traits. As Howe et al. (2004) point out, there is no standard aphasia-friendly environment for all persons with aphasia.

Ylvisaker and Feeney (2000) provide an excellent example of the interaction between Personal and Environmental Factors in a population of difficult-to-serve young adult patients with traumatic brain injury. They discuss the fact that a subgroup of young adult TBI patients have pre-morbid personalities that made them prone to risk taking and oppositional behaviour. These Personal Factors are then treated like Body Functions, which means they must be reduced or eliminated. These authors state that trying to change these traits is really a form of oppression because it does not allow people to be who they are. Ylvisaker and Feeney (2000) state that their therapy programme with this subgroup is "… aimed at helping individuals fashion a self-concept that is emotionally satisfying, offers intrinsic motivation, and is adequately consistent with both their pre-injury understanding of self and the new constraints and possibilities of post-injury life" (p. 408).

Sometimes the environment becomes more oppressive in response to the Personal Factors of patients. Brush, Threats, and Calkins (2001) report a fictional, yet typical, nursing home resident whose Personal Factors and the Environmental Factors of the nursing home had a negative interaction. It is also illustrative of how clinicians can positively influence access within a nursing home setting. The article follows a patient named "Evelyn" on her first week in a nursing home.

One of Evelyn's significant Personal Factors is that she most enjoyed outdoor activities. Now that she is a resident in a nursing home, wanting to leave the building is referred to as "wandering" and could even be "treated" by restricting the resident's movement inside the nursing home. This contributes to anxious behaviour in the resident that is interpreted as being psychiatric and then the patient is medicated to point of sedation, which is the ultimate restriction of access to everything. Brush et al. go on to state that providing a closed outdoor courtyard would offer access to the outside while preserving the safety and mental health of the resident. Since Evelyn previously always walked with friends, the authors state that the facility consider starting a walking club for the residents. This activity of walking with others also serves to increase appropriate social contact. By improving Evelyn's access to being outdoors, the clinicians could thus improve physical, cognitive, and communication functioning.

A second example from the Brush et al. article is the accessibility and appropriateness of the Current Events group at the nursing home. Because this activity is set up to require prolonged attention, passive engagement, and the comprehension of complex material, Evelyn is not interactive and in fact gets up and leaves the room. Thus, the group that is supposed to be a social outlet is not one for her. The authors suggest several ways to improve her access to group socialisation including discussion of personally relevant past events in her life and active encouragement of turn taking.

A third example provided is Evelyn's limited access to meal times and its importance for her physical, psychological, and social well-being. Suggestions of modification of the environments included letting her express her food likes and dislikes, having her name written on her mealtime chair, better lighting, and conversation-conducive seating arrangements. As with walking outside with a partner, increasing Evelyn's ability to fully access the meal place has possible positive effects across the board.

ACCESS, ENVIRONMENTAL AND PERSONAL FACTORS, AND EVIDENCE-BASED PRACTICE

Threats (2002) has stated that personal and environmental factors are under-studied in the evidence-based literature. He states that the relationship between the ICF components of Personal and Environmental Factors needs more study, as well as the relationship between these two contextual factors and Activity/Participation. Studies that measure a group, do something to that group, and then measure the group afterwards are considered to be the basic methodology to prove that therapeutic intervention works. Research into the real-life effects of looking at Personal and Environmental Factors of the ICF and access issues is admittedly more complex to design and measure. However, it may be a necessary task in order to demonstrate the effectiveness of intervention.

Access and environmental factors issues are ones in which the client is not the target of intervention. Advocates for increased access to persons with communication disorders must show that this increased access leads to improved functioning in this population. It must be ascertained which Environmental Factors are amenable to change. If you cannot effectively change certain aspects of the environment, then it is a moot point to discuss it as an intervention. If you can effectively change the environment, then whether this change results in better outcomes must still be proven.

Demographic Personal Factors cannot, of course, be changed. But in working on access issues, these demographic characteristics can be lessened in terms of how they represent additional limitations on persons with disabilities. That these inequities exist in terms of access to services has been demonstrated, and it is often assumed that these inequities lead to the differential outcomes. Is equalising access for all populations enough to produce more comparable outcomes?

Pre-morbid personality characteristics, including coping styles, may or may not be amenable to change. However, they can be studied to help us predict who best benefits from which approach to therapy, especially with regard to self-advocacy. Thus, these characteristics become the independent variables in research looking at therapy efficacy and effectiveness. In addition, research needs to be conducted concerning whether or how pre-morbid personality characteristics and behaviours can be modified in order to help these persons cope and adapt to having a disability.

There is an old joke that has a man coming upon another man under a street lamp who appears to be looking for something he has dropped on the ground. The observer asks the distraught man if he has lost something there under the street lamp. The man replies that he actually lost it across the street, but the light is better here. We researchers in communication disorders have to be careful not to search for therapeutic intervention only where we are most comfortable looking. Issues concerning Personal and Environmental factors and how they affect access to others may turn out to be a crucial aspect to understanding communication disability.

REFERENCES

American Heritage Dictionary of the English Language, Fourth edition Online (2000). Accessed on 10 April 2005 at http://www.bartleby.com/61/91/A0039100.html

Brush, J., Threats, T., & Calkins, M. (2003). Influences on the perceived function of a nursing home resident. *Journal of Communication Disorders, 36*(5), 379–393.

Byng, S., Pound, C., & Parr, S. (2000). Living with aphasia: A framework for therapy interventions. In I. Papathanasiou (Ed.), *Acquired neurological communication disorders: A clinical perspective.* London: Whurr.

Chapey, R., Duchan, J., Elman, R., Garcia, L., Kagan, A., & Lyon, J. et al. (2001). Life Participation Approach to Aphasia: A statement of values for the future. In R. Chapey (Ed.). *Language intervention strategies in aphasia and related neurogenic communication disorders* (4th ed., p. 235–245). Philadelphia: Lippincott, Williams & Wilkins.

Damico, J., & Simmons-Mackie, N. (2003). Qualitative research and speech-language pathology: A tutorial for the clinical realm. *American Journal of Speech-Language Pathology, 12*(2), 131–143.

Duchan, J. F. (2004). Where is the person in the ICF? *Advances in Speech-Language Pathology, 6*(1), 63–66.

Gallois, C., & Pittam, J. (2002, July). *Living with aphasia: The impact and communication of self-stereotypes and other stereotypes.* Seminar presented at the 10th International Aphasia Rehabilitation Conference, Brisbane, Australia.

Garcia, L., Barrette, J., & Laroche, C. (2000). Perceptions of the obstacles to work reintegration for persons with aphasia. *Aphasiology, 14*(3), 269–290.

Howe, T., Worrall, L., & Hickson, L. (2004). What is an aphasia-friendly environment? *Aphasiology, 18*(11), 1015–1037.

Hurst, R. (2003). The International Disability Rights movement and the ICF. *Disability and Rehabilitation, 25*(11–12), 572–576.

Luterman, D. (1991). *Counseling the communicatively disordered and their families.* Austin, TX: Pro-Ed.

Mayberry, R., Mili, F., & Ofili, E. (2000). Racial and ethnic differences in access to medical care. *Medical Care Research and Review*, *57*(1), 108–145.

Oliver, M. (1996). *Understanding disability: From theory to practice*. Basingstoke, UK: Macmillan.

Parr, S., Pound, C., Byng, S., & Long, B. (1999). *The aphasia handbook*. London: Connect Press.

Penn, C., & Jones, D. (2000). Functional communication and the workplace: A neglected domain. In L. Worrall & C. Frattali (Eds.), *Neurogenic communication disorders: A functional approach*. New York: Thieme Publishing.

Preece, J. (1995). Disability and adult education – the consumer view. *Disability and Society*, *10*(1), 87–101.

Reeve, D. (2002). Negotiating psycho-emotional dimensions of disability and their influence on identity constructions. *Disability and Society*, *17*(5), 493–508.

Rioux, M. (1997). Disability: The place of judgment in a world of fact. *Journal of Intellectual Disability Research*, *41*(2), 102–111.

Stone, E., & Priestley, M. (1996). Parasites, pawns, and partners: Disability research and the role of non-disabled researchers. *British Journal of Sociology*, *47*(4), 699–716.

Threats, T. (2005). Culturally sensitive care in the health care setting. *Perspectives on communication disorders and sciences in culturally and linguistically diverse populations*, *12*(3), 3–5.

Threats, T. (2002). Evidence based practice research using the WHO framework. *Journal of Medical Speech-Language Pathology*, *10*(3), xvii–xxiv.

Tregaskis, C. (2002). Social model theory: the story so far … *Disability and Society*, *17*(4), 457–470.

Williams, D., & Rucker, T. (2000). Understanding and addressing racial disparities in health care. *Health Care Financing Review*, *21*(4), 75–90.

World Health Organisation (2001). *International Classification of Functioning, Disability, and Health*. Geneva: WHO.

Ylvisaker, M., & Feeney, T. (2000). Reflections on Dobermans, poodles, and social rehabilitation for difficult-to-serve individuals with traumatic brain injury. *Aphasiology*, *14*(4), 407–431.

APHASIOLOGY, 2007, 21 (1), 81–97

Ψ Psychology Press
Taylor & Francis Group

Access and social inclusion in aphasia: Interactional principles and applications

Nina N. Simmons-Mackie

Southeastern Louisiana University, Hammond, LA, USA

Jack S. Damico

The University of Louisiana at Lafayette, LA, USA

Background: People with aphasia are often excluded from full participation in communicative events and social interactions. Many consider the aphasic language deficit as the cause of social exclusion. However, social exclusion is a complex process that is situated within the wider realm of human social action. While the aphasia literature has provided data on resources and strategies that impact on inclusion and participation, other realms of social science have targeted social action in all its authenticity and complexity, and have focused on how social action is effectively established, negotiated, and sustained. A study of this literature can expand our understanding of issues involved in inclusion, participation, and communicative access of people with aphasia.

Aims: This article will review a selected corpus of social science research that is outside the clinician's typical experience, but that is relevant to the issues of accessibility and social inclusion in aphasia.

Main Contribution: Four interactional principles relevant to the enhancement of social accessibility and social inclusion will be discussed. These four principles concern social constructionism, local negotiation of social action, the collaborative nature of social action, and ways that social dimensions are manifested in social action. Understanding of broad principles of social interaction will improve our ability to enable social participation and inclusion of people with aphasia.

Conclusions: This paper will describe four principles of human social interaction and highlight clinical implications involving various therapeutic strategies and communicative values related to communicative inclusion and social participation.

In the field of aphasiology there has been a growing concentration on quality of life issues in aphasia, especially how aphasia affects an individual's access to communication, people, and social settings. The available literature on these topics suggests that people with aphasia are often excluded from full participation in peer conversation, from obtaining needed information, and from making important life decisions (e.g., Byng, Duchan, & Cairns, 2002; Byng, Farrelly, Fitzgerald, Parr, & Ross, 2003; Kagan, Black, Duchan, Simmons-Mackie, & Square, 2001; Kagan & Leblanc, 2002; Le Dorze & Brassard, 1995; Michallet, Tetreault, & Le Dorze, 2003; Parr, 1994; Parr, Byng, Gilpin, & Ireland, 1997). For example, Byng et al. (2002)

Address correspondence to: Nina Simmons-Mackie PhD, 131 Orchard Row, Abita Springs, LA 70420, USA. E-mail: nmackie@selu.edu describe the observations of a client with aphasia who felt denied from full participation in her therapy because her therapist did not seek her opinions or her participation as a partner. This illustration is typical of the experiences of many people with aphasia both within and outside the therapeutic context. Aphasia results in extensive consequences that transcend the physical and that affect the social lives of all involved parties. Indeed, such social difficulties are ubiquitous in aphasia.

Given how pervasive these social consequences are in aphasia, it is surprising that there has been relatively little focus on this issue until recently. While some earlier publications discussed social consequences (e.g., Artes & Hoops, 1976; Kinsella & Duffy, 1980; Knox, 1971; Malone, Ptacek, & Malone, 1970; Muller & Code, 1983; Oliver, 1983), the vast majority of research in this area has been produced within the past 10 years. One reason for this belated focus is that the issues of accessibility and social inclusion in aphasia are complex, and they involve numerous social, contextual, and cultural considerations. Given this complexity, it is not surprising that the discipline of aphasiology with its medical and experimental orientations has not focused extensively on these issues.

With the recent foci on functional outcomes (e.g., Elman & Bernstein-Ellis, 1995; Enderby & John, 1997; Holland & Thompson, 1998; Worrall & Frattali, 2000) and life participation approaches (e.g., Chapey et al., 2001; Lyon, 1996; Parr, Duchan, & Pound, 2003), and an increase in the application of qualitative research methodologies in aphasia (e.g., Damico, Simmons-Mackie, Oelschlaeger, Elman, & Armstrong, 1999; Ferguson, 1996; Goodwin, 1995; Le Dorze & Brassard, 1995; Perkins, 1995; Wilkinson, 1995), the issues of accessibility and social inclusion have become more prominent. The research conducted over the past decade has suggested that while the aphasic communication disability is a barrier to standard participation, accessible communication and decision making by people with aphasia is possible. Based on our acquired knowledge, a number of strategies and resources that support participation and inclusion have been described in the aphasia literature and have demonstrated that it is possible to provide communicative contexts and resources that enable communicative participation (e.g., Byng, Pound, & Parr, 2000; Garrett & Beukelman, 1995; Kagan, 1998; Kagan et al., 2001; Lyon, 1997; Oelschlaeger & Damico, 2000; Simmons-Mackie & Kagan, 1999). This research is quite promising but more needs to be accomplished.

To continue developing this line of research and its clinical implications, it is important to extend our knowledge base regarding social issues and how they are employed to achieve social action. While the discipline of clinical aphasiology has provided some data in this area, other realms of social science have targeted social action in all its authenticity and complexity and have focused on how social action is effectively established, negotiated, and sustained. Within this literature, social action is defined broadly as human acts carried out in the service of social interaction or social membership. Communication is perhaps the ultimate form of social action including a wide range of interactive events and behaviours such as conversing, flirting, arguing, nonverbal posturing, or negotiating. A study of social action from the perspective of multiple disciplines could enrich our appreciation of social inclusion (or exclusion) in aphasia. Thus, this article will discuss some of the social science research that is outside the clinician's typical experience but that is relevant to the issues of accessibility and social inclusion in aphasia. By surveying sub-disciplines like microsociology, ethnomethodology, interactional sociology, inter-actional aphasiology, and various disciplines focusing on discourse studies, we have chosen a set of important interactional principles that should be employed in research and/or clinical practices regarding the social impact of aphasia, especially as it involves social inclusion and issues of accessibility.

INTERACTIONAL PRINCIPLES FOR CLINICAL APHASIOLOGY

Given the complexity of the social process in all its various manifestations, it is important to have a set of principles available when engaging in data collection, analysis, and interpretation. These principles can guide how data are treated and what importance the data or patterns of data might hold. Further, a set of principles can inform the clinician as she/he attempts to construct values, strategies, and techniques that can assist in increasing access and social inclusion for aphasia. Based on our research and a survey of the literature, there appear to be a number of interactional principles of social action that should be considered. In this article we will highlight four interactional principles. Each will be briefly discussed and then some implications as they pertain to issues of accessibility and social inclusion in aphasia will be provided.

Social constructionism

When surveying the social sciences, one is struck by the pervasiveness of a particular idea that orients our attention to the social world. As such, it is the first principle. Known as "social constructionism", this principle places the primary impetus for human behaviours and beliefs on social interaction and the symbolic context within which an individual operates (Blumer, 1969; Weber, 1946). This principle suggests that people construct the meanings of objects and situations through their interactions with one another. That is, through their face-to-face interactions, individuals socially construct their behaviours, expectations, and beliefs (Blumer, 1969; Durkheim, 1964; Garfinkel, 1967; Gergen & Davis, 1985; Goffman, 1974; Rogers, 1980; Scheff, 1990). Indeed, to a social constructivist, many of the human behavioural traits and psychological processes like self-identity, competence, and the capacity and reactions to intimacy are constructed via social interaction, and human beings develop these internal constructs based on external interactions with others. In their classic sociology text *The Social Construction of Reality*, Berger and Luckmann (1967) emphasise how most societal expectations and social actions are constructed through interactions with one's peers, and that these social interactions are the essential feature of the human condition in order to assist in the construction and establishment of those psycho-social behaviours and constructs that define us as human (Berger & Luckmann, 1967; Blumer, 1969; Kemper, 1991; Shotter, 1984).

The significance of this principle of social constructionism is that this perspective provides one with a theoretical framework from which to view the establishment and maintenance of systematic social and psychological behaviours. Rather than asserting that a particular personality trait or a specific behaviour is due to a psychological construct or neurological module devoid of social influence, this principle places the motivation of any trait, belief, or behaviour squarely within the social sphere. Who we are and how we react is based on our previous and concurrent social interactions. Importantly, as people with aphasia become socially isolated, this condition can have an impact on both their social competence and the numerous other behaviours and traits that are based on social contact. Consequently, re-establishing lost social competence and effectiveness, and establishing various social compensations, requires successful and targeted social contact and interactions.

A concrete example of social constructionism is demonstrated in a sociolinguistic analysis of an aphasia therapy session where the participants constructed social roles through social actions (Simmons-Mackie & Damico, 1999). The authors describe how expectations and beliefs were visible within the therapy discourse and how social roles of "impaired patient" and "expert clinician" were realised and co-constructed through therapy discourse and interaction. These narrowly constructed social roles effectively barred the client from participating in choices regarding therapy materials, goals or tasks (i.e., taking on the role of consumer) resulting in the client walking out of the session and "quitting" therapy.

Local negotiation of social action

Consistent with the first principle, the second interactional principle also places the emphasis on the actual activities that occur during face-to-face interaction. Any successful social action is accomplished at the local level. This means that any social phenomenon as it unfolds is locally and immediately constituted through the observable activities of the participants. This principle is consistent with ethnomethodology (Garfinkel, 1967) and the expectation is that an individual's "common-sense" knowledge of the social world is used on an instance-by-instance basis to construct social action. In this sense, what participants in a social interaction will do in their next interactive turn is related to what their interactive partners have done in the immediate prior turn. This reliance on the immediate and local actions and context, such that one action helps determine the next, creates a *conditional relevance* so that a first action helps determine what may occur as a second action, and the second actually depends on what occurred as the first action (Garfinkel, 1967; Sacks, 1992; Schegloff, 1968). In any social action the importance of this local negotiation can be generally stated as a condition where actions project next actions (Heritage, 1984).

Scheff (1990) has described the importance of this local interpretation by seeing social action at a "micro" rather than a "macro" level and suggesting that the microworld underlies all social occasions. In this microworld, social action is accomplished through the interacting of the immediate context, individuals, and conventions as well as the thoughts, ideas, and emotions imparted by the participants and all of this is negotiated in an immediate instance-by-instance time frame. Consequently, social action is contextually dependent, meaning that it is strongly influenced by the social context in which it occurs. Bruner supports this position when describing "situated action" in *Acts of Meaning* (1990). In this book he stresses the concept that all meaning-making behaviours and all systematic social action exist within both a cultural and a situational context and are negotiated within those contexts.

With regard to issues like accessibility and social inclusion in aphasia, this principle recognises that the context is always highly relevant to data interpretation and to any subsequent actions (Duranti & Goodwin, 1992). Consequently, when considering both the barriers and the solutions to accessibility and social inclusion, these constructs are never treated as isolated or self-contained artefacts. Rather, all social actions are oriented to the contexts and interactions under scrutiny and due consideration should be given to the impact of these variables.

The collaborative nature of social action

The third interactional principle is the logical consequence of the first two—social action is always a collaborative enterprise. If social construction is accomplished at the local level, then all social actions are active and dynamic enterprises wherein (at least) two participants are involved in a process of co-construction. Social actions of all sorts (e.g., conversation, arguments, fights, nonverbal posturing) are not a series of discrete behaviours or messages that pass from an active individual to a passive one. Rather, it is a process of participants actively constructing and negotiating meaning in a coordinated and joint manner as the social action proceeds. This principle has been a focus of social science research for over 40 years in communicative discourse and the findings suggest that conversation is a mutually structured activity between the speaker and the listener to accomplish real and tangible purposes in actual settings and situations (Hymes, 1967; Shotter, 1984). Goffman's work on "participation frameworks" (1969, 1974) and Bell's concept of "audience design" (1984) both demonstrate this co-participation.

For over a decade, as the authors and others have focused on discourse in aphasia, this principle of social action as a collaborative enterprise has been repeatedly documented and verified. Whether in studies of therapy discourse between speech-language pathologists and clients with aphasia (e.g., Damico, Simmons-Mackie, Oelschlaeger, & Tetnowski, 2000; Simmons-Mackie, 1998; Simmons-Mackie & Damico, 1999; Simmons-Mackie, Damico, & Damico, 1999) or studies focusing on natural discourse between people with aphasia and various communicative partners (e.g., Ferguson, 1996; Goodwin, 1995; Klippi, 1996; Laasko, 1997; Milroy & Perkins, 1992; Oelschlaeger & Damico, 1998a, 1998b, 2000; Simmons-Mackie & Damico, 1996a, 1997; Simmons-Mackie & Kagan, 1999), the powerful influence of collaborative discourse management on the participation of the person with aphasia has been a recurrent theme.

The significance of the collaborative nature of social action is very important in clinical aphasiology. Several implications are immediately apparent. In terms of assessment, it is not sufficient to focus only on the person with aphasia. These individuals will be more or less successful as communicators depending on how other individuals in the context collaborate with them. Further, their potential for increased accessibility and social inclusion is often more dependent on their interactional partners than their own abilities (Holland, 1998; Parr, et al., 1997, 2003; Simmons-Mackie, 1998; Simmons-Mackie & Kagan, 1999). To sufficiently assess a person with aphasia, therefore, the process should include a description of both the targeted individual, his/her conversational partner(s) and the interactional contexts within which the individual operates (e.g., Copeland, 1989; Simmons-Mackie & Damico, 2001; Worrall, McCooey, Davidson, Larkins, & Hickson, 2002). For example, observation and interviews have been used with people with aphasia and their significant others to gather qualitative information regarding social networks, collaborative discourse characteristics, and features of relevant context (e.g., Simmons-Mackie & Damico, 1996b, 2001). Simmons-Mackie and Damico (2001) describe such an assessment that resulted in intervention focusing explicitly on improving social participation and communicative access for one woman with aphasia (Simmons-Mackie & Damico, 2001). Assessment involving micro-analysis of conversations has also provided important data on the collaborative construction of meaning between people with aphasia and their regular communication partners (e.g., Booth & Perkins, 1999; Perkins, Crisp, & Walshaw, 1999).

The implications in intervention are even more extensive. First, intervention must involve work with collaborators (i.e., communicative buddies, speaking partners, conversation partners) to provide sufficient communicative and structural support for the individual with communicative impairment if accessibility and social inclusion are to be improved (e.g., Holland, 1998; Kagan, 1998; Kagan & Gailey, 1993; Lyon, 1997; Simmons-Mackie, 1998; Simmons-Mackie & Kagan, 1999). Collaboration by itself, however, may not be sufficient. Due to the deficit nature of aphasia, many people with aphasia are unable to collaboratively negotiate even standard communicative interactions. In such instances, collaboration without sufficient supports can overload formulation demands on the person with aphasia and diminish participation. In the following example, the partner (DR) asks open-ended questions which provide the person with aphasia (PWA) no means of contributing potential responses.

DR: What kind of work do you do?
PWA: Uh ((points up and circles finger in air))
DR: (.4) Um your work um ... what?
PWA: Over here ((points towards the door))
DR: Over here? What do you mean?
PWA: No no ... um ((looks down))
DR: Did you work before?

This dyad never achieves a successful conclusion to this exchange. In effect, the reliance on open-ended questioning of the partner coupled with a lack of partner support and skill excludes the person with aphasia from contributing to the conversation.

In such instances, supportive strategies and resources may be needed to promote participation in conversation and to achieve social inclusion (e.g., Goodwin, 1995; Holland, 1998; Kagan, 1998; Kagan & Gailey, 1993; Lyon, 1997; Simmons-Mackie, 1998). Options suggested in the literature to alleviate this exclusion include using various "speaking for" behaviours, close-ended questions, hint and guess sequences, questions that progressively bracket the answer, joint productions, word search strategies, spontaneous verbal repetition, using resources like written choices, pictographs, or drawing, orienting to nonverbal behaviours to aid guessing, and even non-traditional resources like laughter (e.g., Croteau, Vychytil, Larfeuil, & Le Dorze, 2004; Klippi, 1991, 1996; Laasko, 1997; Madden, Oelschlaeger, & Damico, 2002; Milroy & Perkins, 1992; Oelschlaeger & Damico, 1998a, 1998b, 2000; Simmons-Mackie & Kagan, 1999; Simmons-Mackie, Kingston, & Schultz, 2004). Additionally, the literature suggests that partners orient to multiple layers of information conveyed by people with aphasia since speech might not carry the weight of intent (Davidson, Worrall, & Hickson, 2003; Goodwin, 1995; Ramsberger & Rende, 2001; Simmons-Mackie et al. 2004). In other words people with aphasia, particularly severe aphasia, often use layers of information such as facial expression, prosody, gestures, body language, and minimal verbalisations that convey an idea which is not explicit. For example, Goodwin and colleagues (Goodwin, 1995; Goodwin, Goodwin, & Olsher, 2002) have described the strategic use of gestures, objects in the environment, stereotypic utterances (i.e., yes, no), timing of turns, and prosody by a man with severe aphasia as he negotiated meanings in conversation. By orienting to these multiple layers of information and skilfully employing timely and appropriate resources and support strategies, partners are potentially able to avoid a one-sided interaction and fend off communicative breakdowns and visible trouble.

Manifestations of the social dimensions

The fourth interactional principle concerns how our social interactions correlate with "underlying" social dimensions to influence our identities and placement within the social context. Underlying dimensions such as power, authority, and solidarity do impact on our actions and their interpretations. Who we perceive ourselves to be and how we respond in social contexts is often dependent on the negotiation of these various social dimensions. Consequently, to understand just how we are able to accomplish social actions and to navigate the complexities of accessibility and social inclusion, we must have a functioning understanding of these relations between various social dimensions and their influence on our actions, language, and discourse.

Of course, as objects of discussion, these social dimensions are not easily defined or described. They are complicated values and expectations that are often more metaphorical than tangible. They are relative terms imbued with various qualities that do not lend themselves to clear definitions (Gergen, 1991). Consequently, when focusing on these dimensions, we tend to view them as *social constructions* of reality that are the outgrowth of interactive processes with others and not a simple mirror of *external* reality. Three illustrations of these social dimensions and how they are manifested will demonstrate the importance of this fourth interactional principle for issues of social inclusion and accessibility in aphasia.

Interactional power and asymmetry. One social dimension that influences participation in communicative interactions is the distribution of *interactional power* (Damico, Simmons-Mackie, & Hawley, 2005; Fairclough, 1989; Tannen, 1987). In general, interactional power is created when a participant is perceived by others to be more dominant, hold higher status, or be an expert or an authority. In such instances, power is negotiated and dynamically manipulated during interactions, and one's placement along a relative power continuum may affect numerous conversational behaviours. For example, the distribution of power within an interaction might affect *communicative equality* which is the relatively equal opportunity for participants to contribute to discourse structure and content. Although many believe that communicative equality is simply characterised by equal speaking turns or equal offerings of information, this is not always the case. Rather, communicative equality reflects that a participant is able to negotiate the level of participation that she/he desires within the particular context—in other words, that the participant has equal access to participation. When a power imbalance exists, the more powerful participant might employ behaviours or resources to exert control or constrain the interaction (Damico et al., 2005). Thus, the weaker member of the interaction might be denied full participation.

During conversations involving persons with aphasia, the social dimension of interactional power is frequently employed to the detriment of the person with aphasia. Linguistically, the person with aphasia is typically the less-dominant member of a conversational dyad. In this circumstance the dominant communicator (non-aphasic) is able to constrain who speaks and when. This more-dominant partner sets the topics, allocates the turns and even shifts to new topics while the person with aphasia is less engaged or is a relatively passive member of the interaction. Such asymmetrical discourse limits participation in conversation. This power imbalance has also been documented in aphasia therapy settings. For example, therapists establish themselves as "experts" by providing evaluative feedback ("that was a good one", "try that again") while one rarely hears the person with aphasia evaluating the therapist during therapy interactions with a rousing "nice instruction!" (Simmons-Mackie et al., 1999). Of course, feedback is not the only way that interactional power is manifested in the therapeutic context. Within this setting therapists control speaking turns, select or limit topics, employ questions to control the contributions of the client, employ structured therapy routines like Request-Response-Evaluation (RRE) sequences, and structure the discourse to establish control and authority over the person with aphasia (Damico et al., 2000). In such asymmetrical interactions, one party might control various aspects of speaking rights. For example, Simmons-Mackie and Schultz (2003) found that occurrences of attempts at humour were markedly asymmetrical within the therapy sessions that they studied, with the overwhelming majority of humour attempts (82%) initiated by clinicians. The authors suggested that clinicians held the "joking rights" during therapy sessions.

While these behaviours may be appropriate to the needs and requirements of the therapeutic setting (Panagos, 1996), such control and demonstrations of inter-actional power by therapists can enculturate the client into a relatively passive communicative role that can extend beyond the clinic boundary into real-life interactions. By more fully understanding the negotiation of power within therapy interactions, clinicians might be better equipped to advise the conversational partners of people with aphasia in methods of promoting participation and equality. Thus, the realisation of interactional power might be directly related to the person with aphasia's degree of autonomy and choice in communicative interactions.

Another example of how interactional power is manifested is in the management of repair in interactions with people with aphasia. When people with aphasia encounter difficulties in communicating (e.g., hesitate for word search, produce an unclear utterance), their communicative partners are faced with a range of choices for dealing with this trouble. As the more-dominant conversational partner, the non-aphasic individual might take over the turn at talk or begin to dominate the interaction. Simmons-Mackie et al. (2004, p. 116) describe a violation of speaking rights that occurs when the non-aphasic speaking partner invades the communicative space of the person with aphasia:

> A man with aphasia (Paul) and his wife (Gail) are ordering lunch at a restaurant. The waitress is looking at Paul waiting for him to place his order.
> 1. Paul: Uh uh uh the uh hab [uh ((gazing at the waitress))
> 2. Gail: [He'll have the hamburger.
> 3. Paul: ((Paul shifts his gaze to Gail with a surprised look, then frowns))

Paul's hesitation provides his wife with an opportunity to interrupt and seize Paul's turn and, in effect, answer for him. Gail's violation of her husband's turn at talk could reflect any number of underlying issues and values. Such interruptions might reflect a preference for efficiency, a belief that Paul might not be capable of ordering, or a lack of respect for Paul's right to communicative autonomy. This tactic for negotiating trouble in conversation might be contrasted with more supportive approaches to dealing with conversational trouble. For example, several studies describe collaborative word searches between people with aphasia and their communication partners, and describe strategies used by people with aphasia to invite partners to collaborate in repairs (e.g., pauses, utterances, gaze) as well as strategies used by partners to negotiate repairs (Croteau et al., 2004; Milroy & Perkins, 1992; Oelschlaeger & Damico, 1998a, 1998b, 2000). Such subtle variations in the management of breakdowns can signal differences between communicative inclusion and exclusion. Thus, trouble spots in conversation provide a critical "decision point" at which people with aphasia and their communication partners negotiate the level of participation in social action. However, this decision point must be negotiated with sensitivity to the many factors inherent in the local context. In one interaction maximising client participation might be most appropriate (e.g., discussing therapy goals, informal conversation), whereas in another situation efficiency might take precedence over inclusion (e.g., instructing client during a fire drill). Thus, training of people with aphasia and potential partners must focus on teaching a range of optional strategies that support communicative access and instilling the underlying values that influence inclusion and access.

In addition to overtly controlling discourse structures, therapists and communication partners sometimes employ a dominant interpretive framework to impose their own *interpretations* of utterances. Research on interpersonal communication suggests that expectations and beliefs influence our interpretation of messages. When clinicians or communication partners expect clients to make errors or perform poorly, then potentially appropriate behaviour might be interpreted otherwise (Damico & Damico, 1997; Ulichny & Watson-Gegeo, 1989). In so doing, the partner "denies" persons with aphasia the opportunity to share opinions, make decisions or express their own ideas. Simmons (1993, unpublished data) describes an interaction in which the therapist's expectations mark acceptable client offerings as "inadequate":

> A client with aphasia is completing a treatment task involving picture description. She is describing a picture of a family having a picnic near a lake.
> Client: The people are in the nature.
>   ((spoken slowly and deliberately))
> SLP: Mhm, okay. You could say the people are in nature ... OR ...
>   The people are at the lake.
>   What's the better word?
> Client: Lake?
> SLP: Yea, lake. Good.

Here the therapist has corrected an acceptable word (nature) and offered her own choice (lake). By imposing her own interpretation based on expectations, the therapist has excluded the client with aphasia from sharing her own unique meaning and the therapist has employed her dominant interpretive framework as a manifestation of her interactional power.

Marginality and enculturation of communicative values. A second social dimension that can serve as an illustration involves the process of marginality. As discussed by

Simmel (1950), an individual is marginal if she/he remains on the periphery of a group or context within which interactions are being sought. This marginality may be freely chosen or imposed upon an individual due to various kinds of differences or stigmas (Goffman, 1964; Simmel, 1950). In aphasia, marginalisation occurs when the person with aphasia is oriented to as "different", "damaged", or "less than expected". Others judge the person with aphasia as "outside" of standard membership in the dyad or group, and/or persons with aphasia judge themselves as marginal to social membership. When one becomes a "marginal man" (Park, 1928), accessibility and inclusion are severely curtailed.

Marginalisation might occur when someone in a group or dyad is oriented to as "incompetent". People with aphasia often comment that other people treat them as if they are "stupid" or "mentally deficient". Communication partners who lack knowledge and skill in interacting with someone with aphasia might indeed perceive the person with aphasia as incompetent. As with all other social actors, communicative participation of the person with aphasia depends on an assumption that the person is, in fact, competent to participate (Simmons-Mackie et al., 2004). When communicative partners do not believe in the inherent competence of their communicative participant, then it is unlikely that they will adjust the interaction to support full participation, since communicative interactants often evidence their biases through their discourse. For example, when looking at what made for "good" and "poor" speaking partners during conversational partner training sessions, the aphasic deficit or the role of patient was often made visible within the relationship when the "poor" speaking partners engaged in social action (Simmons-Mackie & Kagan, 1999). During such encounters, the aphasia or stroke as a problem was highlighted and this acted to raise the impairment to the surface of the conversation. For example, one partner focused conversation on aphasia with questions like "Do you ride on special buses?" or asking with surprise "You do it all by yourself?" (Simmons-Mackie & Kagan, 1999, p. 817). The result of comments that "mark" the person as different is potentially the promotion of a disabled identity and a competence asymmetry. A disabled identity can move the person with aphasia to the margins of a social group. In fact, the aphasia literature is replete with examples of people with aphasia who have experienced social isolation or are perceived as "outsiders" (e.g. Parr et al., 1997). Certainly, marginalisation of this nature limits social access.

In addition to explicit language that marginalises the person with aphasia, discourse can implicitly communicate hidden attitudes or rules of behaviour. That is, interactions often enculturate people with aphasia into the rules and values governing particular interactions. For example, Simmons-Mackie and colleagues (Simmons-Mackie et al., 1999) reported instances of mismatch between therapist requests and therapist feedback that communicated subtle biases against non-standard forms of communication such as writing or syntactically incomplete utterances. Similarly, interactions can minimise certain forms of participation that do not fit with the rules (Simmons-Mackie et al., 1999). This sort of attitude leakage can marginalise individuals when they perceive that their communicative contributions are not acceptable. One's self-assessment as an unacceptable communicator can generalise to a self-assessment as " unacceptable person" in the cycle of social marginalisation.

Inclusion in society and in communicative encounters depends on the acceptability of participants and their communicative offerings (e.g., Collins, 1991; Gergen

& Davis, 1985; Goffman, 1964; Shotter, 1984). Speech-language pathologists typically offer people with aphasia a variety of skills, strategies, and resources designed to enhance participation in communication. For example, Kagan (1998) describes pictographic resources used to support communication with individuals with severe aphasia. However, the use of strategies and materials that facilitate participation does not of itself guarantee inclusion. While communicative supports have been widely shown to enhance dyadic communication, it is also possible that such supports could stigmatise and marginalise individuals. For example, Simmons-Mackie and Damico (1995, p. 102) reported that "overt and potentially stigmatising communicative behaviours (e.g. writing, computers) were not used in unfamiliar or public contexts regardless of the need to convey information. In other words, the drive for social acceptability outweighed the need to transmit information in certain situations." People with aphasia appeared to assess the potential acceptability to their communicative partners of certain resources.

Of course, it is possible that the reluctance shown for some adaptive behaviours might be diminished when partners were familiar with and accepting of a variety of communicative modes that facilitate communication in aphasia. Simmons-Mackie and Kagan (1999) found that this was the case with "good" communication partners. As a group these individuals were able to accept and accommodate to the communicative style of aphasic partners. For example, if the person with aphasia tried to write a word, the partner might adopt written supports into his/her own turn. This helped to remove stigma that might be associated with an augmentative style of communicating and indicated a willingness to collaborate with the person with aphasia. It is probable that partners who are knowledgeable and skilled in the use of supports alter their conceptions of what is acceptable, thereby facilitating inclusion. Thus, maximal participation depends on the attitude, willingness, and ability of both the aphasic and non-aphasic participants to adopt nonstandard ways of communicating.

Face saving. A third illustration of how social dimensions are manifested within interaction involves the concept of face saving. Discourse is often tailored to ensure that participants in an interaction engage in *face work* to such an extent that each participant can project an acceptable face or a personal image that is consistent with their own self-identity (Goffman, 1967). When we *lose face* (e.g., feel embarrassed, feel that we are viewed as incompetent, fail to project the image we wish) then motivation to participate can be diminished.

Within the realm of aphasia interaction, the focus on face work is often ignored. Consequently, face-threatening acts in conversation with persons with aphasia may include openly correcting the talk of another, carrying on extended repair, failing to demonstrate attention or interest, using overly complex language, or failing to demonstrate understanding (e.g., Simmons-Mackie & Kagan, 1999). If they are aware of the importance of face, communication partners can engage in a wide range of behaviours that help one another maintain an acceptable social identity or face. For example, one study found that within therapy interactions clinicians used humour to minimise client errors (Simmons-Mackie & Schultz, 2003). Therapists also use self-deprecating humour to remove themselves from the "expert pedestal" thus equalising the therapist–client relationship to some degree, and potentially providing a framework for more equal participation (Simmons-Mackie & Elman, 2004). Similarly, communicative partners sometimes choose to minimise aphasic breakdowns in conversations in order to help the person with aphasia save face (Simmons-Mackie & Kagan, 1999). This decision is negotiated at the local level and considers the possibility that when people make errors in conversation, focusing on fixing the trouble can be embarrassing or face threatening. When repair is potentially face threatening, partners might opt to overlook the trouble, give sufficient time for self-repair, or continue with the conversation despite the trouble. For example, studies have demonstrated that partners might ignore breakdowns, orient the talk away from a misunderstood offering, or pretend to understand the person (Lindsay & Wilkinson, 1999; Simmons-Mackie & Kagan, 1999). While such strategies are probably designed to help the person with aphasia preserve a competent social identity, this could also deny the person with aphasia an opportunity to contribute meaning or be understood. Here the partners must negotiate a delicate interactional and social balance between making meaning and saving face.

IMPLICATIONS FOR CLINICAL APHASIOLOGY

There are many implications pertaining to access and social inclusion in aphasia that we might derive from these four interactional principles of social action. Most obviously, intervention should maximise the knowledge, skill, and attitudes of both aphasic and non-aphasic partners relative to these four principles and how they impact on communicative participation. By recognising that our traits, expectations, and behaviours are primarily negotiated in a collaborative fashion on the give and take of face-to-face interaction, we can be more sensitive to the social dimensions and variables that result in successful social action rather than unsuccessful actions. In the pursuit of communicative equality, however, clinical aphasiologists face several challenges.

The first challenge is that to promote communicative equality, the person with aphasia cannot be treated equally. This is because standard social actions rarely facilitate full communicative access in aphasia. Thus, discourse must be modified in order to layer adaptations and accommodations into the interaction. It is ironic that the non-aphasic partner is required to exert their interactional power in ways that minimise their realisation of such dominance within the interaction in order to maximise the opportunities for the people with aphasia.

A related challenge is that both partners walk an interactive tightrope when they attempt to balance the negotiation of meaning and decision making with social affiliation during communication. On the one hand, people with aphasia should have opportunities to contribute to conversations and make their ideas understood—this is the essence of communicative access. On the other hand, participants in the interaction should maintain face and avoid embarrassment or stigma. If a speaking partner offers significant and visible support or help, overtly verifies understanding, and raises repair work to the surface of the conversation, then the work of providing access could threaten the appearance of competence in the person with aphasia and threaten his/her sense of social inclusion in the conversation. Thus, the speaking partner must make choices about when to follow up on misunderstandings, when to provide supports, when to offer help, and when to gloss over misunderstandings in favour of the appearance of competence. Supporting communicative access is a delicate operation that requires sensitivity to the nuances of communication at the local level.

Finally, promoting communicative access is a demanding task. Partners must not only be knowledgeable, they must be responsive to multiple layers of information and to the potential for trouble in conversation. When this trouble is noted, they must employ behaviours that minimise the trouble and that support participation of the person with aphasia. Paradoxically, as the aphasic communicator gains greater access to communication and communicative equality is maximised, then there is more potential for trouble and more work to do. Promoting communicative inclusion and access can require significant consumption of time and energy for all parties. Participants must have internalised the values to support communicative access and be willing to dedicate the effort required to support participation.

It is difficult to teach a finite set of behaviours that inform potential speaking partners exactly what to do to facilitate access for people with aphasia in every situation. This is because of the complexity of the phenomena and the rapid local management of our behaviours and their interpretations. Dynamic factors influence what is appropriate at any given moment in any given context. Therefore, speaking partners and aphasic clients should learn a range of options for improving access, but more importantly, interactants must develop *values* that support communicative inclusion. Values and beliefs about the importance of communicative access are necessary as the framework upon which to build actual support behaviours. Values might include (1) an assumption that the person with aphasia is a competent person and given the appropriate support, can be a competent communicator, (2) an assumption that the person with aphasia has something to contribute to the conversation, (3) an assumption that all parties within the interaction bear responsibility for supporting participation and access, and (4) an assumption that through cooperative exploration suitable strategies or supports can be identified. In effect, parties promoting communicative access must adopt a new way of being infused with respect for the communicator with aphasia and a belief that the cost of communicative participation is worthwhile.

CONCLUSION

A recurring theme throughout the research described here has been the power of communication to re-establish and/or enhance social inclusion. These findings provide insights that inform our training of communicative partners, and help us to better construct therapy interactions with clients with aphasia. Aphasia therapy is not only a context for improving communication, it is also a context for constructing the person with aphasia's beliefs and values about their own communicative competence, their role in communicative interactions, and their rights to autonomy and communicative access. In order for people with aphasia to uphold their own communicative right to participate, they must develop identities as communicators who have the right to be included in communicative events of their choice. In addition, speech-language pathologists are equipped to ensure that potential speaking partners of people with aphasia gain the necessary skills and values to support access and inclusion. By concentrating on the four interactional principles and their implications as discussed in this article, increased accessibility and social inclusion can become a greater reality.

REFERENCES

Artes, R., & Hoops, R. (1976). Problems of aphasic and non-aphasic patients as identified and evaluated by patients' wives. In Y. Lebrun & R. Hoops (Eds.), *Recovery in aphasia* (pp. 31–45). Amsterdam: Swets & Zeitlinger.

Bell, A. (1984). Language style as audience design. *Language in Society, 13*(2), 145–204.

Berger, P. L., & Luckmann, T. (1967). *The social construction of reality: A treatise in the sociology of knowledge.* New York: Doubleday.

Blumer, H. (1969). *Symbolic interaction.* Englewood Cliffs, NJ: Prentice-Hall.

Booth, S., & Perkins, L. (1999). The use of conversation analysis to guide individualized advice to carers and evaluate change in aphasia: A case study. *Aphasiology, 13*(4–5), 283–303.

Bruner, J. (1990). *Acts of meaning.* Cambridge, MA: Harvard University Press.

Byng, S., Duchan, J., & Cairns, D. (2002). Values in practice and practising values. *Journal of Communication Disorders, 35*(2), 89–106.

Byng, S., Farrelly, S., Fitzgerald, L., Parr, S., & Ross, S. (2003). *Having a say: Involving people with communication difficulties in decisions about their health care.* Research report retrieved from URL http://www.healthinpartnership.org/studies/byng.html) [retrieved on 14 August 2005].

Byng, S., Pound, C., & Parr, S. (2000). Living with aphasia: A framework for therapy interventions. In I. Papathanasiou (Ed.), *Acquired neurogenic communication disorders: A clinical perspective* (pp. 49–75). London: Whurr publishers.

Chapey, R., Duchan, J., Elman, R., Garcia, L., Kagan, A., & Lyon, J. et al. (2001). Life participation approach to aphasia: A statement of values for the future. In R. Chapey (Ed.), *Language intervention strategies in aphasia and related neurogenic communication disorders.* (4th ed., pp. 235–246). Philadelphia: Lippincott, Williams & Wilkins.

Collins, R. (1991). Stratification, emotional energy, and the transient emotions. In T. D. Kemper (Ed.), *Research agendas in the sociology of emotions* (pp. 27–57). Albany, NY: State University of New York Press.

Copeland, M. (1989). An assessment of natural conversation with Broca's aphasics. *Aphasiology, 3*(3), 301–306.

Croteau, C., Vychytil, A-M., Larfeuil, C., & Le Dorze, G. (2004). "Speaking for" behaviours in spouses of people with aphasia: A descriptive study of six couples in an interview situation. *Aphasiology, 18*(4), 291–312.

Damico, J. S., & Damico, S. K. (1997). The establishment of a dominant interpretive framework in language intervention. *Language, Speech, and Hearing Services in Schools, 28*(3), 288–296.

Damico, J. S., Simmons-Mackie, N. N., & Hawley, H. K. (2005). Language and power in the clinical context. In M. J. Ball (Ed.), *Clinical sociolinguistics* (pp. 63–73). Oxford, UK: Blackwell.

Damico, J. S., Simmons-Mackie, N., Oelschlaeger, M., Elman, R., & Armstrong, E. (1999). Qualitative methods in aphasia research. *Aphasiology, 13*(9–11), 651–665.

Damico, J. S., Simmons-Mackie, N. N., Oelschlaeger, M., & Tetnowski, J. (2000, May). *An investigation of therapeutic control in aphasia therapy.* Unpublished paper presented at the Clinical Aphasiology Conference, Waikaloa, Hawaii.

Davidson, B., Worrall, L., & Hickson, L. (2003). Everyday communication activities of older people with aphasia: Evidence from naturalistic observation. *Aphasiology, 17*(3), 243–264.

Duranti, A., & Goodwin, C. (1992). *Rethinking context: Language as an interactive phenomenon.* Cambridge, UK: Cambridge University Press.

Durkheim, E. (1964). *The division of labor in society.* New York: Free Press.

Elman, R., & Bernstein-Ellis, E. (1995). What is Functional? *American Journal of Speech-Language Pathology, 4*(4), 115–117.

Enderby, P., & John, A. (1997). *Therapy outcome measures: Speech-language pathology technical manual.* London: Singular Publishing Group.

Fairclough, N. (1989). *Language and power.* London: Longman.

Ferguson, A. (1996). Describing competence in aphasic/normal conversation. *Clinical Linguistics and Phonetics, 10*(1), 55–63.

Garfinkel, H. (1967). *Studies in ethnomethodology.* Englewood Cliffs, NJ: Prentice Hall.

Garrett, K., & Beukelman, D. (1995). Changes in the interactive patterns of an individual with severe aphasia given three types of partner support. In M. Lemme (Ed.), *Clinical aphasiology, Vol. 23* (pp. 237–251). Austin, TX: Pro-Ed.

Gergen, K. J. (1991). *The saturated self.* New York: Basic Books, Inc.

Gergen, K. J., & Davis, K. E. (Eds.). (1985). *The social construction of the person*. New York: Springer.

Goffman, E. (1964). *Stigma: Notes on the management of spoiled identity*. New York: Simon & Schuster, Inc..

Goffman, E. (1967). *Interaction ritual*. Garden City, NY: Doubleday.

Goffman, E. (1969). *Strategic interaction*. Philadelphia: University of Pennsylvania Press.

Goffman, E. (1974). *Interaction ritual: Essays in face to face behaviour*. Garden City, NY: Doubleday.

Goodwin, C. (1995). Co-constructing meaning in conversations with an aphasic man. *Construction*, *28*(3), 233–260.

Goodwin, C., Goodwin, M., & Olsher, D. (2002). Producing sense with nonsense syllables: Turn and sequence in conversation with a man with severe aphasia. In C. Ford, B. Fox, & S. Thompson (Eds.), *The language of turn and sequence* (pp. 56–80). New York: Oxford University Press.

Heritage, J. (1984). *Garfinkel and ethnomethodology*. Cambridge, UK: Polity Press.

Holland, A., & Thompson, C. (1998). Outcomes measurement in aphasia. In C. Frattali (Ed.), *Measuring outcomes in speech-language pathology* (pp. 245–266). New York: Thieme.

Holland, A. L. (1998). Why can't clinicians talk to aphasic adults? Comments on supported conversation for adults with aphasia: Methods and resources for training partners. *Aphasiology*, *12*(9), 844–847.

Hymes, D. (1967). Models of the interaction of language and social setting. *Journal of Social Issues*, *23*(2), 8–28.

Kagan, A. (1998). Supported conversation for adults with aphasia: Methods and resources for training conversation partners. *Aphasiology*, *12*(9), 816–830.

Kagan, A., Black, S., Duchan, J., Simmons-Mackie, N., & Square, P. (2001). Training volunteers as conversational partners using 'Supported Conversation with Adults with Aphasia' (SCA): A controlled trial. *Journal of Speech, Language and Hearing Research*, *44*(3), 624–638.

Kagan, A., & Gailey, G. (1993). Functional is not enough: Training conversation partners in aphasia. In A. Holland & M. Forbes (Eds.), *Aphasia treatment: World perspectives* (pp. 199–226). San Diego, CA: Singular.

Kagan, A., & LeBlanc, K. (2002). Motivating for infrastructure change: Toward a communicatively accessible, participation-based stroke care system for all those affected by aphasia. *Journal of Communication Disorders*, *35*(2), 153–169.

Kemper, T. D. (Ed.). (1991). *Research agendas in the sociology of emotions*. New York: State of New York University Press.

Kinsella, G. J., & Duffy, F. D. (1980). Attitudes towards disability expressed by stroke patients. *Scandinavian Journal of Rehabilitation Medicine*, *12*, 73–76.

Klippi, A. (1991). Conversational dynamics between aphasics. *Aphasiology*, *5*(4), 373–378.

Klippi, A. (1996). *Conversation as an achievement in aphasics. Studia Fennica Linguistica 6*. Helsinki: The Finnish Literature Society.

Knox, D. (1971). *Portrait of aphasia*. Detroit, MI: Wayne State University Press.

Laasko, M. (1997). *Self-initiated repair by fluent aphasic speakers in conversation. Studia Fennica Linguistica 8*. Helsinki: Finnish Literature Society.

LeDorze, G., & Brassard, C. (1995). A description of the consequences of aphasia on aphasic persons and their relatives and friends, based on the WHO model of chronic diseases. *Aphasiology*, *9*(3), 239–255.

Lindsay, J., & Wilkinson, R. (1999). Repair sequences in aphasia talk: A comparison of aphasic–speech and language therapist and aphasic–spouse conversations. *Aphasiology*, *13*(4–5), 305–325.

Lyon, J. G. (1996). Optimizing communication and participation in life for aphasic adults and their prime caregivers in natural settings: A model for treatment. In G. Wallace (Ed.), *Adult aphasia rehabilitation* (pp. 137–160). Boston: Butterworth-Heinemann.

Lyon, J. G. (1997). Volunteers and partners: Moving intervention outside the treatment room. In B. Shadden & M. A. Toner (Eds.), *Aging and communication* (pp. 299–323). Austin, TX: Pro-Ed.

Madden, M., Oelschlaeger, M., & Damico, J. S. (2002). The conversational value of laughter for a person with aphasia. *Aphasiology*, *16*(12), 1199–1212.

Malone, R. L., Ptacek, P. H., & Malone, M. S. (1970). Attitudes expressed by families of aphasics. *British Journal of Disorders of Communication*, *59*, 174–179.

Michallet, B., Tetreault, S., & Le Dorze, G. (2003). The consequences of severe aphasia on the spouses of aphasic people: A description of the adaptation process. *Aphasiology*, *17*(9), 835–859.

Milroy, L., & Perkins, L. (1992). Repair strategies in aphasic discourse: Towards a collaborative model. *Clinical Linguistics and Phonetics*, *6*, 27–40.

Muller, D. J., & Code, C. (1983). Interpersonal perceptions of psychosocial adjustment to aphasia. In C. Code & D. J. Muller (Eds.), *Aphasia therapy* (pp. 101–112). London: Edward Arnold.

Oelschlaeger, M., & Damico, J. S. (1998a). Joint productions as a conversational strategy in aphasia. *Clinical Linguistics and Phonetics*, *12*(6), 459–480.

Oelschlaeger, M., & Damico, J. S. (1998b). Spontaneous verbal repetition: A social strategy in aphasic conversation. *Aphasiology*, *12*(11), 971–988.

Oelschlaeger, M. L., & Damico, J. S. (2000). Partnership in conversation: A study of word search strategies. *Journal of Communicative Disorders*, *33*(3), 205–225.

Oliver, M. (1983). *Social work with disabled people*. London: Macmillan.

Panagos, J. M. (1996). Speech therapy discourse: The input to learning. In M. Smith & J. S. Damico (Eds.), *Childhood language disorders* (pp. 41–63). New York: Thieme Medical Publishers.

Park, R. (1928). Human migration and the marginal man. *American Journal of Sociology*, *33*(6), 888–896.

Parr, S. (1994). Coping with aphasia: Conversations with 20 aphasic people. *Aphasiology*, *8*(5), 457–466.

Parr, S., Byng, S., Gilpin, S., & Ireland, C. (1997). *Talking about aphasia*. Buckingham, UK: Open University Press.

Parr, S., Duchan, J., & Pound, C. (2003). *Aphasia inside out. Reflections on communication disability*. Buckingham, UK: Open University Press.

Perkins, L. (1995). Applying conversational analysis to aphasia: Clinical implications and analytic issues. *European Journal of Disorders of Communication*, *30*(3), 372–383.

Perkins, L., Crisp, J., & Walshaw, D. (1999). Exploring conversation analysis as an assessment tool for aphasia: The issue of reliability. *Aphasiology*, *13*(4–5), 251–258.

Ramsberger, G., & Rende, B. (2001). Measuring transactional success in the conversation of people with aphasia. *Aphasiology*, *16*(3), 337–353.

Rogers, M. F. (1980). Goffman on power, hierarchy and status. In J. Ditton (Ed.), *The view from Goffman* (pp. 100–133). New York: St. Martin's Press.

Sacks, H. (1992). *Lectures on conversation. Volume I*. Oxford, UK: Blackwell.

Scheff, T. J. (1990). *Microsociology: Discourse, emotion and social structure*. Chicago: University of Chicago Press.

Schegloff, E. (1968). Sequencings in conversational openings. *American Anthropologist*, *70*(6), 1075–1095.

Shotter, J. (1984). *Conversational realities: Constructing life through language*. Newbury Park, CA: Sage.

Simmel, G. (1950). The stranger. In K. Wolff (Ed.), *The sociology of Georg Simmel*. New York: Free Press.

Simmons, N. (1993). *An ethnographic investigation of compensatory strategies in aphasia*. Unpublished doctoral dissertation, Louisiana State University, Baton Rouge, LA.

Simmons-Mackie, N. N. (1998). In support of supportive conversation for adults with aphasia. *Aphasiology*, *12*(9), 831–838.

Simmons-Mackie, N. N., & Damico, J. S. (1995). Communicative competence in aphasia: Evidence from compensatory strategies. *Clinical Aphasiology*, *23*, 95–105.

Simmons-Mackie, N. N., & Damico, J. S. (1996a). The contribution of discourse markers to communicative competence in aphasia. *American Journal of Speech-Language Pathology*, *5*(1), 37–43.

Simmons-Mackie, N. N., & Damico, J. S. (1996b). Accounting for handicaps in aphasia: Communicative assessment from an authentic perspective. *Disability and Rehabilitation: An International, Multidisciplinary Journal*, *18*(11), 540–549.

Simmons-Mackie, N. N., & Damico, J. S. (1997). Reformulating the definition of compensatory strategies in aphasia. *Aphasiology*, *11*(8), 761–781.

Simmons-Mackie, N. N., & Damico, J. S. (1999). Social role negotiation in aphasia therapy: Competence, incompetence, and conflict. In D. Kovarsky, J. Duchan, & M. Maxwell (Eds.), *Constructing (in)competence: Disabling evaluations in clinical and social interaction* (pp. 313–342). Mahwah, NJ: Lawrence Erlbaum Associates Inc.

Simmons-Mackie, N. N., & Damico, J. S. (2001). Intervention outcomes: Clinical applications of qualitative methods. *Topics in Language Disorders*, *21*(4), 21–36.

Simmons-Mackie, N. N., Damico, J. S., & Damico, H. L. (1999). A qualitative study of feedback in aphasia treatment. *American Journal of Speech-Language Pathology*, *8*(3), 218–230.

Simmons-Mackie, N. N., & Elman, R. (2004, May). *The Aphasia Café: Negotiation of identity in group therapy for aphasia*. Paper presented at the Language and Social Interaction Conference, Providence, RI.

Simmons-Mackie, N. N., & Kagan, A. (1999). Communication strategies used by 'good' versus 'poor' speaking partners of individuals with aphasia. *Aphasiology*, *13*(9–11), 807–820.

Simmons-Mackie, N., Kingston, D., & Schultz, M. (2004). Speaking for another: The management of participant frames in aphasia. *American Journal of Speech-Language Pathology*, *13*(2), 114–127.

Simmons-Mackie, N., & Schultz, M. (2003). The role of humor in therapy for aphasia. *Aphasiology*, *17*(8), 751–766.

Tannen, D. (1987). Remarks on discourse and power. In L. Kedar (Ed.), *Power through discourse* (pp. 3–10). Norwood, NJ: Ablex.

Ulichny, P., & Watson-Gegeo, K. A. (1989). Interactions and authority: The dominant interpretive framework in writing conferences. *Discourse Processes*, *12*, 309–328.

Weber, M. (1946). *Theory of social and economic organization*. London: William Hodge.

Wilkinson, R. (1995). Aphasia: Conversation analysis of a non-fluent aphasic person. In M. Perkins & S. Howard (Eds.), *Case studies in clinical linguistics* (pp. 271–292). London: Whurr.

Worrall, L. E., & Frattali, C. M. (Eds.). (2000). *Neurogenic communication disorders: A functional approach*. New York: Thieme.

Worrall, L., McCooey, R., Davidson, B., Larkins, B., & Hickson, L. (2002). The validity of functional assessments of communication and the Activity/Participation components of the ICIDH-2: Do they reflect what really happens in real life? *Journal of Communication Disorders*, *35*(2), 107–137.

APHASIOLOGY, 2007, 21 (1), 98–123

Ψ Psychology Press
Taylor & Francis Group

Living with severe aphasia: Tracking social exclusion

Susie Parr

Connect – The Communication Disability Network, London, UK

Background: Little is known about what happens to people with severe aphasia in the years after stroke when rehabilitation comes to an end, or about day-to-day life for this group.

Aims: This study aimed to track the day-to-day life and experiences of people with severe aphasia, and to document levels of social inclusion and exclusion as they occurred in mundane settings.

Methods and Procedures: Ethnography was chosen as the qualitative methodology most suitable for studying the experience of people with profoundly compromised language. 20 people who were judged to have severe aphasia following stroke agreed to be visited and observed three times in different domestic and care settings. The observer documented environments, protagonists, events, and interactions. Field notes were elaborated with personal, methodological, and interpretative notes. Written material (for example information leaflets) was also documented and described. Data were subject to thematic analysis.

Outcomes and Results: The study revealed how social exclusion is a common experience for this group, played out in a variety of ways in a range of domestic and care settings. Social exclusion occurs at infrastructural, interpersonal, and personal levels.

Conclusions: The study suggests that the social exclusion of people who struggle to communicate could be addressed through training, for professional and lay carers, that promotes support for communication; opportunity and access; respect and acknowledgment; and attention to the environment.

Social exclusion is a complex concept. The UK government definition refers to *"what can happen when people or areas suffer from a combination of linked problems, such as unemployment, poor skills, low incomes, poor housing, high crime, bad health and family breakdown"* (http://www.socialexclusionunit.gov). Some definitions take a wider view. People are thought to be excluded when they are not part of the networks that support most people in ordinary life—of family, friends, community,

Address correspondence to: Susie Parr, Connect – The Communication Disability Network, 16–18 Marshalsea Road, Southwark SE1 1HL, London, UK. E-mail: susiepparr@btinternet.com

This study would not have been possible without the support and backing of a number of people. First, thanks are due to the people with severe aphasia and their families who allowed the research to take place. We are most grateful to the therapists and voluntary sector workers who suggested participants and made initial contact on our behalf. Thanks go to all the staff working in the day centres, nursing homes, and respite centres for their cooperation and support for the study. The project was enriched by the guidance and contribution of members of the advisory group and the co-researchers, Sally Byng of Connect and Colin Barnes and Geoff Mercer of the University of Leeds. We are indebted to The Joseph Rowntree Foundation for supporting this study, and particularly to Alex O'Neil for his patient and constructive input at every stage of the project. Finally, the author would like to thank Carole Pound, Alan Hewitt, and Judy Duchan for their contribution to the preparation of this paper.

http://www.psypress.com/aphasiology   DOI: 10.1080/02687030600798337

and employment. Thus, exclusion is a very broad concept: it includes not only deprivation but also problems of social relationships, including stigma and social isolation. Initiatives to promote social inclusion, for example by The Scottish Office, acknowledge that the complicated multi-faceted nature of social exclusion demands action on a number of levels to promote integration, prevention, understanding, inclusiveness, and empowerment (www.scotland.gov.uk).

The concept of social exclusion is familiar within social policy, and sociological and disability-related research. It is prominent within the field of learning disability (Fyson & Ward, 2004), underpinning for example the Valuing People White Paper in the UK (Department of Health, 2001). Within this field, there is sophisticated debate concerning the relationship between social capital and social inclusion, and how both concepts must influence services for people with learning disability (Bates & Davies, 2004).

Despite its proliferation elsewhere, the notion of social exclusion does not seem to have impacted on stroke-related research. It has been little explored with reference to the experience of people with aphasia, although some attention has been paid to the social impacts of loss of communication and how these might be addressed to enhance the individual's level of participation (LeDorze & Brassard, 1995; Lyon, 2000; Simmons Mackie, 2000). One study, Parr, Byng, Gilpin, and Ireland (1997), has discussed the socially constructed barriers that disable people with aphasia.

People with severe aphasia rarely feature in stroke research, other than as subjects of experimental studies. This may be because it is so difficult to ensure their comprehension and enable their contribution. In the earlier study (Parr et al., 1997) 50 people with aphasia, of different ages and backgrounds, were interviewed about their experiences. Supported by the interviewer, most were able to express themselves in some way, using a combination of speech, writing, and gesture. A small number of people with profound communication difficulties were also interviewed. Their contributions were sparse in comparison with the rich accounts given by other respondents. In effect, people with severe aphasia could not contribute fully to the research because the methodology was not suitable.

Clinical experience suggests that impairment-focused therapy, as well as research, is often limited for people with severe aphasia, and yet this group can live with profoundly compromised language for many years after therapy ends. They enter different settings such as nursing or residential homes, day centres, and volunteer-run support organisations. This group is "difficult to reach" and what happens to them is a source of considerable concern to clinicians (Hersh, 1998). Their experiences, thoughts, feelings, and concerns are largely unexplored and unknown. We (the group of co-researchers cited on the opening page) planned a study that would try to document the day-to-day experience of this group of people and explore their perspectives on life with aphasia (as far as possible), tracking the processes of social exclusion or inclusion as they occurred.

Considering different qualitative methodologies that might be suitable to the endeavour, ethnography seemed to have the most potential. Ethnography has its provenance in the field of social science. Once the tool of Western anthropologists exploring remote and exotic communities, in recent decades it has been used to analyse the nature of groups and practices closer to home and to document the experience of vulnerable and marginalised people (Hammersely & Atkinson, 1995). It is an eclectic and flexible methodology, combining observation, interaction, analysis of artefacts, and interview. It allows experience, behaviour, and meaning to be explored in naturally occurring contexts. Ethnography has been identified as a useful means of studying healthcare: "As a detailed way of witnessing human events in the context in which they occur, ethnography can help healthcare professionals to solve problems beyond the reach of many research approaches, particularly in the understanding of patients' and clinicians' worlds" (Savage, 2000, p. 1402).

Simmons-Mackie and Damico (1997, 1999) have demonstrated the strengths of ethnographic methods in the study of aphasia, exploring compensatory strategies and what goes on in therapeutic interactions. Ethnography raises numerous complex ethical issues, particularly around consent, transparency, and representation. However, the emphasis on observing and documenting settings, activities, and artefacts (in this study, written documents), as well as interactions, made ethnography seem a suitable method for exploring the day-to-day life of people with severe aphasia, for whom verbal communication is extremely problematic.

The ethnographic component of this study was complemented by a UK-wide survey of speech and language therapists, support groups, organisations of disabled people, and self-help groups with the purpose of eliciting views of the long-term outcomes for people with severe aphasia. Informal and paid carers also took part in in-depth interviews. These are reported elsewhere (Parr, 2004). The focus of this paper is the ethnographic study itself.

METHOD

Ethnographic data capture naturally occurring phenomena in rich detail, collected from multiple sources, and analysed at different levels. These data are drawn from different methods: participant observation, complemented with interview, inter-action, and analysis of artefacts. The data provide a microcosmic picture of everyday experience. Minute description of the mundane, taken-for-granted world can "illuminate the habitus of socially constructed values as these are embodied and played out" (Edgar & Russell, 1998, p. 10). It is a labour-intensive method and for this reason tends to be best used with small samples. In this study, the sample comprised 20 people living in one inner-city area in the UK.

Gaining access to participants

Participants were sought through networks of speech and language therapists, voluntary and self-help groups, and organisations dedicated to supporting people after stroke. As in any small-scale qualitative study, the aim was to access a cross-section of people with severe aphasia who would represent a range of different factors and experiences. A sampling matrix was set up. Quotas were set for sampling criteria including age, gender, type of aphasia, home circumstances, level of physical impairment, and ethnic origin. Like Allen (2000), we were unwilling to put people through testing and so we asked our contacts to consider those who, in their opinion, had major difficulties with communication as a result of aphasia.

This strategy seemed effective in prompting speech and language therapists and some of the voluntary sector contacts to think about possible participants. However, day-centre and residential- and care-home staff found it difficult to identify people with aphasia-related communication difficulties. None of these contacts referred to medical or care notes. None knew the term "aphasia". People recommended did have severe communication difficulties but these were often associated with motor impairments, or dementia, not aphasia. The process of locating possible participants took several weeks. Not only are people with severe aphasia "hard to reach", they can also be hard to find.

Eventually, 20 people who met our sampling criteria were identified by our contacts as having severe and intractable communication difficulties following stroke, and as people who seemed interested in the project. As far as possible, it was ascertained by a qualified speech and language therapist that they did indeed have aphasia, and that no other major influences were affecting their communication (such as deafness, dementia, or severe motor speech impairment). This was done informally, without recourse to testing. Informal assessment included observing and documenting the nature of the person's difficulties with communication and talking to carers about the history and onset. This process was more difficult in the institutional and some voluntary settings, as often nobody knew much about the people concerned. Consent was gained using specially designed materials (Parr, 2004). Table 1 shows some of the characteristics of the 20 people with severe aphasia who agreed to take part in this study. They comprised 11 men and 9 women, of different ages and backgrounds. Time elapsed since stroke ranged from 9 months (Tom) to 15 years (Miss Silver). All names have been changed to protect confidentiality.

In this study, the type of aphasia was divided into two broad categories: those with fluent "empty" speech, and non-fluent speakers, for whom every utterance was a struggle. All the participants had marked receptive impairment, which meant they struggled to follow conversations, requests, and instructions and to interpret written material. Within the two broad categories of fluent and non-fluent aphasia, everybody was different. Styles of communication varied. Each person had adapted to aphasia in different ways, finding their own means of communicating and using various devices and means of support. Some used drawing, gesture or mime, intonation, facial expression, and bits of writing to supplement their speech. Some were able to use word lists to some effect. Three were trying out a portable communication aid, with varying degrees of success. Some had no resources to draw on.

Participant observation: Organising visits

Each of the 20 people with severe aphasia was visited three times during the course of the study in a range of different settings and situations (see Table 2). This was in line with the time-sampling strategy described by Hammersley and Atkinson (1995). Each visit lasted between 1 and 3 hours.

Participant observation involves the observer entering a situation, watching, and recording whatever is going on. However, the observer is not always detached or removed from what is going on, but becomes a part of the activity as and when appropriate (Hammersley & Atkinson, 1995). Sometimes it was possible to sit and make notes unobtrusively, and without much interaction. This was particularly the case when something else was going on, for example therapy or computer sessions, or in recreational activities such as quizzes. On several occasions the researcher became involved with activities, for example helping to carry in shopping from the car, or joining a swimming session. Often, she engaged in conversations and interactions, particularly when visiting a person who was on their own. Documentation of these conversations fed into the data.

TABLE 1
Information about the participants

Name and age (years since stroke)	Type of aphasia	Physical impairment	Domestic situation	Work pre-stroke	Source of contact
Roger, 50 (3)	Non-fluent Poor comprehension	None	Home with family	Director	Voluntary organisation
Pete, 53 (2)	Non-fluent Poor comprehension	Hemiplegia Ambulant with help	Home with wife	Company director	SLT
Ruth, 33 (1)	Fluent Poor comprehension	None	Home with family	Student	Person with aphasia
Donald, 71 (2.5)	Non-fluent Poor comprehension	Hemiplegia Non-ambulant	Home with wife	Retired teacher	SLT
Gill, 55 (12)	Non-fluent Poor comprehension	Hemiplegia Ambulant with help	Home with husband	Hairdresser	Voluntary organisation
Brenda, 72 (3)	Non-fluent Poor comprehension	Hemiplegia Non-ambulant	Nursing home	Retired	SLT
Ivy, 72 (5)	Non-fluent Poor comprehension	Hemiplegia Non-ambulant	Home with husband	Retired	SLT
Frank,79 (6)	Non-fluent Poor comprehension	Hemiplegia Non-ambulant Dysphagia	Home with wife	Retired	SLT
Albert, 91 (1)	Non-fluent Poor comprehension	Hemiplegia Non-ambulant Dysphagia	Nursing home	Retired	SLT
David, 60 (2)	Non-fluent Poor comprehension	Hemiplegia Non-ambulant Dysphagia	Home with wife	Unemployed	Voluntary organisation
Jean, 74 (1.5)	Non-fluent Poor comprehension	Hemiplegia Non-ambulant	Home with husband	Retired	SLT
Charles, 59 (4)	Non-fluent Poor comprehension	Hemiplegia Ambulant with help	Home with wife	Hospital Porter	Day centre
Harry, 81 (1)	Fluent Poor comprehension	None	Home alone	Retired	Voluntary organisation
Terry, 54 (12)	Fluent Poor comprehension	None	Home with wife	Joiner	Voluntary organisation
Anthea, 80 (2)	Fluent Poor comprehension	Hemiplegia Non-ambulant	Nursing home	Retired	SLT
Mary, 53 (6)	Non-fluent Poor comprehension	Hemiplegia Ambulant	Home alone	Executive	SLT
Miss Silver, 77 (15)	Non-fluent Poor comprehension	Hemiplegia Ambulant with help	Home with family	Retired	Day centre
Fred, 78 (12)	Non-fluent Poor comprehension	Hemiplegia Non-ambulant	Nursing home	Retired	GP
Christine,74 (1.5)	Non-fluent Poor comprehension	Hemiplegia Ambulant with help	Home with husband	Unemployed	SLT
Tom, 38 (9 months)	Fluent Poor comprehension	Hemiplegia Ambulant Seizures	Home with partner	Electrician	SLT

TABLE 2
Settings and situations observed in the study

Person	Settings and situations
Roger	1. Going to the local post office alone to buy cards and stamps
	2. Playing in a bowls match
	3. At home with wife and family
Pete	1. At home with paid carer, then going to the pub with family
	2. In day centre
	3. At home with wife
Ruth	1. In day centre
	2. Shopping at Tesco
	3. At home with family
Donald	1. At home with wife
	2. Occupation therapy session in hospital
	3. Visit from friends, doing singing practice
Gill	1. At home, and at a local stroke club
	2. Local shopping and visit to Lidl supermarket
	3. Swimming
Brenda	1. Having lunch in dining room of nursing home
	2. In room, watching TV
	3. Meant to be bingo, but cancelled. Watching TV in room.
Ivy	1. At home with husband
	2. Taking part in a stroke group at a day centre
	3. Having hair done by a home care worker
Frank	1. At home with family
	2. In respite care setting
	3. At home with family
Albert	1. Having lunch in the nursing home
	2. Sitting in alcove in nursing home
	3. In own bedroom at nursing home, unwell
David	1. In day centre doing cookery
	2. At home with wife and visitor
	3. At local stroke club
Jean	1. At home with husband
	2. At home, daughter and grand-daughter visit
	3. At home with husband
Charles	1. At day centre, having lunch and taking part in a quiz
	2. Physiotherapy session in hospital
	3. At home with wife
Harry	1. At home alone
	2. At stroke club
	3. Shopping in Sainsbury's with son-in-law
Terry	1. At day centre, working on computer
	2. In respite centre
	3. At home alone
Anthea	1. In room at nursing home
	2. In room at nursing home
	3. In room at nursing home
Mary	1. At home alone
	2. At Different Strokes meeting
	3. At home alone
Miss Silver	1. In day centre, doing crafts
	2. In day centre, eating lunch
	3. In day centre, taking part in Christmas service

(*Continued*)

TABLE 2 (*Continued*)

Person	Settings and situations
Fred	1. Having lunch in dining room of nursing home
	2. In room, watching TV
	3. In room at nursing home, unwell
Christine	1. At home with husband
	2. At home with husband
	3. At home with husband
Tom	1. At home with partner
	2. Out-patient occupational therapy
	3. Going to the pub with partner

Participant observation: Writing field notes

Throughout the observation sessions the researcher wrote field notes. Comments and conversations were noted down verbatim. Audio and video recordings were not made. The issue of making audio or video recordings during observational visits is discussed in depth by Hammersley and Atkinson (1995). Disadvantages include the inevitably selective focus; the loss of vital information (perhaps not recording something happening in a corner out of earshot or audio view); attention to the recording or filming process interfering with observation and participation; possible negative impact on participants; and the huge resources needed to analyse such data adequately. For these reasons, visits were not video-recorded, although consent for this had been gained.

Several hours immediately following each visit were spent expanding the hastily scribbled notes, writing a detailed account of the events that had just been observed. At this stage, a very preliminary form of analysis was begun, as points that seemed of possible theoretical interest in the text were highlighted in a set of interpretative notes. There was no attempt to classify such issues at this point, simply to note them and raise questions about them. At the same time, important methodological issues, such as an idea that should be followed up in carer interviews, were noted. The research process was reflexive, and the researcher incorporated personal notes into the text. These concerned worries about her own health, her family, and reflections on her personal and professional experiences. Rather than try to obliterate these personal perspectives, ethnographers are encouraged to be explicit. Reflexivity adds to the authenticity and transparency of ethnographic work, underlining the premise that there is no external reality, only multiple representations and meanings, and that any form of investigation is subject to bias (Davies, 1999). The observations resulted in 60 sets of expanded and detailed notes, annotated with interpretative, methodological, and personal comments. An example of one page of the notes is given in Appendix 1, and some excerpts from them appear in this paper.

Analysing ethnographic data

Analysis of ethnographic data begins with the organisation of field notes into categories. Data are scrutinised and sorted into themes, in a way that provides an important infrastructure for searching and retrieval. This can be done in numerous ways using different forms of indexing and coding. Computer software (such as

Ethnograph and Nudist) can be useful, but as Hammersley and Atkinson (1995) comment, manual sorting is still perfectly appropriate and often a more flexible means of beginning analysis. Generally, the types of categories developed undergo some changes as the research proceeds and the process takes on the characteristic "funnel" structure: starting wide and progressively narrowing towards interpretative themes.

Data were first sorted in terms of categories suggested by Layder (1993), which provided the first conceptual framework and guided the analytical process. Analytical charts were developed using the Framework method (Ritchie & Lewis, 2003), and data from the notes sorted under different headings and sub-headings: actors and activities; settings; interactions; identity and narrative; and the exercise of power and ideology in all these domains. The charts formed the basis for a set of chapters that explored the data in terms of these domains. Finally, returning to the original research question, markers of social exclusion and inclusion were identified, and illustrated from the notes. These fell into four broad interacting categories: infrastructure and resources; the behaviour of other people; settings and environments; and personal identity and narrative.

This last analysis provided the basis for returning the findings to members of the aphasia working group (who were part of the project advisory panel) and to participants. At this point, the focus fell on issues of social exclusion and inclusion, and attempts were made to represent these concepts in an accessible format. The discussions that occurred in these consultations constituted another form of data and led to a further simplification and revision of themes, with suggestions for implementing change.

Hammersley and Atkinson (1995) suggest that artefacts in the form of written documents provide a rich source of information. A range of such artefacts in the form of written documents was therefore collected where possible or transcribed verbatim, whenever they were encountered in the day-to-day context of people with severe aphasia. These included: written information produced by institutions such as nursing homes, respite, and day centres, and by different services; letters from different agencies; notices; written instructions; mission statements. Analysis of these data fed into the discussion of social exclusion and inclusion.

The varied methodologies, the intricacies of data production and analysis, the complexities of representation and validation, and the endeavour to make the research process inclusive raised numerous questions and challenges for the research team, reported in more depth in Parr (2004).

FINDINGS

An extract from the expanded notes (below) gives a taste of the nature of ethnographic writing. The field-notes constitute a comprehensive narrative concerning everyday life with severe aphasia.

> During the quiz, the nurse suddenly turns to Pete. "Can you write it down?" she says. "Do you want to? You can join in." "No no no" he says "Yes, but no." "It'll take too long?" "No yes, but ..." "It's too much trouble? " "No yes, but um .." "It's not too much trouble for me. I'll fetch a pen and paper." She goes out. Pete looks at me, still the same smile. She comes back in with one small piece of paper and a pencil. "There you are." "No no no" he says smiling and shaking his head. "What about yes yes yes?" she

says. Everyone starts to laugh and there is a chorus of "No no no" and "Yes yes yes ..".
Pete takes the pencil and sits with it poised over the paper on the table, leaning forward,
his gaze on the nurse. He is smiling.

Discussions of social exclusion suggest it occurs at three levels: infrastructural,
interpersonal, and personal (Table 3). There follows a summary of the key issues
arising from analysis of the ethnographic notes, in terms of these three levels of social
exclusion. There are few clear-cut boundaries between these levels. Each influences
and affects the others. For example, how a therapist or care attendant behaves may
be affected by resource and infrastructural issues, and also have an impact on the
confidence levels and self-esteem of a person with aphasia.

Infrastructural aspects of the social exclusion of people with severe aphasia

Findings relating to infrastructural aspects of exclusion are reported here in terms of
eight issues: work; making ends meet; housing; services; information; training;
information and communication technology; and geography.

Work. Even within a relatively small group, there was evidence of major
restrictions in terms of return to work. The youngest participant, Ruth, was the only
person in the group of 20 people who was in paid employment. She worked as a
cleaner, an occupation at odds with her aspirations to train as a teacher or a nurse.
Also young, Tom was still hoping to resume work as a self-employed electrician.
However, the likelihood of this seemed remote, given his limited language and the
physical restrictions, including epilepsy, that had started with the stroke. Even
though he continued to attend speech and language therapy and occupational
therapy, opportunities for re-entering the workplace or for retraining were not
addressed. Long-standing problems with national insurance payments consolidated
the financial difficulties facing Tom and his partner Jaqui (she had stopped work to
look after him). Most days, he lay in bed till noon, then watched TV, lying on the
sofa with a cigarette in one hand and the remote control in the other. Constantly

TABLE 3
Indicators of social exclusion

Level of social exclusion	Indicators
Infrastructural exclusion	Limited access to employment; inadequate income; services (health, housing, education, leisure); communications media; information and communication technology; information; the location of resources and services; the nature of the place.
Interpersonal exclusion	Limited association with groups and places in society: family; neighbours; friends; workmates; people of similar age or gender or culture or religion. People can feel excluded because they are no longer part of a group to which they once belonged, or because they belong to a group that they have always perceived as being excluded.
Personal exclusion	Alienation; isolation; lack of identity; low self-esteem; passivity; dependence, bewilderment, fear, anger, apathy, low aspirations, hopelessness.

Information from: The Library and Information Commission (www.lic.gov.uk/publications/policy-reports/inclusion)

spending time together was starting to have a negative effect on the couple. Terry, a cabinet-maker, had tried to return to work some weeks after his stroke, full-time and with no modifications in his working conditions or hours. He had quickly become ill and exhausted, and had to stop. His workshop at home was still orderly, with the tools laid out in neat rows. During one visit he wrote the word "jops" and then said "All gone", with a sorrowful expression. Like many of the other participants who had been working he regretted not only the loss of income, but also the major change of lifestyle and identity that stroke had brought. Gill frequently referred to her work as a hairdresser and expressed through gesture and facial expression her regret for the status and pleasure of working in a skilled job. Mary also expressed her sense of loss of influence and power, comparing the activity, travel, prestige, and excitement of her working life as an executive with the boredom and restriction of her current existence. Those like Donald who had retired from paid employment indicated that they missed engagement in the voluntary and community work they once enjoyed.

Making ends meet. With a few exceptions, people who took part in this study experienced financial hardship. Relatives described shopping from charity shops and catalogues, forgoing holidays, and "robbing Peter to pay Paul". In many cases, families with two incomes were reduced to relying on benefits (the partner having also given up work to care for the person affected by the stroke). The welfare and benefit systems seemed difficult to negotiate. Access to benefits, information, and support was unpredictable. The struggle for benefits had taken their toll, particularly in the early days when the chaos and uncertainty of acute illness were compounded by worry and hardship. A few years post-stroke, some people were well supported and organised, and had enough to live comfortably. Others were still economising, with little prospect of things improving. Relatives described how the inability to discuss financial issues with their loved one exacerbated anxiety and tension.

Housing. Of the 20 people who took part in the project, 5 lived in poor or inadequate housing. They were experiencing significant problems with the house itself (damp, cold, dereliction, noise) and were also worried about crime in their locality. One carer described having been mugged, and during one observation session there was an aggressive verbal assault on Gill and her husband, in the car park of a supermarket.

Of course, the financial and housing hardships and employment worries experienced by the participants are not solely related to aphasia. Other factors, such as mobility difficulties, fatigue, and seizures, also had an effect on the person's ability to resume work and restore previous levels of income. However, difficulty in communicating, as well as being a major barrier to effective functioning in all but menial work settings, meant that negotiation, discussion of alternative courses of action, and access to information, support, and training opportunities were also limited. This meant that tasks that might previously have been shared (for example asking the authorities to consider a change of council flat) fell to the person who could talk and write. Although some people tried to ensure their partners with aphasia were involved in decisions, in practice this was often very difficult.

Services. This small sample of participants had patchy and inequitable access to services. Most people had input from support services such as home care, enabling them to continue living at home, but only one couple had obtained funding from the Independent Living Foundation ensuring continuous, high-quality care. Some people, years after their stroke, were continuing to receive physiotherapy, occupational therapy, and speech and language therapy. Others had no continuing input. It was clear that many of the participants would have benefited from a particular health or social care service that was not available. For example, Christine was living in constant pain, her right arm swollen and difficult to move. Yet she did not see a doctor or physiotherapist. She could not ask for this herself, relying on her husband who had health worries of his own, to raise her predicament in his own consultations. His concerns about Christine's arm were not followed up. They were both anxious about her safety and comfort during his increasingly frequent visits to hospital. As it was, she spent up to 6 hours alone each time, with no way of getting help should she need it.

Another need was for support in dealing with communication breakdown. Several episodes of frustration and tension within families and institutions were documented. Some family members described moments of aggression when a message could not be expressed or understood. Yet none could recall having received guidance on dealing with communication problems. Wendy spoke for many when she said she acted on instinct when trying to help Roger during his frequent struggles with communication.

The issue of access to services was prominent in the survey. A number of respondents indicated that their services for people with aphasia were not accessible to those with severe difficulties. Sometimes this was because information about the service was not understood, and sometimes because the service itself was unsuitable, for example focusing on pencil and paper activities. This perception was supported in the ethnographic study. In day centres and in volunteer-led groups, people with severe communication problems sat through question and answer sessions and pen and paper games in which they could not participate.

Some services seemed unrelated to the needs or concerns of the person with aphasia. For example, Tom (who was desperate to return to work as an electrician) spent occupational therapy sessions sanding a member of staff's garden furniture and painting wooden toys. The therapist, seemingly unaware of Tom's concerns, perceived his indifferent attitude to these activities as "lack of motivation". This meant that he was going to be discharged soon with no further treatment or support. Ruth reluctantly joined in with quizzes and arts and crafts at her day centre, feeling such activities would be more suitable for her young daughter.

In some cases, services that were provided clearly missed the mark. At one day centre, a worker had spent a considerable amount of time making a wooden communication aid for David. He could not use it. It was awkward to handle (he had a right hemiplegia), and displayed words and images that he could not understand and that were not relevant to him. In addition, the assistant was trying to teach him to use Amerind, a form of sign language. She had little training and no input from anyone with knowledge of aphasia and of communication aid technology, yet she had been given special responsibility for supporting people with communication difficulties.

Because he could not use the stairs and had no stair-lift, Charles was confined to a tiny ground-floor living room, all the space taken up with his bed, armchair, commode, and the sofa. His physiotherapist had not seen his home situation for herself and chastised him for not practising walking, something he had no space to do. He often misunderstood her and could not tell her about the problems he was experiencing. She commented that, with Charles, what she said to him went "in one ear and out the other", but she did not feel his marked aphasia had any significant impact on his response to her treatment. At home, Charles and his wife managed as best they could. People adapted, problem-solved, and worked out their own ways of doing things to get around mobility and communication problems. Often their solutions were pragmatic and idiosyncratic, bearing little relation to therapists' guidance.

The quality of services such as these seemed severely compromised by a lack of integration: between the real-life issues faced and the activities of day centres and rehabilitation units; and between service providers with different expertise and skills (for example day centre or nursing home staff working with people with aphasia on a day-to-day basis commented that they had no contact with speech and language therapists). These issues were also highlighted in the survey. People with severe communication difficulties are commonly described by service providers as "hard to reach", but perhaps this description could apply to the services themselves.

Information. Information and explanation make services accessible. People with aphasia need information to be adapted so that it is easier to understand. Yet the study suggests that little or no account is taken of aphasia by providers of health, social care, or voluntary or public services. In the study, no one was given any information about the different therapeutic activities they were involved in. There were few explanations of rationale, benefits, or limitations, and these were often loaded with jargon, as when one therapist told Donald she was going to explore his "range of movement". People who perhaps didn't understand were considered "unmotivated". Inaccessible information was also evident in written communications. For example, one participant could not understand an official letter concerning her return to driving.

Clear, accessible, written and spoken information about services is now a requirement under the Disability Discrimination Act (1995). Yet it seems that some providers of health, social care, and other services may have little concept of the possible barriers faced by someone who struggles to talk, write, read, and understand. Another infra-structural problem concerns time as a resource. Many workers in rehabilitation units, day centres, and nursing homes described their full workloads and rapid pace of work. It seemed unlikely that they would be able to fit the labour-intensive process of adapting written and spoken information into their schedules. Again, these issues accord with points raised in the survey.

Training. According to people working in the different service contexts, methods of communicating and different techniques for "managing" were mostly transmitted informally, passed on from one worker to another. In Anthea's nursing home, for example, more experienced people worked alongside newcomers to pass on their skills, and tips for managing Anthea's day-to-day care and avoiding upset. Idiosyncratic theories and ways of working often developed unchecked. Fred's keyworker, for example, made him repeat the names of items of food or drink before she gave them to him, thinking this was good for him. Within these service contexts, there was no evidence of anyone using any methods for supporting communication.

A number of people within residential and social services settings commented that they had no training regarding communication. A staff nurse in Brenda's nursing home observed that training priorities concerned crisis-management techniques, and the physical handling of patients.

Despite many examples of communication breakdown, few service providers expressed concern about their own skills and competence. Therapists, day centre staff, volunteer helpers, nursing home attendants, and respite staff often seemed confident about what they were doing. The underpinning rationale for a service was embedded in the culture of the various institutions, often unarticulated and unquestioned.

In some cases professional confidence was overwhelming, manifested in an authoritative style of communication, extensive use of expert jargon, and continuous directed activity. Rather than viewing this critically in terms of individual practice, it would perhaps be fairer to think in terms of infra-structural constraints, pressures, and culture. Lack of training and support is clearly an issue here, for workers at every level in the different care professions.

Information and communication technology (ICT). Access to ICT was very limited for the group taking part in the study. Only Terry and Roger had access to home computers. Wendy carefully nurtured Roger's computer skills and he learned to print out digital photographs and place files into folders that she had created. Terry spent one day a week in the computer suite at the day centre (using it to try and improve his speech). The time and support he needed were simply not available. At the day centre, the worker who was helping clients with the computer could only spend a few minutes each session with him. By setting up Terry's activities so quickly, he inadvertently ensured that Terry would constantly need to return to him for help. At home, Terry used the computer for entertainment, and his wife, working full time, found returning to his constant requests for help an added drain on her energy and good will. Again, access to ICT for people with major communication problems means dedicated time and training—a resource that seems in short supply.

Geography and "the nature of the place". Even in an urban setting, the small-scale ethnographic study showed how much time people spent travelling to or from services, or waiting to be picked up.

Lack of respect and value for people often seemed to be embodied in environments that contrasted with people's home settings. Some institutional environments were shabby and poorly cared for, with broken equipment and unwatered plants. In some cases the way in which space was organised and used consolidated isolation and exclusion. Albert sat for hours in the small alcove off the main room, silent, in contact with no one, the TV murmuring in the corner. There was continuous background noise: the amplified office phone ringing constantly, often unanswered; music playing loudly; the crash of equipment from the kitchen; the staff calling back and forth to each other. Frank and Terry's respite settings were hospital-like, filled with clinical equipment suggesting they were ill. These environments were also shabby, with ill-fitting curtains, dirty walls, neglected plants, broken TVs and radios with no remote control.

Institutional environments often rendered participants bored and powerless, unable to turn the TV or radio on or off, or switch channels, or to control lighting and heating levels. The environments also seemed to express the value and esteem, or lack of it, with which clients were regarded. Even table-settings demonstrated this. At Fred's home, run by Social Services, tables were set with knives and forks, mats, napkins, salt and pepper, jugs of water and glasses, and fresh flowers. At Brenda's private nursing home, soup was served out in plastic bowls, and economy lemonade dispensed from big bottles. There was no salt and pepper on the tables, and no napkins, no jugs of water. Often the reality of the institutional environments was at odds with the rhetoric of publicity material. The brochure for Brenda's home described the use of fresh produce at every meal, yet she was eating catering-pack soup, fish, chips, and frozen peas, and tinned mandarin oranges with evaporated milk. In Albert's case, the brochure described an inclusive and friendly ethos in the home that was not apparent during observations.

Notice boards were particularly revealing, as they expressed aspects of staff attitudes towards service users in a direct, unmediated fashion. At Pete's respite centre, authoritarian instructions were pinned on every wall. A notice on his door conveyed stark details of Fred's physical needs, and methods of "handling" him. Strikingly, there were no equivalent instructions concerning communication. The way in which the notice was phrased demonstrated how Fred had been depersonalised: *"Movement in bed: independent. In/out bed: assistance to sit. On/off chair: independent. On/off toilet: Independent. Assistance with trousers. No of carers: 1. In/out bath. Parler bath. Standing walking: N/A. Sitting: independent. In/out car/ vehicle: balance and legs and feet. Build: medium. Height: medium. History of falls: none."*

Interpersonal exclusion

Findings relating to interpersonal aspects of exclusion are reported in terms of three issues: close personal relationships; relationships with service providers; and relationships with other service users.

Close personal relationships. Within the small group of people who took part in the study, there was much evidence of interpersonal exclusion. While couples and families generally held together (although not without tensions and difficulties), many relatives described how friends and workmates had fallen away, because they did not know how to communicate and seemed to feel awkward and even frightened. Some interlocutors developed strategies that were also profoundly excluding: issuing a string of single word commands; talking *about* rather than *to* the person; teasing; insisting on words and phrases being repeated; or simply not acknowledging the person. Wendy's descriptions of awkward conversations with friends and family indicate how commonly such strategies were deployed, and the ways in which she tried to deal with them:

> One chap came, he did come a couple of times, but they seemed to sort of, they bossed Rog about and I hated that. Now come along, I'm sure you could say more than that, and I wanted to slap them quite honestly. I hated it when people told him what he could say and what he couldn't say, I felt as if he was being bullied.

Not everyone in the study had someone like Wendy to take their part. Most chose to withdraw from contact. Jean was very reluctant to leave the house, even to go on an outing with her husband. He felt she was frightened and expressed his own frustration at being cooped up. Mary rarely saw people and spent many hours sitting alone. No one visited Tom, and his only social contact occurred during his weekly trip to the pub. Thanks to closed-circuit security TV, Christine was able to watch her friends from the block of flats coming in the main entrance and riding in the lift. This was the sum of her contact with them. Generally, people with severe aphasia lost contacts that they had enjoyed through work, sporting, or other interests. Everyone in the study seemed to experience some social constriction, a narrowing of social contact that contrasted with life before the stroke.

There is no doubt that other factors such as physical impairment and financial problems also contributed to difficulties in maintaining personal relationships. It was hard for Tom and Jaqui to visit the local pub. They took over an hour to cover a route they had previously walked in 10 minutes. They couldn't afford a taxi and had to face the prospect of the uphill return journey. The lifts were quite often broken, so Tom would have to end his outing by climbing up seven flights of stairs.

However, some exceptional episodes showed the potential for social inclusion and cohesion as people with aphasia entered new social groups or were absorbed into communities. Miss Silver seemed to enjoy the church service held at her day centre, an event that attracted many people from her local community and gave her a chance to catch up with old friends and acquaintances. Wendy had spent months encouraging Roger's forays into the bowling club. She had joined too and accompanied him to every game for nearly a year. He now attended matches on his own. His team-mates looked out for him, and had learned from Wendy about aphasia and ways of supporting Roger's communication. Mrs Fell organised a weekly visit from Donald's friends from church and the choral society. They followed a strict routine, staying for only 1 hour and trying out a few minutes of singing exercises with Donald. The social inclusion of Roger and Donald in this way had demanded a lot of careful work and attention on the part of their wives. Wendy thought deeply about how people communicated with Roger, and would often demonstrate how to involve him in the conversation. Many relatives, aware of their role, expressed concerns about what would happen were they to become ill or to die before the person with aphasia.

Relationships with service providers. Although social attachments based on friendship or work or interest dwindled for people with aphasia, everyone in the study had entered into new relationships with providers of health, social care, and voluntary services. Everyone became the recipient of some service: day care, respite care, nursing care, therapy, and stroke club. Within these settings, as within families and partnerships, other people's attitudes and the quality of their communication varied. In some cases, service providers were attentive, respectful, and able to communicate in a way that both supported and included the silent person. The attendant at Fred's nursing home, for example, chatted to the residents in a friendly, natural way as she served their meal. She sat down with them until they had finished and she could remove their plates. She offered residents choice and support ("*Have you finished? Shall I take that?*") easing their difficulties with gentle humour. The home help who visited Ivy engaged Ivy in a conversation about her family, even though Ivy could not say a word. Such examples of successful and respectful communication seemed to be a matter of individual style and instinct, rather than being a result of training.

But at every level there were also examples of poor communication and lack of respect. Sometimes these had potentially serious implications. Frank's respite care team only discovered by chance that he had swallowing problems, and needed a specially modified diet to minimise the possibility of choking. They did not know how to communicate with him, not having read the notes his wife had sent. It was a matter of trial and error as to whether he got his message across. Charles could not let his therapist know about his significant problems with mobility at home. Pete struggled without success to convey some information to the manager of the day centre.

Strategies for managing the communication difficulties varied. Albert's nursing assistant addressed him using single- and two-word commands ("*Come on. Back.*") before dragging him backwards on a dining chair across the lounge towards the table for lunch. In Pete's case, the manager made little attempt to understand what he was trying to convey, and within a couple of minutes she had left him in the corridor, saying she would phone his wife and ask her.

Sometimes, people with communication problems were teased or treated in other disrespectful ways. People working at Anthea's nursing home laughingly imitated her idiosyncratic way of speaking as they walked away from her room. One nurse repeatedly stuck out her tongue at Brenda. One therapist told Charles she would show him some "pretty pictures" of the exercises she wanted him to practise. People with aphasia were told to "behave". Sometimes people were patronised: the support worker bent over Gill, patted her, and spoke to her as if she was an infant. David had to sit silently as stroke club volunteers said of him: "*He's got a lovely wife.*" People became invisible, talked about as if they were not there.

Relationships with other service users. Perhaps unsurprisingly, Pete did not enjoy his trips to the day centre, and expressed this with sighs and a weary facial expression. He seemed an unwilling member of a new social group. Ruth, who had more language, had little to do with other day centre clients, most of whom had physical and cognitive impairments. She preferred to talk to staff and students, many of whom were similar to her in age and background. She consolidated her distance from the other clients by taking on tasks around the centre: laying tables and removing plates. She didn't want to eat with the group and sat away from the tables while other clients dined. Although she acknowledged the profoundly serious nature of her difficulties with communication, Ruth saw herself as being in this situation on a temporary basis.

Ruth's aphasia was the major long-standing consequence of her haemorrhage. Her physical problems had mostly resolved. But her word-finding difficulties and her problems with taking in complex written or spoken information meant that her career plans were jeopardised and her sense of herself severely altered. Yet her troubles were invisible, and often not evident to others until she spoke. She was acutely aware of being different, not being right. She was unable to revisit her plans and unwilling to enter new communities until things improved for her. She was similar to Terry, whose wife described how he had become increasingly isolated and reluctant to venture out because of other people's reactions to him:

> I mean he still gets this stuff now up at the shops, if he sees somebody he used to work with he'll look at them and they'll walk away, they can't cope with it you know, they walk away

... He doesn't go out as much as he used to. Yea, he used to go out a lot more, but he seems to be drawing back, getting more and more isolated as time goes on.

Personal aspects of exclusion

It would be wrong to suggest that everyone in the study experienced feelings of personal exclusion. Some, like Ivy and Christine, seemed to have become accustomed to the life-changes brought by stroke, and to find enjoyment and pleasure in day-to-day things like being with family, eating meals, and watching TV. Harry relished his vegetable plot. Ivy also continued to enjoy going out, and travelled with her husband to visit relatives in Italy. Gill, too, seemed to enjoy many aspects of her life: the company of her daughters and husband, drinking in the social club and at home, swimming. Roger clearly adored his wife and family, and enjoyed the companionship of the bowling club. Terry loved using the computer, despite the frustrations it brought him. He and his wife took holidays in the Isles of Scilly and he appreciated the peace and beauty of this setting.

However, the study provided plentiful evidence of personal exclusion. Findings are documented in terms of four issues: isolation, boredom, and depression; identity and personhood; lack of control; and frustration and anger.

Isolation, boredom, and depression.. The sense that participants were lonely and bored was conveyed by them through facial expression, body language, sighing and vocalisation, and often voiced by carers. Many participants seemed to be isolated. Even in situations in which contact with others was still plentiful, people with aphasia were being disparaged, teased, patronised, or ignored. A number of respondents chose to stay put, rather than venturing out. Some people seemed low-spirited and depressed, particularly those who were alone for long stretches of time, and who had little to do other than watch television. Boredom seemed common. Previous means of entertainment and relaxation, such as reading or doing crosswords, were no longer possible. Access to information and communication technology was limited. Malfunctioning sets without remote control meant that some people, like Frank and Charles, were unable to watch television when in institutional settings. Three people in the study now spent the majority of each day smoking.

Identity and personhood. Although this was often hard to address directly, it was clear that everyone had faced major changes in terms of identity and life plans. Reconfiguration of self, one's past and future, was unmediated by language. There could be little discussion and negotiation of the subtler aspects of change and loss. Many of those who had been working or studying before their stroke found themselves confronting a constriction of their plans and hopes, but with little acknowledgement and no support. Personal histories seemed to be lost, particularly in the case of those participants who were in nursing homes, where no one knew much about them other than the most basic information.

There were many examples throughout the study of participants being treated as if they were not quite a person: being referred to in their presence; being ignored or talked over; being sidelined; being given commands. There seems to be a danger that if a person cannot communicate they may be perceived as less than human: their personhood is lost. It is not hard to imagine the impact of this on one's sense of self for all but the most robust. Language is a primary means of self-expression. For Wendy, this was a critical issue, although difficult to capture in words. She found she could deal better with moments of tension or difficulty when she identified with Roger and put herself in his place:

> *To me its a way of controlling what's going on between the two of you, to try and put yourself in that person's position. I think it helps you not to get, not to get out of patience with it, how can I explain it?*

It is commonly acknowledged that institutional settings can have a depersonalising effect on clients, patients, and residents. In such settings, pressure of work means that staff often have to be concerned *"with the mass not the individual"* as a nurse at Brenda's home put it. In such settings, in which large numbers of people are managed, perhaps it is inevitable that individuality is subsumed. The presence of aphasia makes it more difficult for service providers to apprehend someone's individuality, character, personality, and history. People with severe aphasia who enter institutional settings seem particularly vulnerable to depersonalisation.

Lack of control. Although some families endeavoured to include the person with aphasia in decisions, the study revealed very little evidence of people with severe aphasia exercising choice and control in their day-to-day lives, other than at the most basic level. The most powerful manifestations of this control were often nonverbal. Donald closed his eyes to shut out other people in the room, sometimes for 10 minutes at a time. Anthea would focus her gaze on what she was eating rather than continuing an interaction. Jean kept her eyes fixed on the television rather than turning to greet her visitor.

People with aphasia were often over-ruled, and unable to express their opinions, or object to what was happening or what other people said. Lack of language rendered many relatively powerless in the face of the verbal strengths of others. Nevertheless, one or two people continued to make a point of communicating in a confident way, despite the difficulties. Gill would often initiate exchanges with other people, using gesture and facial expression, and enquire after the health of a member of their family. Ironically, at one point she was asked to do this by a volunteer driver, as some kind of performance of her communication skills: *"Go on, ask me how my wife is"*. Like Gill, Roger would often persist and continue in his efforts to convey an idea or make an enquiry, even when the going was very difficult. But many would give up, worn out by the effort of trying convey some point, or sometimes embarrassed by the struggle. In addition, those around seemed to have little idea of how to support people with aphasia in getting their message out.

Participants with aphasia often seemed bewildered and uncertain when in service settings. Relatives described feelings of "being all at sea", particularly in the early days following stroke. This highlights an important point. While it is possible to trace the manifestations of social exclusion in the lives of people with aphasia, many relatives and family members also shared aspects of this experience, and found their lives changed and themselves excluded and undermined in similar ways. As Pete's wife put it:

> *It's all very well to dwell on what he has lost, but you lose it by proxy. You're almost disabled by proxy. You have to suffer all the lack of access that the disabled person has to*

suffer if you're with them. The lack of freedom, when you could go off and do as you please, but you've got to be there for that person. So your activities are curtailed as well.

Frustration and anger. Frustration was commonly expressed by participants and carers. Some family members described how communication trouble would commonly spill over into anger and sometimes violence.

DISCUSSION

This small-scale but in-depth study of the day-to-day lives and experiences of people with severe aphasia reveals evidence of social exclusion, at three different levels: infrastructural, interpersonal, and personal. It also shows that social exclusion is not a fixed, immutable state. A person with aphasia might be socially excluded one moment as a situation unfolds, and included the next. One moment, a person with aphasia might be engaged in a conversation, and the next undermined with teasing or criticism, a brief, impenetrable comment, or a pitying expression. This dynamic was apparent on many occasions in the study. People with aphasia who attended the feedback meetings reinforced this point, indicating that their sense of exclusion or inclusion varied from situation to situation, and from moment to moment. The study also suggested that carers can experience similar levels of isolation and social exclusion.

Can the experiences of a small group, documented in this study, be relevant and true for the wider community of people with severe aphasia? Although they were difficult to recruit, this small sample was selected to represent a range of different ages and backgrounds. What was striking was the commonality of experience across a diverse group, particularly concerning the communication strategies employed by other people. In addition, many of the themes emerging in the ethnographic component of the study were echoed and reinforced by findings from the nationwide survey of support groups and service providers. This suggests that, while not everyone with severe aphasia will have exactly the same experiences as participants in the study, they may well experience similar aspects and levels of exclusion, played out in different ways in their day-to-day settings. The strength of ethnography lies in the mundane evidence it provides, exposing the gap between policies and intentions and what actually happens in day-to-day life.

What would make a difference to the experience of severe aphasia?

Social exclusion is clearly evident in the details of everyday experience documented in this study. Encouragingly, there are also some examples of social inclusion. With support, people with aphasia can become engaged in meaningful and pleasurable conversations, interactions, and activities, and be involved in making or sharing decisions. The source of exclusion or inclusion lies largely within other people: how they communicate and attempt to understand; how they organise and use the environment; their manner and approach; their resourcefulness and energy; their values. This in turn is embedded in and influenced by the social groups, cultures, and institutions within which individuals operate. While it may be easy to identify ways in which, say, a therapist, a residential care attendant, a volunteer supporter, an employer, or a family member might improve their communication skills, to focus on these aspects of inclusion alone would oversimplify the issue. It would deny the influence of infrastructure, resources, tradition, habit, and culture. Similarly, feelings of isolation, boredom, or depression (the personal aspects of exclusion) cannot be addressed in isolation from the influences that bring them about.

Tackling the social exclusion of people with severe aphasia therefore needs to be a multi-faceted, multi-dimensional process appropriate to the complicated, mercurial nature of the experience. Social exclusion is manifest within infrastructural, interpersonal, and personal contexts. Within each of these contexts, possibilities for bringing about social inclusion hinge on four things: support for communication; acknowledgment and respect; opportunity and access; attention to the environment. Within this small sample, there was sporadic evidence of social exclusion being tackled on these levels by carers, both paid and unpaid.

Support for communication. In the study, difficulties with communication were evident across entire social networks: family members and friends; highly trained professionals; poorly trained or untrained workers in care settings who often have prolonged, day-to-day contact with people with aphasia. In some cases, breakdowns in communication were not perceived to be problematic by service providers.

Much could be done to support those who come into contact with people with aphasia in every context in developing practical skills and creative strategies for recognising and dealing with communication breakdown. Means of supporting communication and conversation are well understood and can be effectively taught (Kagan, 1998). The study suggests that there is an urgent need to equip those around people with aphasia with these basic skills and strategies so that communication and conversation can be enhanced. These skills should be afforded as much priority as the manual and "handling" skills that currently seem to be privileged in training.

Acknowledgement and respect. The study highlights many subtler forms of discrimination and interpersonal exclusion. Such attitudes can be manifested in body language, gesture, facial expression, turn of phrase, and even tone of voice. Consequently, they can be extremely difficult to identify and to influence. Mercurial though they may be, such behaviours are a powerful source and means of exclusion. The potential for exclusion is manifest in every interaction with people at every level of power and influence: family members, friends, rehabilitation experts, tea-ladies, benefits personnel, drivers, and voluntary helpers. The way in which the nurse, attendant, hairdresser, or therapist addresses the person with aphasia can increase isolation and low self-esteem, or consolidate inclusion and engagement. Fleeting moments and subtle aspects of communication and behaviour can make a profound difference.

Training is therefore needed not only to teach the mechanics of supporting communication, but also to highlight and enable the expression of acknowledgement and respect. Changing cultures, institutions, ways of speaking and behaving that have perhaps been taken for granted for decades is no easy task, however motivated the personnel might be. Therefore, training at the grass roots should not be conducted in isolation from efforts to influence policy and planning, perhaps within the context of anti-discriminatory legislation.

Encouragingly, within the context of healthcare services, attention is increasingly being paid to the processes of service delivery and to the social relations underlying care. Particular emphasis falls on the need for inclusive practices, underpinned by respectful and competent communication. The move towards partnership and shared decision making in the delivery of health and other services will in time change the power-balance of relationships within these domains. Health policy signals a move towards providing services that are more geared to the concerns of service users, more relevant, and therefore more effective. Charles's experience in the physiotherapy department suggests that, although listening to people with severe aphasia is not easy, understanding their perspective would enable service providers to be more effective and efficient. Those who cannot communicate cannot advocate for such changes, but there is a clear need for audit of communication practices at every level of provision, in every type of service.

Considering the personal response and the inner state of people affected by severe aphasia, the need for different levels of acknowledgement and support is clear. Counselling can be made accessible, enabling people with marked communication difficulties to articulate and address emotional issues (Clarke, 2003). Exploring personal history and life stories with people who cannot communicate, and enabling people to share their perspectives and experiences with others, might also support the maintenance of a robust sense of personal identity, integration with family and community life, and continuity with the past. This seems particularly important for people with aphasia in residential or nursing care, who may not have family members around them acting as guardians of their life stories. Inevitably, this kind of work on personal narrative would demand considerable skill and delicacy, another useful focus for training. Methods of supporting the identities of people with aphasia through narrative and portfolio work are currently being developed (Pound, Parr, Lindsay, & Woolf, 2000).

Accessible work, education, and leisure opportunities would also strengthen and affirm identities, as would access to opportunities for contact with other people in similar situations. Members of the project advisory group emphasised the importance of providing and fostering opportunities for people with severe language impairments to meet, to share experiences, and to engage in purposeful activity. Aphasia self-help organisations and some voluntary sector organisations may be starting to address these issues, but the survey suggests that many have some way to go before people with severe language difficulties have access to their activities and can be fully included and engaged. Practical ideas for promoting communication access can be found in Pound and Hewitt (2004).

Relatives and friends of people with severe aphasia identified a need for training in the practical skills of supporting communication. Alongside this, they articulated a desire for acknowledgement of their own life changes and support in surmounting the barriers they face, for example in accessing benefits.

Opportunity and access. Communication access to opportunities for employment, training, and education could be enhanced, thereby making it possible for the person with aphasia to meet their potential and contribute their expertise and knowledge in paid or voluntary work (Hewitt & Byng, 2003; Parr, Paterson, & Pound, 2003). Clearly, there is much work to be done with employers, trainers, educators, policy makers, and providers of health care, social care, and voluntary and public services to raise awareness of aphasia and the disabling barriers faced by those who struggle to communicate. A useful focus for services currently expending energy and resources on activities that seem to miss the mark could involve the identification of relevant work, educational, and financial opportunities with people who have aphasia, and working together to enhance their accessibility.

The study indicates that people with severe aphasia are faced with long periods of enforced "leisure time", yet their access to leisure pursuits such as information and communication technology and reading may be very limited. Boredom seemed to be an issue for a number of participants. Attention needs to be given to exploring and enhancing physical and communication access to a range of different leisure pursuits such as sporting activities, enjoying literature and art, cooking, and using computers. Services need to connect with the day-to-day lives of people with aphasia, the problems and restrictions that they and their families face, and the issues of access that are raised across the spectrum of work, education and leisure (Pound & Hewitt, 2004).

The study highlighted a disconnection between the various services used by people with aphasia. Thus, occupational therapists had no contact with disability employment services even though their treatment focused on vocational activities. There was little communication between aphasia therapists and day centre staff or residential home personnel working on a day-to-day basis with people with severe aphasia. Voluntary sector groups providing services for people with aphasia had little to do with other community enterprises or with aphasia self-help groups. It is possible to live for many years with aphasia, entering into different care settings during that time. More active and purposeful coordination between providers of health, rehabilitation, welfare, community, voluntary, and social services would enable good practice to be shared, and aims and values to be articulated, and have a beneficial impact on the long-term experience of people with aphasia.

The fact that discrimination against disabled people in employment and the delivery of services is now against the law within the UK (Action for Dysphasic Adults, 1998) may prove a useful vehicle for change. By law, disabled people, (including people with aphasia) have equal access to employment, to services, and to information about services. When service users have aphasia, this means service providers need to learn how to support communication, and to invest time in adapting information. This raises a number of resource issues: the process of supporting communication and enhancing access takes time and skill, and depends on training (Pound & Hewitt, 2004).

Attention to the environment. Other changes might facilitate the inclusion of people with severe aphasia. Institutional geography, the way in which space is laid out, organised, maintained, and used, can effect isolation and disempowerment, or increase respect, engagement, and control. Re-arranging seating and tackling background noise are simple processes that could make a big difference. Sitting down and talking with people who have severe communication problems is a simple but significant activity that could be prioritised in various health, institutional, and voluntary care settings. While physical access to public and institutional space has improved, attention now needs to be paid to how environments can be designed and used in such a way as to maximise communication access.

People with aphasia who enter hospital, respite, or residential care may not be able to ask someone to switch the lights or TV on or off, to change channels, or to work the radio, and they may not be physically able to do this for themselves. Other forms of entertainment and passing time, such as reading, may be impossible. Frank's control of his environment and how he passed his time in respite care was profoundly compromised. Attention to these seemingly small details, being mindful of what someone like Frank might want, need, or enjoy, could make a big difference to the quality of his experience.

Attention to the environment also means ensuring that institutional spaces are cared for and well maintained. Attention to the "nature of the place" also means thinking about the message, quality, and tone of notices, signs, and other written material, with the purpose of ensuring that they are physically and communicatively accessible, and that they express respect. Small environmental changes of this kind could be effected with relative ease, yet have a massive impact.

CONCLUSION

This project identified a number of influences that combine to constitute people's experience of severe aphasia. It suggests that severe aphasia, as well as being a profile of linguistic difficulties or inabilities, is an experience that is largely shaped by how other people react and behave within different settings. Language and communication may be severely restricted by aphasia. However, *the severity of the impact* for the individual is determined by the response and behaviour of families, friends, statutory and voluntary service providers, communities, and institutions. This small-scale study shows how the social inclusion, and social capital, of people with severe communication disabilities can be enhanced or undermined and diminished. The documentation of day-to-day experience of people with severe aphasia suggests that there is an urgent need to address such issues within the discipline of aphasiology. We can look to sophisticated discourses within the field of learning disability for guidance in developing our own discourse and practice (for example, Bates & Davies, 2004).

In a paper that anticipated the *National Service Framework for Long-Term Conditions* (Department of Health, 2005), Simmons-Mackie (2000) makes a plea for support for managing the long-term consequences of aphasia to be expanded, intervention being offered at relevant periods as the individual's life with aphasia unfolds, and barriers to participation rise up. She suggests that the role of therapists should expand beyond traditional confines towards collaboration with a constellation of health, welfare, employment, education, and leisure services. This study offers support for such developments. It suggests that, even though it seems to be a regrettably common experience and one that may permeate the detail of daily life in the years after stroke, social exclusion is not an inevitable consequence of severe communication impairment. People with severe aphasia can have access to choice, opportunity, engagement, and enjoyment. The challenge to service providers lies in creating the conditions for this to happen.

REFERENCES

Action for Dysphasic Adults (1998). *Open hole the stony wall: Report of the ADA Working Party on the Disability Discrimination Act, 1995*. London: ADA.

Allen, K. (2000). *Communication and consultation: Exploring ways for staff to involve people with dementia in developing services*. Bristol, UK: The Policy Press and The Joseph Rowntree Foundation.

Bates, P., & Davies, F. (2004). Social capital, social inclusion and services for people with learning disabilities. *Disability and Society, 19*(3), 195–206.

Clarke, H. (2003). Doing less, being more. In S. Parr, J. Duchan, & C. Pound (Eds.), *Aphasia inside out* (pp. 80–91). Buckingham, UK: Open University Press.

Davies, C. (1999). *Reflexive ethnography*. London/New York: Routledge.

Department of Health (2001). *Valuing people: A new strategy for learning disability for the 21st century*. London: Department of Health.

Department of Health (2005). *The National Service Framework for long-term conditions*. London: Department of Health.

Edgar, I., & Russell, A. (1998). *The anthropology of welfare*. London: Routledge.

Fyson, R., & Ward, L. (2004). *Making "valuing people" work*. Bristol: Policy Press.

Hammersley, M., & Atkinson, P. (1995). *Ethnography: Principles in practice* (2nd ed.). London/New York: Routledge.

Hersh, D. (1998). Beyond the plateau: Discharge dilemmas in chronic aphasia. *Aphasiology, 12*, 207–243.

Hewitt, A., & Byng, S. (2003). From doing to being: From participation to engagement. In S. Parr, J. Duchan, & C. Pound (Eds.), *Aphasia inside out* (pp. 51–65). Buckingham, UK: Open University Press.

Kagan, A. (1998). Supported conversation for adults with aphasia. [Clinical Forum.] *Aphasiology, 12*, 816–830.

Layder, D. (1993). *New strategies in social research*. Oxford, UK: Polity Press.

LeDorze, G., & Brassard, C. (1995). A description of the consequences of aphasia on aphasic persons and their relatives and friends, based on the WHO model of chronic diseases. *Aphasiology, 9*, 239–255.

Lyon, J. (2000). Finding, defining and refining functionality in real life for people confronting aphasia. In L. Worrall & C. Frattali (Eds.), *Neurogenic communication disorders: A functional approach* (pp. 137–162). New York: Thieme.

Parr, S. (2004). *Living with severe aphasia – the experience of communication impairment after stroke*. Brighton, UK: Pavilion Publishing.

Parr, S., Byng, S., Gilpin, S., & Ireland, C. (1997). *Talking about aphasia*. Buckingham, UK: Open University Press.

Parr, S., Paterson, K., & Pound, C. (2003). Time please! Temporal barriers in aphasia. In S. Parr, J. Duchan, & C. Pound (Eds.), *Aphasia inside out* (pp. 127–144). Buckingham, UK: Open University Press.

Pound, C., & Hewitt, A. (2004). Communication barriers: Building access and identity. In J. Swain, S. French, C. Barnes, & C. Thomas (Eds.), *Disabling barriers – enabling environments* (2nd ed.). London: Sage.

Pound, C., Parr, S., Lindsay, J., & Woolf, C. (2000). *Beyond aphasia*. Bicester, UK: Winslow Press.

Ritchie, J., & Lewis, J. (Eds.). (2003). *Qualitative research practice*. London: Sage.

Savage, J. (2000). Ethnography and health care. *British Medical Journal, 321*, 1400–1402.

Simmons-Mackie, N. (2000). Social approaches to management of aphasia. In L. Worrall & C. Frattali (Eds.), *Neurogenic communication disorders: A functional approach* (pp. 162–189). New York: Thieme.

Simmons-Mackie, N., & Damico, J. (1997). Reformulating the definition of compensatory strategies in aphasia. *Aphasiology, 8*, 761–781.

Simmons-Mackie, N., & Damico, J. (1999). Social role negotiation in aphasia therapy: Competence, incompetence and conflict. In D. Kovarsky, J. Duchan, & M. Maxwell (Eds.), *Constructing (in)competence: Disabling evaluations in clinical and social interaction* (pp. 313–342). Mahwah, NJ: Lawrence Erlbaum Associates Inc.

WEBSITES

British Government Social Exclusion Unit (n.d.) Retrieved 3 August 2005 from http://www.socialexclusionunit.gov.

Library and Information Commission policy (n.d.) Retrieved 3 August 2005 from http://www.lic.gov.uk/publications/policyreports/inclusion

Scottish Office (n.d.) retrieved 3 August 2005 from http://www.scotland.gov.uk

APPENDIX

EXCERPTS FROM ETHNOGRAPHIC FIELD NOTES

Terry in respite care

I reach Terry's room, a single room with a single hospital bed in it (it is high, has wheels and ratchets and side bars which are dropped down). His name is written in biro on a piece of paper sellotaped to the wall just above the bed. There is an anglepoise lamp over the bed, a locker, an old brown Parker Knoll armchair with a pair of underpants and a baseball hat on it, a small TV. The window looks onto a patch of grass and a wall. A wire coathanger hangs from a hook on the wall. The room feels odd. It is shabby, bare, flaking light pink paintwork, yet with a gaily coloured geometric frieze around the top and similarly gaily patterned duvet on the unmade bed. An open door leads into another room, a long tiled room with a washbasin and a disabled toilet at the end, with grab rails and bars around it. It feels dingy.

> *Interpretation: The wallpaper and duvet can't hide the hospital feel. It is a place for people who are sick or with motor impairments, unlike Terry. The dinginess and shabbiness adds another aspect. It makes the room feels like a hostel for homeless people.*

> *Personal: I would so hate having to stay here, were I in Terry's position.*

I think Terry has been having a rest, his bed is rumpled, the duvet thrown back. "Come on then" says Terry, smiling. He is rather shaky, his hands trembling and I wonder if this is because he has just woken up. Or does he need to take some medication? He pats his duvet, but I move the underpants and hat and sit on the armchair facing the bed. He sits on the bed. "How are you getting on here Terry?" I ask. He's been here nearly two weeks. "It's alright, it's alright" he says with an uncertain intonation … "but" .. long drawn out … "but'" .. He trails off. I look round the room. "When are you going home?" He struggles: "Um .. um … come on come on .." "Tomorrow?" I ask. "No." He picks up a TV Times and searches through the pages until he comes to Monday and shows me. "Looking forward to going home?" "Oh yes" he says.

Terry at home

I can see on the planner (and remember from my phone conversation with his wife) that he has just been in Meerwood House again for respite. I check this with him. He nods and I ask how it was. He grimaces. "It's alright, it's alright" he says doubtfully. "But …" and this word trails off uncertainly and he shrugs. Was his friend Steve there? "Yes, yes." He writes: "13 Nov." I look at November 13 on the planner and the same tiny writing reads: "Terry respite." He says: "Him and me" pointing to the chair where Jane his wife sat last time I visited. "Alright, alright. But …" then he mimes a conflict, grabbing at his own throat and grimacing and saying "Oooh." Then he says in a conciliatory tone: "It's alright though. Him and me. But …" and he clenches his two fists and bangs them together. I say: "You get on ok, you and Jane but you need a rest, from each other?" and he says: "That's it. That's it."

I remember the stark, dingy bedroom at Meerwood House and say: "Do you prefer to be at home?" He grimaces again: "Well" again with an uncertain intonation. He jumps up again, goes out and comes back with a spiral bound notebook and a biro. He writes: "JOPS." and says: "Better, this. It's all gone you see. All gone." "You want to work?" I venture. "That's it. That's it. But it's all gone." He points round the room to all the furniture, which his wife had told me he made before his stroke. "It's gone." He mimes sleeping, by resting his cheek on the back of his hand. "Over there, that's it. That's it." I ask what he will do today and he shrugs and then makes a pulling movement with his hand and points to the window. "Over there." I think for a minute. "Fishing?" No. He makes a repetitive, side to side movement with his hand and points out of the window: "That." The hedge is waving wildly and I say: "Trim the hedge?" and he says: "That's it that's it." "With an electric trimmer?" I ask. "Yes." What will he have for lunch? He mimes a chicken by tucking his hands into his armpits, raising and lowering his elbows and clucking. "Chicken?" "That's it." What sort of chicken? He shrugs, he doesn't know. He says: "Fried chicken?" He points to Jane's chair and says: "Him." "Something Jane has left for you?" "Yes." Then what? TV? He smiles and says: "Yes" and leaning forward grabs a TV Times and shows me the write up of a film about Grace Kelly, on Channel 5 at 3pm. "Good. Good?" He mimes sleep again and I say: "Will you go to sleep?" and he says "Yes." He points to his head with a finger and makes a circular movement, then mimes eating something from his hand, then sleep. "You take tablets that make you sleepy?" "That's it" and in he goes to the kitchen again, coming back with a Flora margarine container full of tablets that he shows me. Epilin, Lamital, Fluoxetine, Baclofen (when he shows me this he rubs all down his right side) and Aspirin (he pats his heart). "When do you go to sleep?" He points to his watch, to the 3 and then the 4. "Him and him. More or less." "Is it ok being here on your own? It seems like a long day." He frowns and says: "It's alright, but …" and then he points to JOPS in his notebook. "It's all gone."

APHASIOLOGY, 2007, 21 (1), 124–136

Ψ Psychology Press
Taylor & Francis Group

Developing an evidence-base for accessibility for people with aphasia

Linda Worrall, Tanya Rose, Tami Howe, Kryss McKenna and Louise Hickson

The University of Queensland, Brisbane, Australia

Background: Discrimination on the basis of disability is prohibited in many countries and therefore research on communication accessibility for people with aphasia has become a priority.
Aims: The aim of this paper is to summarise and discuss the results of a series of research studies, carried out in one Centre, into accessibility issues for people with aphasia, focusing on the accessibility of community environments and the accessibility of information.
Main Contribution: When asked about the accessibility of the community generally, people with aphasia reported both physical and societal barriers and facilitators, as well as barriers and facilitators related to other people. Many people with aphasia still do not receive written health information about aphasia and, when they do, the information is often written at a level too high for them to read. In terms of the accessibility of written information on websites about aphasia, high-quality websites may not be easily accessible to people with aphasia. For accessible websites to be delivered, the involvement of people with aphasia is paramount.
Conclusions: There are three common themes emerging from this series of research studies. First, accessibility is an important and often emotive issue for people with aphasia. Second, people with aphasia are marginalised by a communicatively inaccessible society. Third, there is considerable diversity among people with aphasia about their perceptions of the barriers and facilitators to communication in the community.

Discrimination on the basis of disability is prohibited by law in many countries of the world. Services and products are therefore required to be accessible by all, including people with aphasia. However, people with aphasia report that communicative accessibility is a significant problem for them (Parr, Byng, Gilpin, & Ireland, 1997). Accessibility is often only viewed from the restricted perspective of physical accessibility, such as ramp entry to buildings for people in wheelchairs. While people with aphasia often experience accessibility issues because of their physical impairments, little attention has been given to the issues of accessibility specifically related to the communication impairments of people with aphasia.

Address correspondence to: Linda Worrall, Communication Disability in Ageing Research Centre, School of Health and Rehabilitation Sciences, The University of Queensland, Brisbane, QLD 4072, Australia. E-mail: l.worrall@uq.edu.au

http://www.psypress.com/aphasiology   DOI: 10.1080/02687030600798352

DEFINITION OF ACCESSIBILITY

Accessibility is defined as something "that can readily be reached, entered, or used" (Oxford University Press, 1999). For a service or product to be "readily reached", an individual must first be aware that it exists. For example, to reach services that are specifically relevant to the person's health condition(s), he/she will need to know the services that are available. This process requires that the person knows such fundamental information as the name of his/her own health condition(s) to be able to connect with the most appropriate services. Hence, one aspect of accessibility relates to whether the person with aphasia receives information in the first place. For example, are brochures about stroke, aphasia, and relevant services available in general medical wards, stroke units, and general practitioner waiting rooms? To "readily be reached" also requires that the person be able to travel to or link up with the service or product. The second aspect of accessibility, to be "readily ... entered", would include policies and attitudes that encourage the participation of the person with aphasia in the service. The third component of accessibility, to be "readily ... used", would include services in which people with aphasia may easily participate, and products and materials, such as written information, that they may easily read.

This definition of accessibility may be extended by referring to the person–environment fit models. Within most of these models, an accessible environment is conceptualised in terms of "fit", where "fit" is derived from the everyday use of the term (e.g., "clothes that fit"), referring to a match between the environment and the abilities of the people for whom it is intended to be used (Steinfeld & Danford, 1999). Combining this idea of accessibility with the Oxford American Dictionary definition of the term, accessibility may be conceptualised as how well an environment "fits" the intended users, so that it can be readily "reached, entered, or used". This conceptualisation views accessibility as a complex relationship between the environment and the person or people using it. As a result, accessibility cannot be assessed without considering both the environment and the person or people who are the intended users.

The World Health Organisation's *International Classification of Functioning, Disability, and Health* (ICF) (WHO, 2001) can help to operationalise the concept of accessibility, particularly in relation to the environment. The ICF is a conceptual framework that views functioning and disability as a dynamic interaction between the person's health condition, his/her personal factors, and environmental factors. Within this framework, personal factors refer to characteristics such as the person's age, gender, personality, and social background (WHO, 2001), while environmental factors refer to all aspects that are external to a person's control. Environmental factors can have either a positive (facilitative) or negative (barrier) effect on functioning. Within the ICF, the three levels of environmental factors are immediate personal environment (e.g., family, work), services (e.g., rehabilitation services, government agencies), and cultural/legal systems (e.g., cultural beliefs, laws). Hence, environmental factors not only include the physical environment, but also the attitudes of other people, the communicative accommodation of other people in the person's environment, and policies and laws that influence society as a whole. Using this framework to operationalise the concept of accessibility, it is evident that to improve accessibility for a person or people with aphasia, a thorough understanding of the environmental and personal factors that influence their participation is needed.

EVIDENCE ABOUT ACCESSIBILITY FOR PEOPLE WITH APHASIA

Evidence-based practice is a core principle of modern health care. While many speech pathologists are primarily concerned with evidence surrounding treatment, there are several different types of clinical questions that require evidence (Sackett, Strauss, Richardson, Rosenberg, & Haynes, 2000). Accessibility issues for people with aphasia need evidence about the experiences and perceptions of people with aphasia in the community, ways to validly assess accessibility, and the effectiveness and cost-efficiency of interventions that aim to improve accessibility.

Howe, Worrall, and Hickson (2004) used the ICF terminology and constructs to review existing research in this area. Their analysis reviewed aphasiology articles in the environmental factors component of the ICF, which is divided into five domains: support and relationships; attitudes; products and technology; natural environment and human-made changes to environment; and services systems and policies. The review indicated that although there is some research in each of the domains of ICF environmental factors, there is much more research to be undertaken. Illustrations of studies that have been completed include, in the support and relationships domain, a study that examines the communication accommodation shown by conversational partners of people with aphasia. In the attitudes domain there is research that has found negative attitudes towards people with aphasia, and in the products and technology domain there is evidence that supports modified written information that facilitates comprehension of people with aphasia. Within the natural environment and human-made changes to environment domain it has been found that background noise may be a barrier to people with aphasia, while in the services, systems, and policy domain the provision of psychosocial support and counselling services has been found to be a facilitator. Howe et al. (2004) also found that aphasiologists have generally not conceptualised the communication of other people within the environmental factors domain of the ICF, although they do recognise it as an important influence on the communication of people with aphasia. In addition, the influence of environmental factors such as attitudes and values, social systems and services, and policies, rules, and laws has been acknowledged in some of the aphasiology literature (see Byng, Duchan, & Cairns, 2002; Jordan & Kaiser, 1996), but the influence of these factors on people with aphasia has not been investigated or systematically subjected to change. That is, there is little research evidence about the nature of the environmental factors that affect people with aphasia, and there is as yet no evidence about the effectiveness and outcomes of modifying the environment to improve accessibility for people with aphasia.

Researchers at The University of Queensland Communication Disability in Ageing Research Centre have undertaken a number of studies to address some of these gaps in the accessibility literature. This article will present findings from these studies under two headings: (1) Evidence about the accessibility of the community for people with aphasia and (2) Evidence about the accessibility of information for people with aphasia. In the first section, preliminary data from a study exploring the nature of the barriers and facilitators for people with aphasia in the community are presented (Howe, Worrall, & Hickson, 2006). In the second section, a series of Communication Disability in Ageing Research Centre studies about the accessibility of information for people with aphasia is described. These studies include investigations into the following areas: the availability of information to people with aphasia in an acute stroke ward (Knight, Worrall, & Rose, in press); the nature and readability of written information for people with aphasia (Rose, Worrall, & McKenna, 2006); the accessibility of written information on aphasia websites (Ghidella, Murray, Smart, McKenna, & Worrall, 2005); and the effectiveness of specific features of "aphasia-friendly" formatting of written information (Brennan, Worrall, & McKenna, 2005). This latter programme of research has been in collaboration with occupational therapy colleagues.

EVIDENCE ABOUT THE ACCESSIBILITY OF THE COMMUNITY FOR PEOPLE WITH APHASIA

Howe, Worrall, and Hickson (2006) conducted a qualitative study with 25 people with post-stroke aphasia to investigate their perceptions of the accessibility of the community. Specifically, semi-structured in-depth interviews were used to obtain participants' perspectives regarding the environmental factors that influence the participation of people with aphasia in the community. Participants were aged 34 to 85 years with varied aphasia severity as measured by the *Western Aphasia Battery* (Kertesz, 1982). Maximum variation sampling was used to select participants purposefully for characteristics such as gender (15 males), self-reported absence/presence of marked physical impairment, time post-onset of aphasia (10 to 137 months post-onset), living situation (i.e., alone vs with others), current driving status compared to pre-aphasia (i.e., changed vs unchanged), current working status compared to pre-aphasia (i.e., changed vs unchanged), years of education, and self-reported satisfaction with current community participation. Analysis revealed a wide range of environmental factors that may influence the community participation of people with aphasia. Findings fell into a number of broad categories including: (1) barriers related to other people, (2) physical barriers, (3) societal barriers, (4) facilitators related to other people, (5) physical facilitators, and (6) societal facilitators.

Barriers related to other people include other people's actions, attitudes, and characteristics. Examples of barriers mentioned by individual participants related to other people's actions were "not listening", "(the person) doesn't look at you" when communicating, and correcting the person with aphasia when he/she used a paraphasia (e.g., saying, "that's not a magazine, it's a book" after the person with aphasia used the incorrect word). In addition, other people's attitudes such as treating the person with aphasia "like a child", or as if he/she was "stupid" or "mentally deranged" were identified by some participants as barriers. Communication characteristics of other people such as having a foreign accent were also reported to make it more difficult for some people with aphasia to participate in the community. Noise and visual distractions in the environment and objects such as automatic ticketing machines and automated teller banking machines where "every one of them are different" were examples of physical barriers identified by a number of participants.

Societal barriers such as procedures and policies and the cost and location of services formed another broad category of environmental factors. Examples of these types of barriers included procedures that required specific communication (e.g., having to state the exact location the person was travelling to on a bus), procedures that required reading and writing (e.g., having to read a form and write on it to make a complaint to an organisation), and policies that involved time pressure (e.g., "They [bank tellers] got 5 minutes ... to get the ... transaction"). Other societal barriers such as a lack of opportunities for leisure and social activities for people with aphasia and a lack of awareness of aphasia in society were also reported.

The broad category of facilitators that people with aphasia perceived related to other people included their familiarity with the person with aphasia, their actions, and their attitudes. Other people's familiarity was frequently cited as a facilitator, with many participants reporting that it was easier to participate in environments where the other person or people knew them. "Suggest(ing) a few things" when the person had difficulties saying a word and "giving more time" were examples of facilitative actions of other people reported by some participants, while "patience" was frequently reported as a facilitative attitude. The category of physical facilitators included objects and auditory aspects of environments. Some participants reported that having an object available in the environment to which they could point (e.g., a drink the person wants is displayed on the counter at a food outlet) and the presence of clear signs, were facilitators.

Societal facilitators included services, procedures, and societal awareness of aphasia. A few participants reported that having a specialised driving instructor for people with aphasia and having an advocate in organisations such as government departments and legal agencies would be facilitators to participation. Improving society's awareness of aphasia was identified as a key facilitator for community participation (e.g., "Education about aphasia is the most important one") by many participants.

In addition to environmental barriers and facilitators, some participants emphasised the importance of their own communication disability on their ability to participate in the community (e.g., "The BARRIERS ... got nothin' to do with it ... I just can't TALK"). One interpretation of this finding may be that these participants mainly perceived the influences on their participation in terms of the prevailing medical model which focuses on the deficits of the individual (Lock, Jordan, Bryan, & Maxim, 2005), rather than in terms of a fit between the person and his/her environment.

Generally, however, this study found that people with severe through to mild aphasia perceived a wide range of environmental factors as influencing community participation, and that several of these factors were different from those identified in previous research about people with other types of health conditions. Some of the findings were also much more specific than the current environmental factor codes within the World Health Organisation's ICF (2001). For example, various specific actions of other people were reported to play an important role in influencing the community participation of individuals with aphasia (e.g., other people "not listening" as a barrier), yet the current version of the ICF only provides broad support and relationship environmental factor codes such as "e310 Immediate family" and "e320 Friends". Future versions of the ICF may need to incorporate more detailed environmental factor codes in a number of areas to address the needs of people with aphasia. The investigation also highlighted that community participation is not an all-or-none phenomenon, but rather varies along a continuum, and that some factors such as the availability of a support person may be a barrier for one individual, yet a facilitator for another.

In addition to this investigation, researchers in the Communication Disability in Ageing Research Centre are currently conducting two other studies focusing on the accessibility of the community for people with aphasia. Howe, Worrall, and Hickson are using the method of participant observation with adults with aphasia to investigate barriers and facilitators to community participation, while Alkhaled, Brown, McGahan, Seah, Howe, and Worrall are conducting focus groups to identify community service providers' perceptions (e.g., bank tellers, travel agents, shop assistants, and information-counter receptionists) of barriers and facilitators to community participation for adults with aphasia. Once completed, the findings from these three studies will contribute to the evidence-base needed to develop future interventions to make community environments more accessible for adults with aphasia.

EVIDENCE ABOUT THE ACCESSIBILITY OF WRITTEN INFORMATION

In the current era of increased consumer awareness and consumer rights, information accessibility has become a hot topic. While information can be provided verbally (e.g., live presentations and videos), much information is provided in written format. More questions than answers remain in the quest to make written information, particularly written health information, accessible for people with aphasia. Developing and providing optimally effective written information is an involved process. There are issues concerning content choice. What information do people with aphasia need and want to know? Are the medical terms aphasia/dysphasia routinely documented and explained in written information? The medium chosen to convey health information also warrants investigation. For example, do people with aphasia have significant preferences for receiving information via brochures, booklets, information sheets, or the Internet? Do factors such as hemipareses, visual neglect, and severity of reading disability impact on their choice of medium?

Research investigating the timing and frequency of the provision of health information is also essential. Studies that involve listening to the experiences of those living with aphasia are vital in determining when and how often health information should be supplied. Do health professionals provide the same amount of information to stroke patients without aphasia as they do to stroke patients with aphasia? Due to the multiple health conditions that frequently co-occur with aphasia, issues regarding the amounts and different types of written information also exist. Are speech pathologists aware of the written information supplied beyond their own discipline? Are systematic processes in place that encourage a reliable and organised approach to health information distribution? Finally, is the written health information provided to people with aphasia consistently designed with knowledge and consideration of their associated reading difficulties? Evidence-based research investigating modifications to written information (i.e., "aphasia-friendly" text formatting) is another crucial component to providing accessible written information.

Researchers within the Communication Disability in Ageing Research Centre have investigated these issues. This paper shares findings from studies that have examined the provision of both verbal and written health information to people with aphasia post-stroke. Research that highlights the amount and types of information given to people with aphasia is described and evidence about the effectiveness of modifications to written information is discussed.

Do people with aphasia receive health information?

Inadequacies in the provision of health information to stroke survivors have been well documented in the literature. First, studies have repeatedly found that stroke patients are not satisfied with the amount of stroke-related information provided (Lomer & McLennan, 1987; Pound, Gompertz, & Ebrahim, 1994; Wellwood, Dennis, & Warlow, 1994). Lomer and McLennan (1987) reported that 93% of stroke patients in their study stated that they received little or no information about stroke. Wellwood et al. (1994) also found that 88% of stroke patients did not receive any stroke-related health information. Second, the research has identified that when health information is provided, specific gaps in information content exist. For example, O'Mahony, Rodgers, Thomson, Dobson, and James (1997) reported inadequacies in information about psychological problems associated with stroke. Of participants in that study, 72% stated that they did not receive enough advice and information concerning the emotional problems related to stroke. A lack of stroke-related information about community support has also been identified in the literature (Hanger & Mulley, 1993). Third, studies have found that current practices in providing health information to stroke patients are flawed. Wiles, Pain, Buckland, and McLellan (1998) reported that when information was supplied, stroke patients did not always feel that the information made sense. It has also been documented that booklets discussing general stroke information "appear to be of limited efficacy" for stroke patients (Rodgers, Bond, & Curless, 2001, p. 130). More recently, Olofsson, Andersson, and Carlberg (2005) reported that stroke patients tended to take a passive role while in hospital. They did not know what information to ask for, tended to blame themselves when desired information was not obtained, and felt that nursing staff had no time for information.

Given these difficulties, people with aphasia post-stroke are particularly vulnerable to lack of information. The seminal work by Parr et al. (1997) highlighted that the skills required to request and comprehend health information are significantly reduced by the language difficulties associated with aphasia. A more recent study by Eames, McKenna, Worrall, and Read (2003) reiterated the finding that despite similar information needs, people with aphasia post-stroke continue to be less likely to receive information from health professionals than stroke patients without aphasia.

Knight et al. (in press) recently completed a study to explore whether patients with aphasia do in fact receive less health information than patients without aphasia post-stroke. This study aimed to determine the frequency of health information provision within an acute stroke unit and to investigate patients' knowledge of stroke and aphasia post-discharge. Participants in this study were two patients with aphasia and five stroke patients without aphasia, recruited from one acute stroke unit in an Australian hospital. The study used extensive participant observation (during which time spent communicating with health professionals was recorded) and semi-structured interviews to explore the realities of participants' time in the acute stroke setting, as well as participants' perspectives during their stay in the acute stroke setting. The study found that when communicating with stroke patients without aphasia, 22% of health professionals' communication time was related to the exchange of health information. This finding is in stark contrast to the 7% of time spent conveying health information to patients with aphasia. Five of the seven participants (both patients with and without aphasia) conveyed anxiety in relation to the lack of health information they received. When asked, "Can you tell me what a stroke is?" participant responses were coded on an ordinal scale using the criteria of whether the participant was able to indicate that a stroke was both damage to the brain and was caused by interruption of blood flow. The rating of "complete understanding" was given when both criteria were met. Only one of the seven participants in this study was able to demonstrate a complete understanding of stroke. Participants with aphasia did not demonstrate an understanding of stroke and conveyed no understanding of aphasia when similar criteria were applied. It is acknowledged that caution must be taken when drawing conclusions from this small-scale study. In addition, participants in an acute stroke unit may have comprised levels of awareness and alertness. Despite this, hospitals and hospital staff are main sources of health information for patients. As such, this study again calls into question whether the health information needs of people with aphasia are currently being met.

As part of a larger-scale study, Rose et al. (2006) interviewed 40 participants with aphasia post-stroke to determine if they received written health information about stroke and aphasia since their stroke. Participants were recruited from university-run aphasia therapy groups and metropolitan and rural hospitals within southeastern Queensland, Australia. Participants had a range of aphasia severities, with Western Aphasia Battery Aphasia Quotients (Kertesz, 1982) ranging from 6.58 to 93.1 (mean = 74.96, SD = 20.48). Participants were aged from 32 to 84 years (Mean = 65.8, SD = 12.02), 60% were male, and the time post-onset of aphasia ranged from 2 months to 14 years 10 months (mean = 2 years 10 months, SD = 3 years 5 months). Data were collected using semi-structured in-depth interviews and surveys. Two-thirds (66%) of participants confirmed that they had received written health information about stroke, while half reported that they had received written health information about aphasia.

These findings could be viewed positively, considering the bleak findings of Lomer and McLennan (1987) and Wellwood et al. (1994) whose studies, discussed above, both reported that a very high percentage of stroke patients received no literature about their stroke. However, it is important to consider that findings may reflect a sample bias, as this population was possibly more interested in health information, evidenced by their involvement in this study. While this study did not seek out information about the reasons why information was not reported as being received by participants with aphasia (e.g., memory difficulties, person was not ready to receive information), findings strongly suggest that people with aphasia continue to be uninformed about stroke and aphasia. Some participants reported first hearing the word "aphasia" when they received the information sheet inviting them to participate in the study. Health professionals still have a long way to go in ensuring written health information about aphasia and stroke is accessible at all times to all people with aphasia. Speech pathologists must ensure that the profession educates as well as treats people with aphasia.

What health information do people with aphasia receive?

As part of the study by Rose et al. (2006), the 40 participants with aphasia were asked to provide copies of the written health information they had either received or self-collected. The collected artefacts revealed substantial variety in the amount of written health information received. Some participants had received large amounts of written information (not necessarily discussing stroke and aphasia), while others had received limited amounts of or no written health information, a result that concurs with the findings of Olofsson et al. (2005). In the Olofsson et al. (2005) study, the different rate of distribution of written information was not correlated with the patients' ability to "grasp the information" (p. 436). Factors including patient personality, patient desire and interest in health information, health professional knowledge and work ethic, type of healthcare facility, discharge location, aphasia severity, severity of reading disability, recency of stroke, and memory may have contributed to the variability in the amount of health information received by participants.

In addition to individual variation in quantity and source of information, people with aphasia are also exposed to written health information discussing an array of different health topics. For example, participants in the Rose et al. (2006) study reported receiving written information about stroke, resource centres for people with stroke, stroke and depression, aphasia, memberships to stroke and aphasia support groups, options for providing donations to stroke groups, and strategies for communication. Additional health information provided addressed dyspraxia, dysarthria, dysphagia, communication cards, outpatient-allied health appointments, preadmissions information, hospital-specific information, hand exercises, sequencing instructions, enduring power of attorney, dementia and incontinence, personal exercise programmes, positioning, hemiplegic home programmes, falls prevention, return to work options, disability services, medical aids, hearing loss, home visits, medication guides, coping strategies, exercise classes, research information sheets inviting participation, carer information, nursing services, information discussing complaints and compliments, and transport options. Due to the multiple symptoms that result from stroke, people with aphasia require written health information about a variety of topics. To avoid unnecessary repetition and confusion, health professionals need to develop systematic ways of providing health information. For example, in an acute stroke unit a staff member could be nominated to provide best-practice information on a range of topics in an accessible format for each patient. It is also imperative to recognise that accessible health information extends beyond information about stroke and aphasia. If speech pathologists are serious about providing accessible health information to people with aphasia, advocacy at both a multidisciplinary and health policy level is required.

From the written health artefacts collected in the Rose et al. (2006) study, almost half were foldout brochures/pamphlets (47.6%) while the same percentage were either A4 booklets, information sheets, or newsletters. Eames et al. (2003) also found that after verbal information, pamphlets and information sheets were common media for health information delivery. Health information can be provided in many formats such as pamphlets, information sheets, newsletters, books, handwritten notes, videos, cassette tapes, computer programs, and the Internet, as well as in verbal format (Eames et al., 2003). Research is currently taking place to determine if people with aphasia have a preference for how they receive written information.

As Griffin, McKenna, and Worrall (2004) note, web-based stroke education resources are potentially enormously beneficial for people with stroke, particularly those living in the community, because of their ease of access. Internet access through home computers is becoming more common, and Internet facilities are available in most public libraries. This provides an unprecedented opportunity for consumers to access health information. Ghidella et al. (2005) conducted a study to examine the quality, communicative accessibility, and readability of websites that were designed to inform people with aphasia about aphasia. Two participant groups (18 speech pathologists and 6 people with aphasia) assessed five aphasia websites. A subsequent aim of this study was to determine if websites preferred by people with aphasia were those that scored well on published measures of accessibility and quality, and if preferences were comparable to those of speech pathologists. This study concluded that accessible websites do not necessarily equate to high-quality websites, and that high-quality websites were not always easily accessible. Speech pathologists and people with aphasia did not agree about what makes a good website, a finding which strongly suggests that people with aphasia need to be involved in the design of aphasia websites.

How can text be modified to improve accessibility?

Developing written health information with a readability level that matches or is lower than the reading skills of the target audience is one factor in improving access to health information. However, several studies have repeatedly found considerable discrepancies between the readability levels of health information compared to the reading skills of the patients who read them (Albert & Chadwick, 1992; Eames et al., 2003; Griffin, McKenna, & Tooth, 2006; Sullivan & O'Conor, 2001). Eames et al.'s (2003) study found that most of the written stroke information received by stroke patients both with and without aphasia exceeded participants' reading abilities. Inappropriate readability levels continue to be used in written health information given to people with aphasia.

To illustrate this point, text from an artefact collected as part of the study by Rose et al. (2006) is shown below. The paragraphs below formed part of an allied health appointment letter given to a patient with aphasia.

TRANSPORT:
If you require Ambulance Transport, you are a subscriber, and, you meet the QAS transport criteria, please contact the Day Hospital 24 working hours prior to your appointment and we will order the ambulance for you.

LOCAL MEDICAL OFFICER (GP)
It is important that you have a local Medical Officer whom you see on a regular basis after discharge. The Hospital Medical Officers are not always available for consultations.

Both of the above extracts are written at a Flesch-Kincaid reading grade level of 12 (Flesch, 1948), which is equivalent to the reading level expected after 12 years of education. The literature generally recommends that a reading grade of 5–6 be used when developing written health information for patients whose reading abilities are unknown (Doak, Doak, & Root, 1996; Estey, Musseau, & Keehn, 1991). Because tools for calculating readability statistics are now available in commonly used word processing software and are also readily available on the Internet, it seems inexcusable that documents with such inappropriate readability levels continue to be created and given to people with aphasia.

An appropriate readability level is only one aspect of accessible document design. Formatting parameters such as layout, typography, and graphics also need to be considered when developing accessible health information. Recommendations for designing effective written health information based on stroke research have been published (Hoffman & Worrall, 2004). However, no such recommendations or text formatting guidelines presently exist specifically for people with aphasia. This could be viewed as problematic when more and more speech pathologists are claiming to produce "aphasia-friendly" information. As speech pathologists become more aware of the need to produce aphasia-friendly written information, research that actually defines aphasia-friendly formatting and investigates its effectiveness is both warranted and timely. Particularly when research has shown that (1) not all people with aphasia welcome the exaggerated simplification of written health information (Rose, Worrall, & McKenna, 2003), (2) people with aphasia post-stroke appear to have more specific design preferences compared to people without aphasia (Eames et al., 2003), and (3) the perceptions of people with aphasia and speech pathologists about communicative accessibility can be considerably different (Ghidella et al., 2005). It is essential that text-formatting guidelines are developed based on evidenced-based research involving participants with aphasia, rather than solely relying on professional opinion.

Studies specifically addressing text formatting for people with aphasia are scarce. Rose et al. (2003) found that 12 people with mild to moderately severe aphasia were able to comprehend significantly more health information when the information was modified using simple words and short sentences (Flesh Kincaid reading scores below 6.7), large font size (size 18), standard font (Times New Roman), ample white spacing, and pictures (Microsoft ClipArt). In this study, knowledge test scores increased by 29.6% after the modified (aphasia-friendly) versions were read, compared to the 18.4% increase in knowledge after participants read the original unmodified information. Hence, 11.2% more information was comprehended when the modified aphasia-friendly versions were read. Brennan et al. (2005) found that simplifying text, using large font, incorporating increased amounts of white space, and using pictures allowed greater comprehension of information by people with aphasia. However the addition of Microsoft ClipArt pictures to paragraphs alone did not significantly improve reading comprehension. These results suggest that pictures may have the potential to cause distraction to people with aphasia and that purpose-drawn illustrations and photographs may be a more appropriate graphic choice to supplement text (Brennan et al., 2005; Worrall et al., 2005). Accessible document design continues to be a focus of research within the Communication Disability in Ageing Research Centre. Text-formatting guidelines specifically for people with aphasia are in the process of being developed. In addition, the effectiveness of aphasia-friendly formatting and reactions to aphasia-friendly information are being analysed according to participants' aphasia severity, reading ability, and time post-onset.

In summary, current research investigating information accessibility for people with aphasia has suggested that they do not receive the same amount of information as people without aphasia post-stroke. Despite apparent improvements in the provision of written health information, many participants with aphasia still do not receive written health information about aphasia. Due to the complex nature of stroke, people with aphasia may be exposed to many sources of health information and receive written health information about a wide range of topics. Systematic methods in providing health information need to be developed, as does an appreciation for the types and amounts of written health information that are required and supplied beyond the discipline of speech pathology. Pamphlets are one of the most commonly used media for conveying health information—however, text continues to be written at reading levels too high for people with aphasia. This persists despite research findings confirming that the modification of written health information by using simple words, large and standard font, and white space assists comprehension by people with aphasia. Ongoing research into the design and layout of written health information, particularly with respect to graphic choice, is warranted. In addition, high-quality websites are not easily accessible to people with aphasia and, for accessible aphasia websites to be delivered, the involvement of people with aphasia is paramount. Further research that provides practical and evidenced-based recommendations, to ensure that information provided to people with aphasia is routinely presented in comprehensible and welcomed formats, is currently in progress.

CONCLUSION

Focusing on accessibility issues for people with aphasia is relatively new. This paper has summarised some of the past, current, and future research projects in this topic area within our research centre. There are three commonalities to the findings. First, accessibility is an important and often emotive issue for people with aphasia. Second, even though people who have had a stroke face a disabling society every day, people with aphasia are marginalised even further by a communicatively inaccessible society. Third, there is considerable diversity among people with aphasia about their perceptions of barriers and facilitators to communication in the community.

The University of Queensland Communication Disability in Ageing Research Centre is collecting research evidence about the nature of aphasia-friendly environments and aphasia-friendly written material in particular, but there is also a need for evidence about the effectiveness (including the cost-effectiveness) of interventions that modify the environment to make it more accessible for people with aphasia. This is a major challenge that needs to be undertaken. Potentially, interventions that modify the environment so that it is more communicatively accessible to people with aphasia will have widespread benefits to a number of stakeholders (e.g., conversational partners in society in general, other communicatively disabled populations, and non-English-speaking individuals in an English-speaking environment), not just people with aphasia. However, there is an urgent need for speech pathologists and other professionals to work with people with aphasia to overcome some of the significant barriers that people with aphasia face on a daily basis.

REFERENCES

Albert, T., & Chadwick, S. (1992). How readable are practice leaflets? *British Medical Journal, 305*, 1266–1268.

Brennan, A. D., Worrall, L. E., & McKenna, K. T. (2005). The relationship between specific features of aphasia-friendly written material and comprehension of written material for people with aphasia. *Aphasiology, 19*(8), 693–711.

Byng, S., Duchan, J., & Cairns, D. (2002). Values in practice and practising values. *Journal of Communication Disorders, 35*, 89–106.

Doak, C. C., Doak, L. G., & Root, J. H. (1996). *Teaching patients with low literacy skills.* Philadelphia: J. B. Lippincott.

Eames, S., McKenna, K., Worrall, L., & Read, S. (2003). The suitability of written education materials for stroke survivors and their carers. *Topics in Stroke Rehabilitation, 10*, 70–83.

Estey, A., Musseau, A., & Keehn, L. (1991). Comprehension levels of patients reading health information. *Patient Education and Counselling, 18*, 165–169.

Flesch, R. (1948). A new readability yardstick. *Journal of Applied Psychology, 32*, 221–233.

Ghidella, C. L., Murray, S. J., Smart, M. J., McKenna, K. T., & Worrall, L. E. (2005). Aphasia websites: An examination of their quality and communicative accessibility. *Aphasiology, 19*(12), 1134–1146.

Griffin, E., McKenna, K., & Worrall, L. (2004). Stroke education materials on the World Wide Web: An evaluation of their quality and suitability. *Topics in Stroke Rehabilitation, 11*, 29–40.

Griffin, J., McKenna, K., & Tooth, L. (2006). Discrepancy between older clients' ability to read and comprehend and the reading level of written educational materials used by occupational therapists. *American Journal of Occupational Therapy, 60*, 70–80.

Hanger, H. C., & Mulley, G. P. (1993). Questions people ask about stroke. *Stroke, 24*, 536–538.

Hoffman, T., & Worrall, L. (2004). Designing effective written health education materials: Considerations for rehabilitation professionals. *Disability and Rehabilitation, 26*, 1166–1173.

Howe, T., Worrall, L., & Hickson, L. (2004). What is an aphasia-friendly environment? A review. *Aphasiology, 18*, 1015–1037.

Howe, T., Worrall, L., & Hickson, L. (2006). *Environmental factors that influence the community participation of adults with aphasia.* Manuscript in preparation.

Jordan, L., & Kaiser, W. (1996). *Aphasia: A social approach.* London: Chapman & Hall.

Kertesz, A. (1982). *The Western Aphasia Battery.* New York: The Psychological Corporation, Harcourt Brace Jovanovich.

Knight, K., Worrall, L., & Rose, T. (in press). The provision of health information to stroke patients within an acute hospital setting: What actually happens and how do patients feel about it? *Topics in Stroke Rehabilitation.*

Lock, S., Jordan, L., Bryan, K., & Maxim, J. (2005). Work after stroke: Focusing on barriers and enablers. *Disability and Society, 20*, 33–47.

Lomer, M., & McLennan, D. L. (1987). Informing hospital patients and their relatives about stroke. *Clinical Rehabilitation, 1*, 33–37.

Olofsson, A., Andersson, A., & Carlberg, B. (2005). If only I manage to get home I'll get better: Interviews with stroke patients after emergency stay in hospital on their experiences and needs. *Clinical Rehabilitation, 19*, 433–440.

O'Mahony, P., Rodgers, H., Thomson, G., Dobson, R., & James, F. W. (1997). Satisfaction with information and advice received by stroke patients. *Clinical Rehabilitation, 11*, 68–72.

Oxford University Press (1999). *The Oxford American dictionary of current English. Oxford Reference Online.* Retrieved 14 May 2005, from http://www.oxfordreference.com/views/ENTRY.html?subview=Main&entry=t21.e173.

Parr, S., Byng, S., Gilpin, S., & Ireland, C. (1997). *Talking about aphasia: Living with loss of language after stroke.* Buckingham, UK: Open University Press.

Pound, P., Gompertz, P., & Ebrahim, S. (1994). Patients' satisfaction with stroke services. *Clinical Rehabilitation, 8*, 7–17.

Rodgers, H., Bond, S., & Curless, R. (2001). Inadequacies in the provision of information to stroke patients and their families. *Age and Ageing, 30*, 129–133.

Rose, T. A., Worrall, L. E., & McKenna, K. (2003). The effectiveness of aphasia-friendly principles for printed health education materials for people with aphasia following stroke. *Aphasiology, 17*, 947–963.

Rose, T., Worrall, L., & McKenna, K. (2006). *Written health information for people with aphasia. Is it received and is it accessible?* Manuscript in preparation.

Sackett, D., Strauss, S., Richardson, W., Rosenberg, W., & Haynes, R. (2000). *Evidence-based medicine: How to practice and teach EBM.* London: Churchill Livingston.

Steinfeld, E., & Danford, G. S. (1999). Theory as a basis for research on enabling environments. In E. Steinfeld & G. S. Danford (Eds.), *Enabling environments: Measuring the impact of environment on disability and rehabilitation* (pp. 11–33). New York: Kluwer Academic/Plenum Publishers.

Sullivan, K., & O'Conor, F. (2001). A readability analysis of Australian stroke information. *Topics in Stroke Rehabilitation, 7*, 52–60.

Wellwood, I., Dennis, M., & Warlow, C. (1994). Perceptions and knowledge of stroke among surviving patients with stroke and their carers. *Age and Ageing, 23*, 293–298.

Wiles, R., Pain, H., Buckland, S., & McLennan, L. (1998). Providing appropriate information to patients and carers following a stroke. *Journal of Advanced Nursing, 28*, 794–801.

World Health Organisation (2001). *International classification of functioning, disability and health.* Geneva: WHO.

Worrall, L., Rose, T., Howe, T., Brennan, A., Egan, J., & Oxenham, D. et al. (2005). Access to written information for people with aphasia. *Aphasiology, 19*(11), 923–929.